IMAGES
of America

CANBY

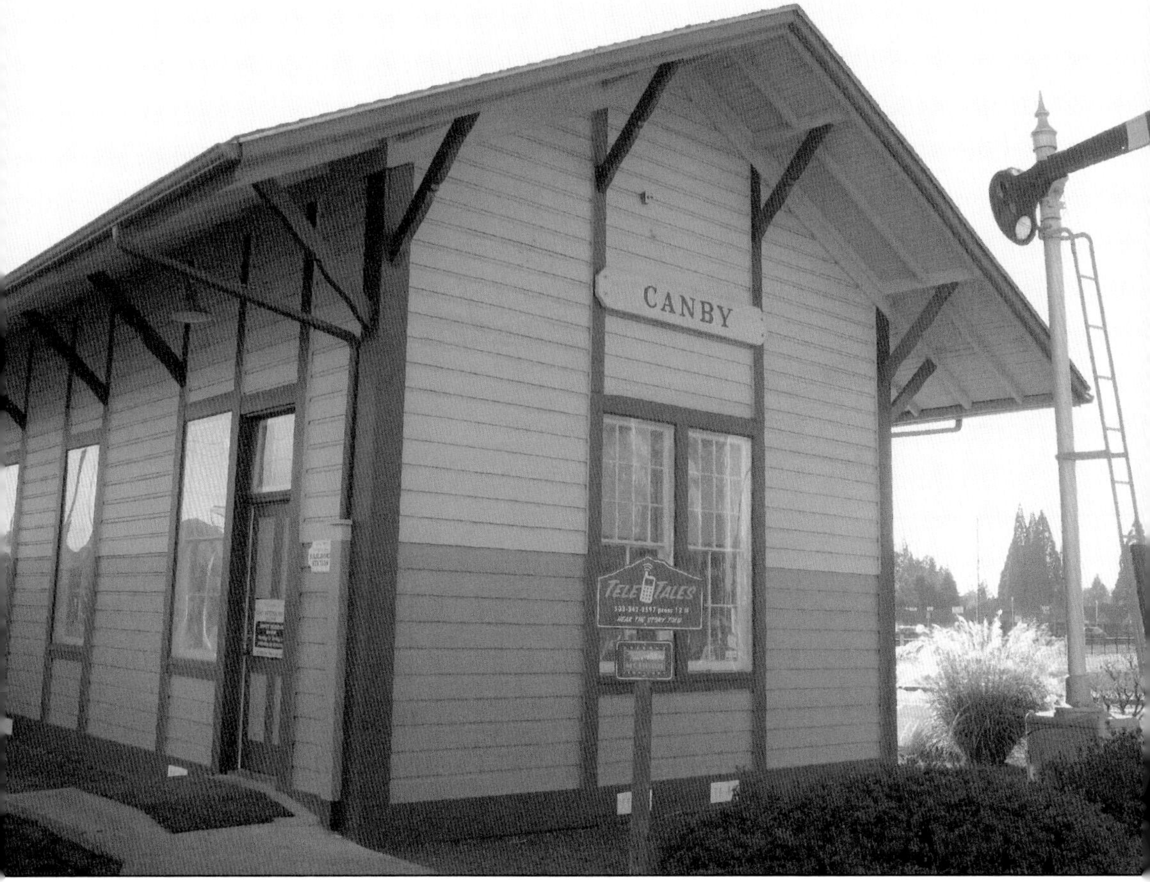

The Canby Depot, located at the intersection of North First Avenue and Grant Street, had been a functioning train station during the development of the city. The first steam train traveled through Canby in 1871. The railroad planned to demolish the building unless it could be moved. The Canby Historical Society raised funds to save it. The Canby Depot is now located near NE Fourth Avenue and Pine Street in Canby, Oregon. (Courtesy of Canby Historical Society.)

ON THE COVER: Workers at the Canby log dump on the Willamette River in 1950 pose between loads. (Courtesy of Canby Historical Society.)

IMAGES
of America

CANBY

Rebecca Harrison and Daniel Cowan

ARCADIA
PUBLISHING

ISBN 978-1-4671-1704-3

Published by Arcadia Publishing
Charleston, South Carolina

Printed in the United States of America

Library of Congress Control Number: 2016932900

For all general information, please contact Arcadia Publishing:
Telephone 843-853-2070
Fax 843-853-0044
E-mail sales@arcadiapublishing.com
For customer service and orders:
Toll-Free 1-888-313-2665

Visit us on the Internet at www.arcadiapublishing.com

For Hanna Hofer, program coordinator at the Canby Public Library; thanks to her, or we would not have written this book

Contents

Acknowledgments

This book was initiated by the City of Canby's public library. It became a reality when the president and finance officer of the Canby Historical Society, Nora Clark, gave us full access to the Canby Depot Museum. The museum has a vast collection of photographs, archival materials, and historical images of the Canby area. We deeply appreciate Sara Kirkpatrick and Anne Hulit, for their experience and help with the photographs, and the Gribble and Kraxberger families, who offered pictures for this book from their private collections and shared their stories as well as their books.

All photographs are from the Canby Historical Society unless otherwise credited.

Introduction

The city of Canby is located in Clackamas County, Oregon, nestled deep within the North Willamette Valley. Bordered by the Willamette and Molalla Rivers, Canby was the seasonal meeting place for local tribes of Native Americans.

In 1838, James Baker, one of the first white men to live in Oregon, settled north of the town with his cattle, driven up from the California region. Baker married a woman from the Kalapuya tribe; they began operating a huge farm just north of the city. Other people arrived, including Philander and Anna Lee, who acquired squatter's rights alongside a spring-fed stream (where SE First Avenue is now) in 1848. Through the Donation Land Claim Act, in 1850, the Lees gained title to 647 acres, which encouraged many families to trek over the Oregon Trail.

Joseph Knight and his family moved to Baker Prairie (named after James Baker, and Canby's first regional name) in 1868. The Knights opened a general store and constructed buildings, and family members served as postmaster, school clerk, sheriff, druggist, blacksmith, and carpenter. To export their goods, they used dirt roads and the Willamette River, which supplied the main transportation. Steamboats took their harvest into Oregon City and Portland.

The Oregon & California Railroad was incorporated on March 17, 1870, after its predecessor, Oregon Central, had completed the first 20 miles of rail line from East Portland to Parrott Creek. As the line from Portland to San Francisco was expanding, developers contacted Philander Lee for some of his land in 1870. Lee sold 111 acres for the 24-block town, 12 lots per block, for $2,960. Other landowners, such as the Knight family, sold an additional 300 acres to the railroad. Canby's city plat was filed in Oregon City on August 9, 1870. Heman A. Lee, Philander's second son, served as the first mayor. Rails were laid across the prairie and a bridge was built over the Molalla River to the west from 1870 through 1873. The first Oregon & California Railroad steam train whistled up along the Willamette River heading south from Portland to Salem and through Canby on September 29, 1870. A railway yard was built close to what is now NW First Avenue and Grant Street. Philander's eighth child, Albert H. Lee, was the first railroad agent. The first freight train ran from Portland to Albany the following December, and passenger service began early in 1871. For 90 years, mail in and out of Canby and nearby post offices moved through the station. Trains were frequent, carrying supplies for stores, farms, and passengers.

By 1890, Canby had three hotels and a bank and was ready for a proper name. The city was named after Brig. Gen. Edward Richard Sprigg Canby, a Civil War hero who had arrived in Oregon just a week before the original platting of the city in 1870 to take control of the US Army's Department of the Columbia. (Captain Jack, a Modoc warrior, and his men killed General Canby in the Modoc War. Jack was hanged on October 3, 1873, for the murder of General Canby—the only US general killed by American Indians.) The Oregon Legislative Assembly incorporated the town of Canby on February 15, 1893, making it the second-oldest city in Clackamas County.

The population grew to 587 people by 1910. The railroad tracks were rapidly framed with warehouses as the agricultural industry grew in the area. Local crops included grain, hay, potatoes, dairy products, turkeys, flax, prunes, rhubarb, asparagus, berries, nuts, livestock, lumber, bulbs, flowers, and nursery stock. For many years, three covered bridges crossed the Molalla River from Canby, and in 1914, local capitalists established a ferry service across the Willamette River. Before 1920, the "Road of a Thousand Wonders" (now NW First Avenue), was the main route through Canby, running northeast to Oregon City and west to Barlow and up the valley. That year marked the arrival of the Pacific Highway (Highway 99E) to the south of the railroad tracks, bringing a new wave of transportation and development to Canby. The town had grown from 998 people in 1940 to 1,286 residents by 1945. Canby now has a population of over 15,800, and the city covers a three-square-mile area. Many of the early buildings and homes in the original townsite still exist, and early farmhouses and barns border the city. William Knight's 1874 home still stands at 525 SW Fourth Avenue, as does the Knight Building, built in 1890 on NW First Avenue, which served as the early meeting place of the city council. The Knight Building was also the first home of Carlton & Rosenkrans, then the largest department store in Clackamas County.

Canby is the home of the Clackamas County Fairgrounds, where the annual Clackamas County Fair and Rodeo has been held since 1907. The fairgrounds, located north of Oregon Route 99E, are used in August for the fair and year-round for other events. The Canby Depot Museum is housed in the oldest train station in Oregon. The depot originally stood at the intersection of North First and Grant Streets; on August 4, 1983, it was moved to its current location at the corner of NE Fourth Avenue and Pine Street and converted into a museum by the Canby Historical Society.

Volunteers demolished the 1907 warehouse addition and used its materials in restoration of the tattered depot. Sitting now several blocks distant from its original site, the station still occupies a small portion of the Philander Lee Donation Land Claim. The restored station began new life October 6, 1984, as Canby Depot Museum, which keeps the city's heritage dating back to the 1870s, as well as the history of the mapping of the town and construction of the first 100 miles of main line railroad southward to link with the transcontinental system. The Canby Ferry, north of the city, stills crosses the Willamette River daily. A variety of light industrial companies lie within the city and nearby. Outside of the town, agricultural and nursery products, along with fruits and other crops, are produced for markets in Clackamas County and beyond. Today, folks who prefer a small-town atmosphere in the Willamette Valley's moderate climate inhabit the city of Canby.

One

Founding Families
Where the Fertile Ground Grew Plantations

The Willamette Valley was a prosperous land for the Native Americans. The Lewis and Clark Expedition of 1804–1806 was the first the new Americans had heard about this northwest country. When the Lewis and Clark journals were published in 1817, they invited exploration. By 1838, James Baker, one of the earliest pioneers to arrive in the Oregon Country, began farming in what would become Canby. Entrepreneurs such as John Jacob Astor and Dr. John McLoughlin, the principal factor of the Hudson Bay Company, started new settlements along the Willamette River close to Portland, including in the Canby area. Philander and Anna Lee acquired squatter's rights on land next to a spring-fed creek in 1848.

The Donation Land Law of 1850 followed the Great Migration that began in the 1840s. This new government grant provided 640 acres free to any homesteaders in these new territories. In 1850, the Lees gained title to their 647 acres through this new land entitlement.

The area grew, with new roads, buildings, and a dock for steamboats; an area within the Baker Prairie land claim was evolving into a city. In 1870, Baker Prairie's original 24-block townsite was platted on land bought by the Oregon & California Railroad from Philander Lee, the Knight brothers, and a few others. Twenty-three years later, Canby was incorporated on February 15, 1893, with a population of 200. By 1910, the population had increased to 587.

Agriculture was the main economy in Canby. Fresh vegetables, berries, and dairy products, along with flax and livestock, were sold both nearby and well beyond the Willamette Valley. The depot sent trains filled with local farm products to destinations throughout the United States. In 1918, a paved road, the Pacific Highway (now Oregon Route 99E), opened Canby to everyone.

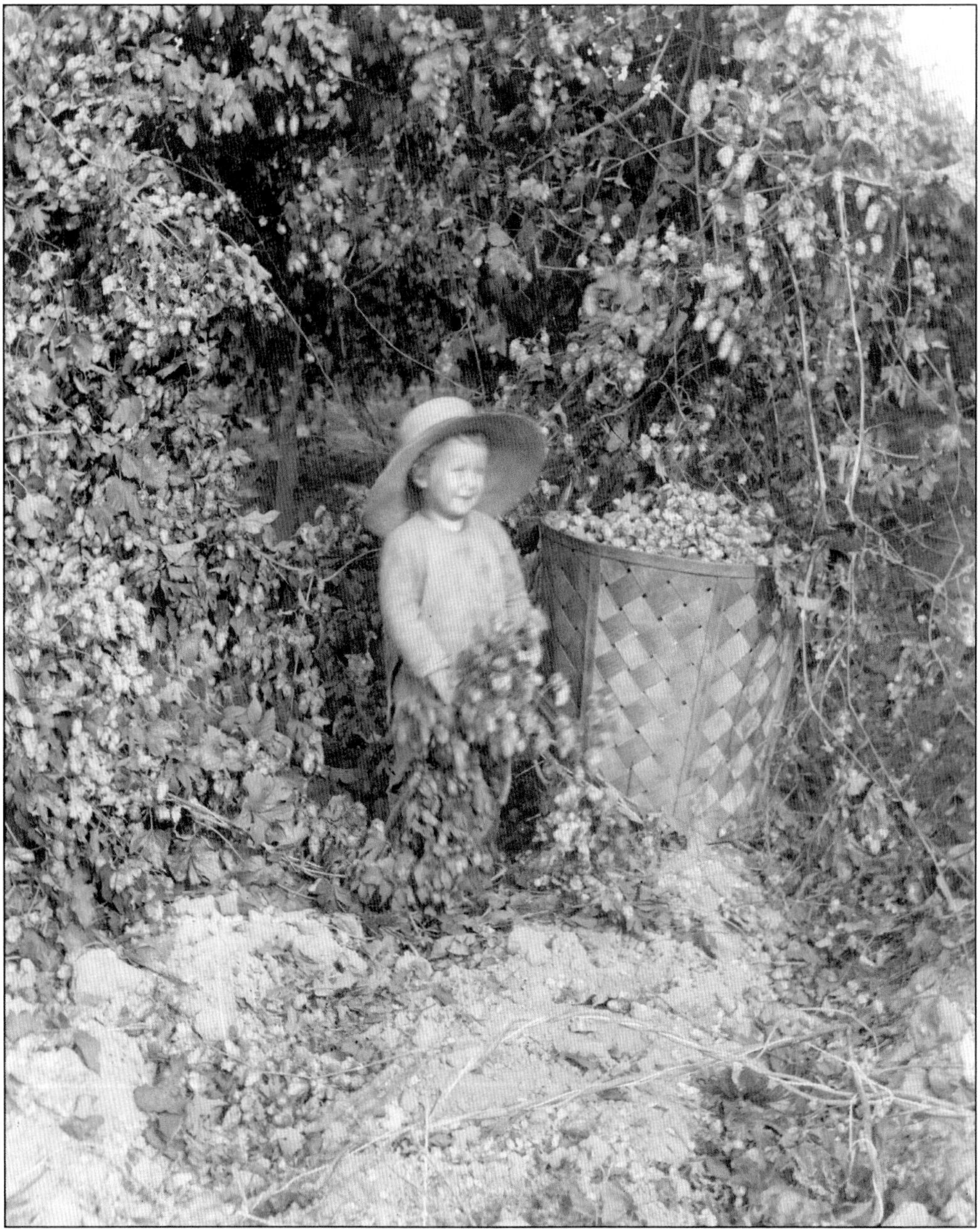

The practice of growing hops to flavor beers, as well as for other beverages and herbal medicine, has been ongoing since the Middle Ages. Hops have a long history of use as a sleep aid. They are used in medicine, they also can be made into a useful fiber, and they can be used as a food source. They were actively produced along America's east coast by English and Dutch farmers, but because of the harsh weather and mildew infestations, the markets became very dismal in the late 1700s. Once the Pacific Northwest began to grow, hop farms thrived with the favorable climate. The air was drier, and there was easy access to irrigation for these flowers. Hopyard picking was a family business. The hops were planted and picked without the use of machines. Filling a hop basket as quickly as possible was the goal of every picker through the busy fall season. Families often camped several weeks in the hopyards, many of which were in the Canby area.

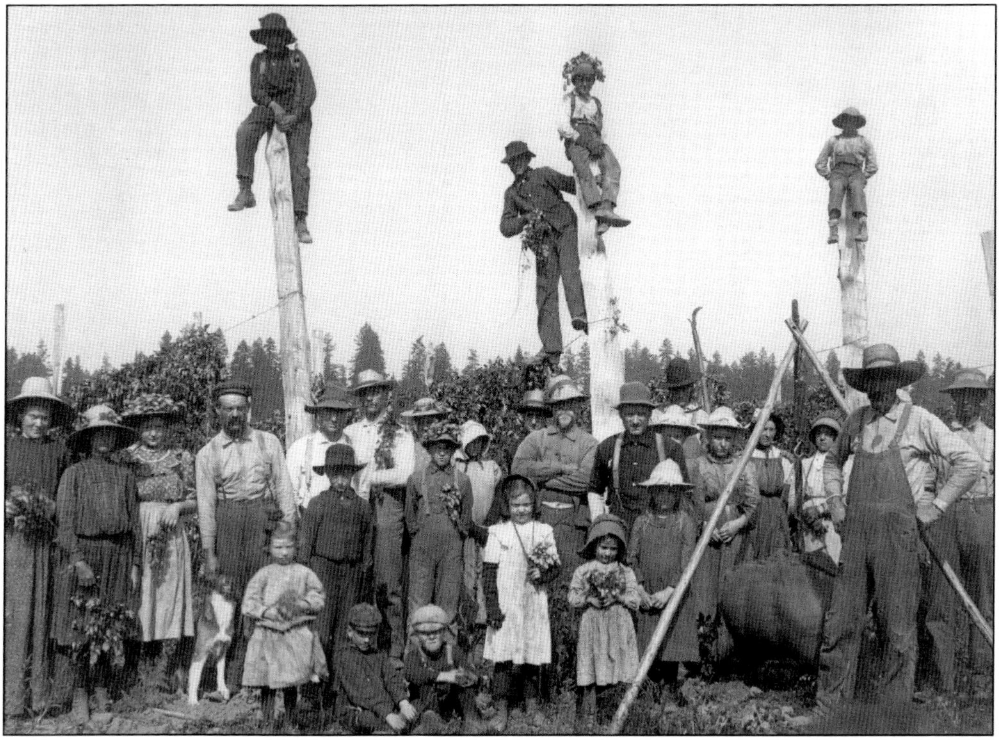

This 1907 image of the John Daley hopyard shows Daley standing with his arms folded. Many hopyards in the Willamette Valley brought in pickers from small towns, including Canby. With such fertile, sandy soils, hops were an easy harvest. Almost every farmer had his own dock along the river, which acted as shipping points for crops. There were 38 landings in the eight-mile stretch between Canby and Butteville.

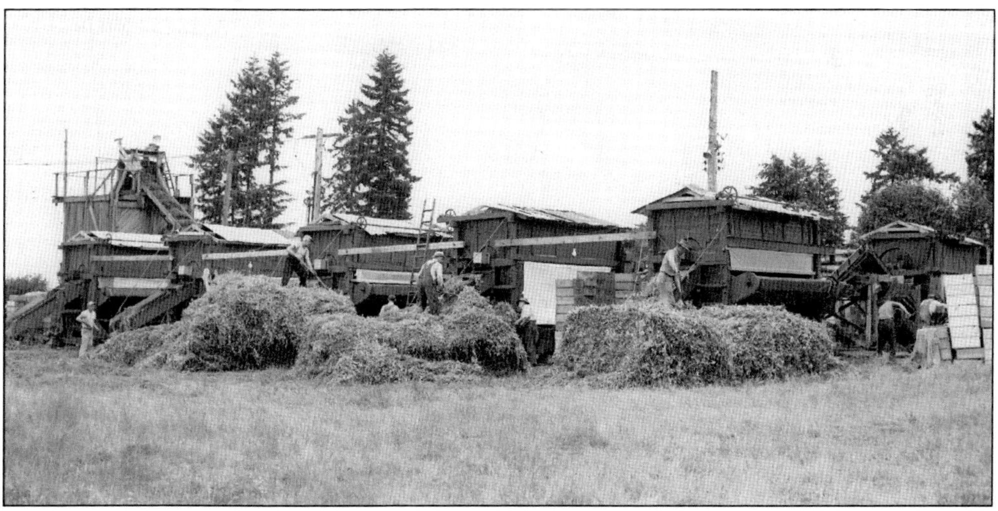

Green pea farms were plentiful in Canby from the late 1930s through the 1950s. These "pea viners" are loading peas to take to the "pea viner corner" of South Ivy Street and SE Thirteenth Avenue. The viners would then manually separate the peas from the vines. The work was performed until nightfall, as the season was short. The peas were then trucked to the town of Woodburn for processing and packing.

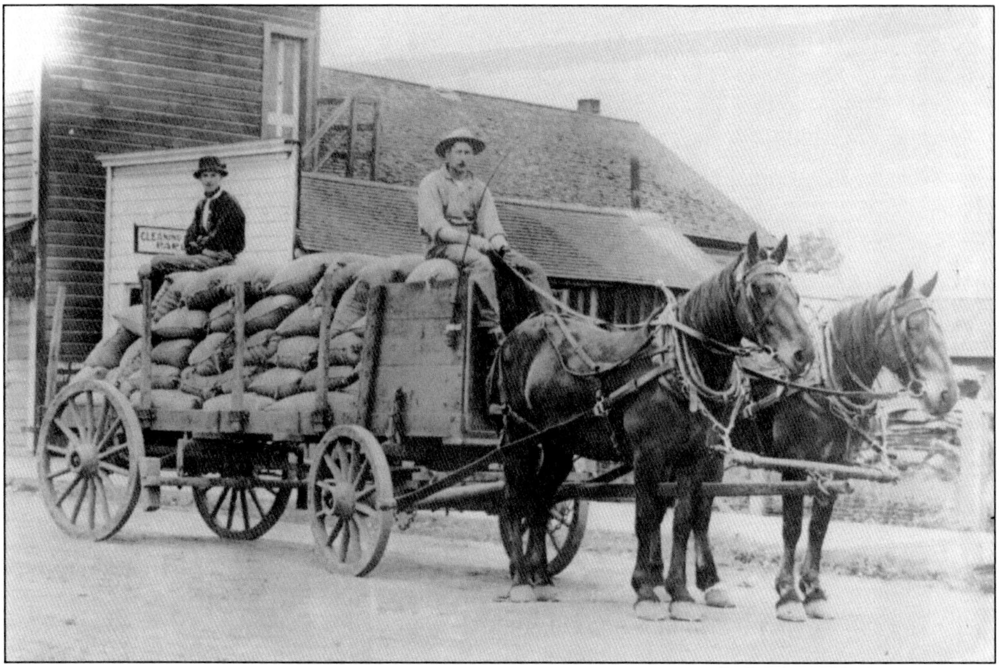

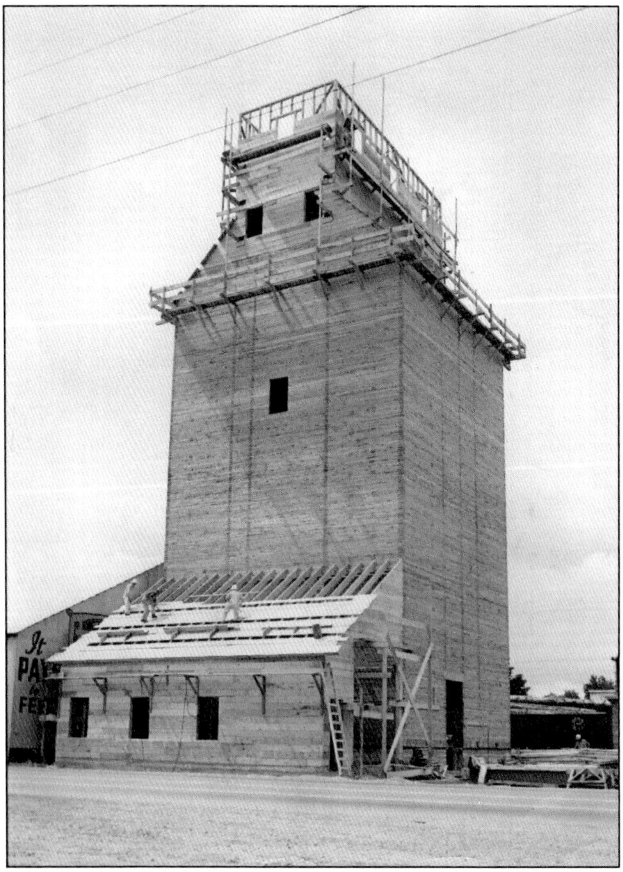

Grain was hauled to a gristmill or sent for shipping by rail. This kept teams and draymen busy for many years. Ensley W. Gribble (1889–1982) is the driver of this team, probably on Main Street around 1910. Ensley was the grandson of a family that helped settle this area. He had a livery stable and was a drayage business operator in 1913–1914 at NW Holly Street and First Avenue.

Grain elevators were essential to the growth of Canby. A grain elevator is monolith containing a bucket elevator or a pneumatic conveyor that scoops up grain from a lower level and dumps into a silo or other facility. In 1951, this Buchanan-Cellers grain elevator was under construction. It was located on the northwest corner of Grant Street and Highway 99E, where today sit many shops and a gas station.

Agriculturalists have worked the area around Canby since the first settlers arrived in the middle of the 19th century. Farms offered opportunities for countless types of employment. Growers realized the importance of their land and worked to create new ways to promote the area's farming industry to insure the community's sustainability in the future. Here is Carl Schaarschmidt, owner of the Canby Green Market, holding an overgrown squash in 1955.

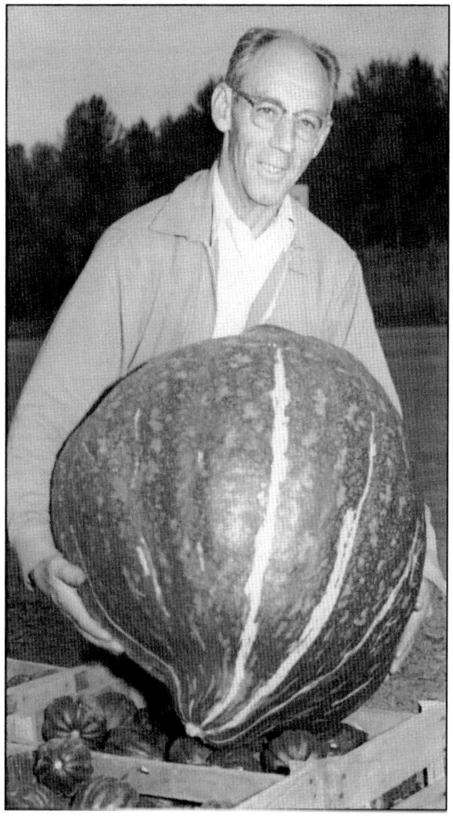

The combine harvester, also called a combine, is a machine that harvests grain crops. The name originates from its intermixing of three separate operations of gathering—reaping, winnowing, and threshing—into a single machine. It is used for many types of crops, such as wheat, rye, barley, corn, oats, soybeans, and flax.

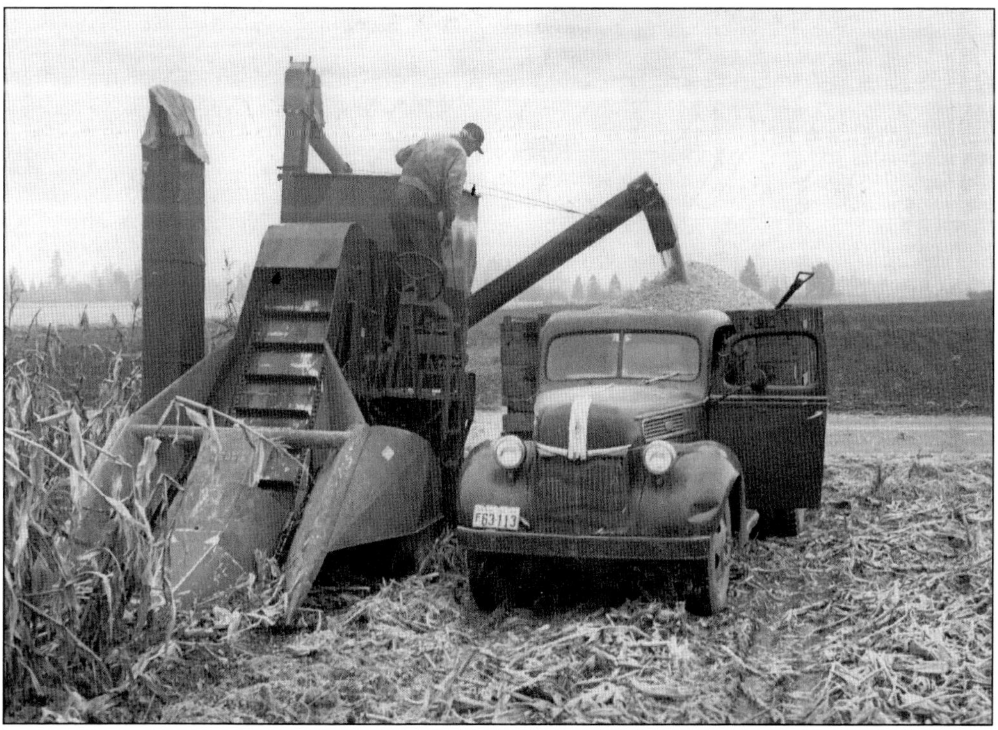

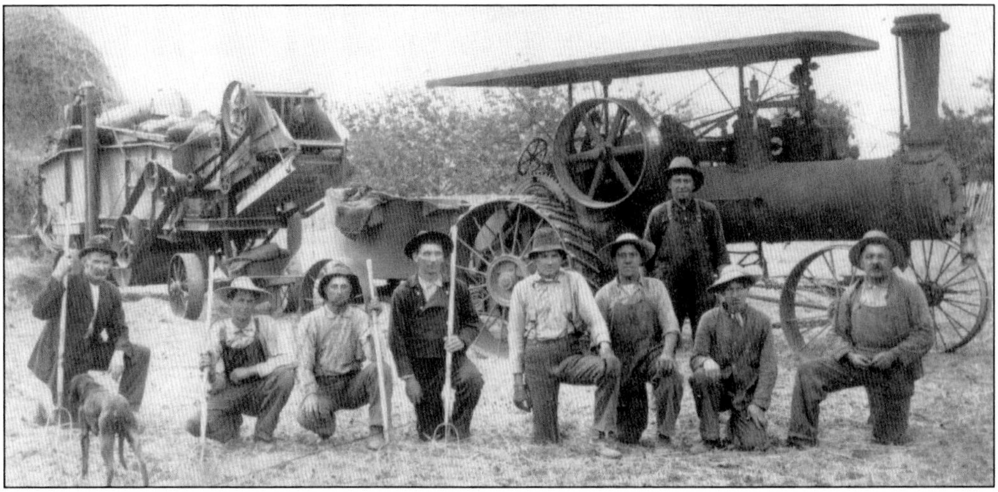

This is Charles Harnack's threshing crew at the Scramlin Farm in Macksburg in 1913. From left to right are George W. Scramlin, Ed Rupp, John Brusch, Leonard Wehner, Marshall Scramlin, Alfred Cents, Alfred Harnack, Charles Harnack Jr., and Charles Harnack Sr., owner of the 10 x 10 (-inch cylinder diameter and stroke) Case steam tractor and a 32 x 54 separator, or combine. Engineer Alfred Harnack is standing. George Washington Scramlin was a longtime storekeeper in Macksburg.

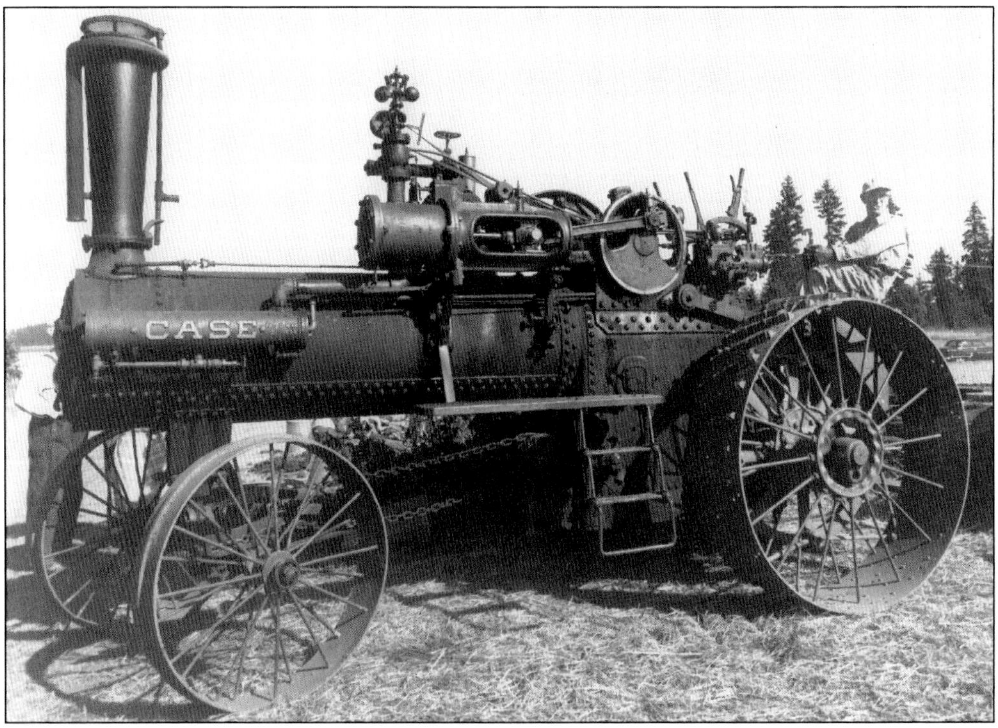

The Case tractor was used to aid in threshing. The operator of a threshing machine might travel from farm to farm threshing grain. Oats, wheat, and other grains were common items to be threshed. On a threshing day, all the neighbors would cooperate at that day's farmstead to complete a massive job in one day. Here is Ted Whitehead in 1956.

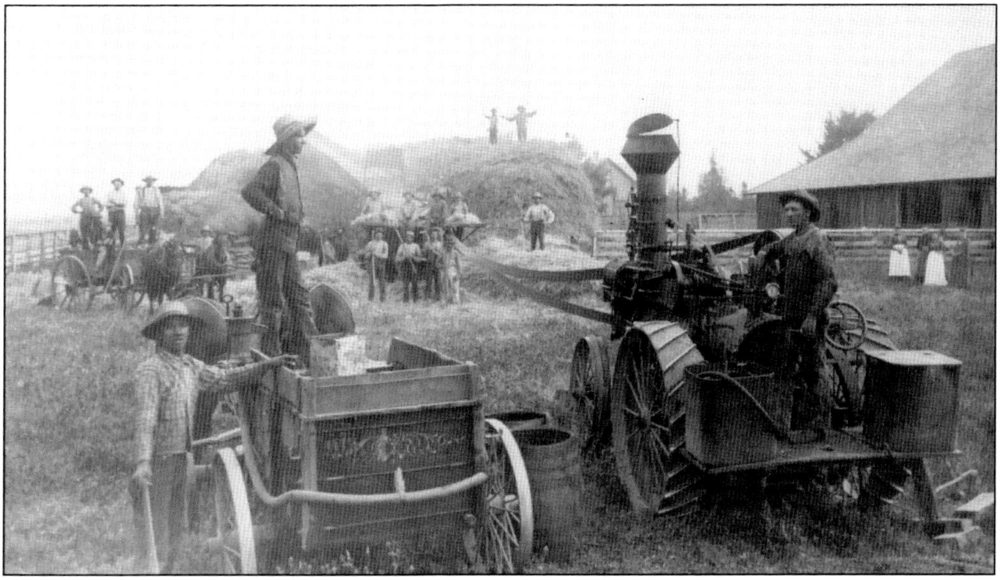

The men seen above are threshing the spring oats on Jim Smith's farm in Macksburg in 1897. They are using a 10-horse Russell engine and mostly likely a 36-inch Russell separator with a hand feed and swinging stacker, owned by John Barth. Harry (left corner), his son, is the footboard "popper," with oilcan on hand. Jim Smith (on the right) holds the reins on his grain wagon team. The helper with his arms on his belt is Ross Feyrer. The wagon sitting on the right side of the pitcher tanker was used for hauling water for the engine. The pitcher pump is there for filling the tank. This photograph shows at least 23 men on the farm's working crew. Below is Dave Sheppard hauling a water tank at the 1955 Steam Up Day at the Pitts farm. The photograph below was taken by Bill Wagner.

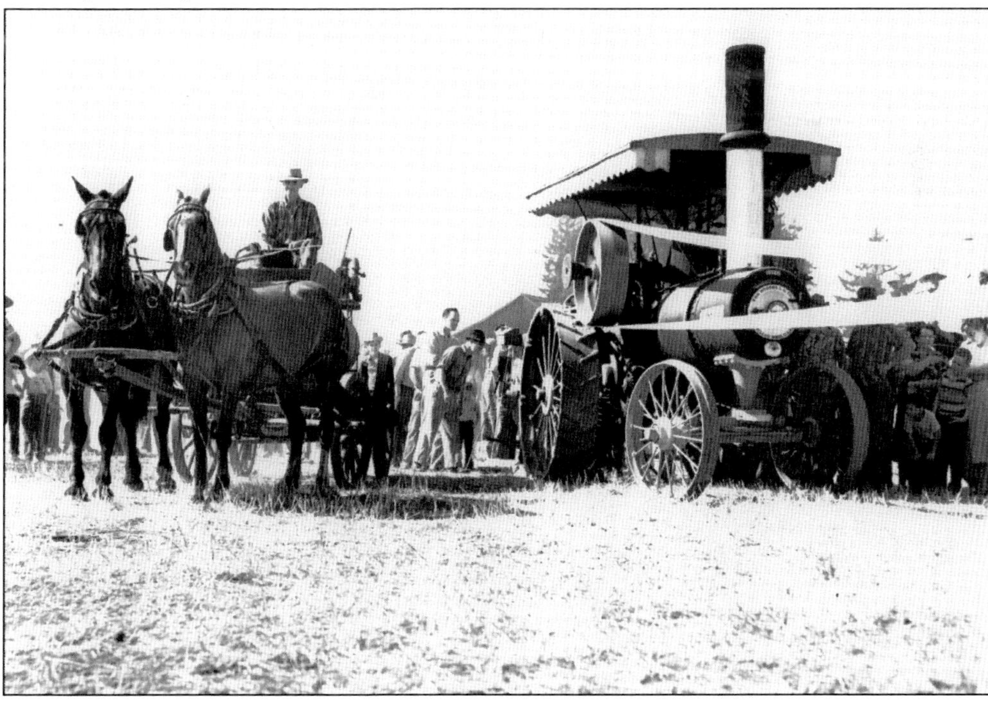

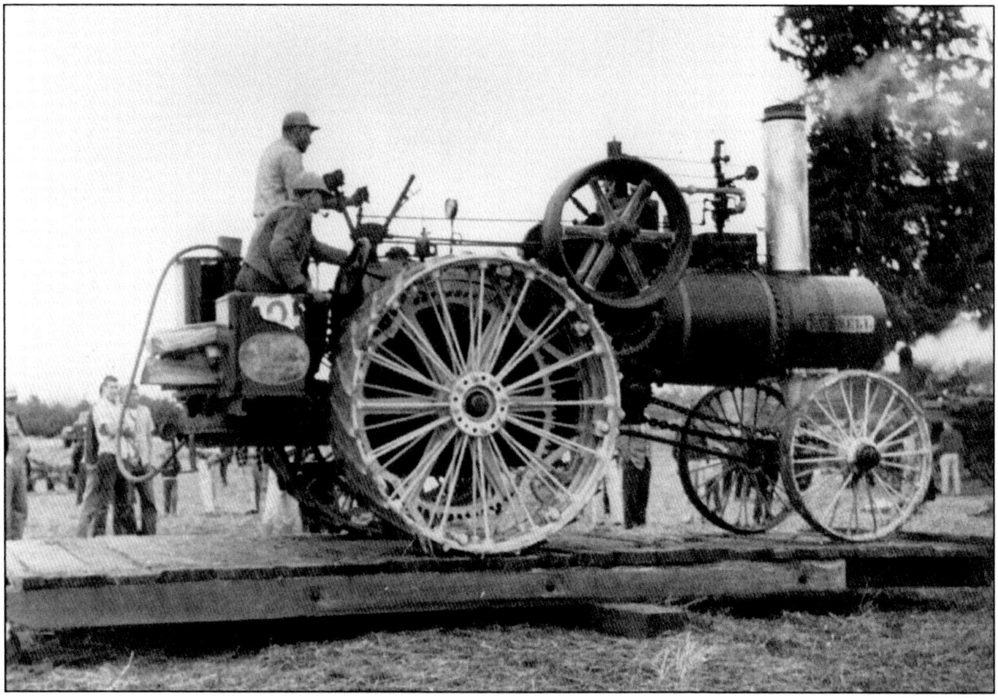

This Russell steam engine on the teeter-totter was built in 1916. Here, it is shown looking brand-new at the Fourth Steam Up Day in August 1959 at the Pitts farm in Canby. Rodney Pitts made Steam Up Day famous throughout the entire West and lured thousands of steam engine enthusiasts to his farm each year. Harvey Livesly is steering and the owner, Harvey Mikkelsen, is helping him.

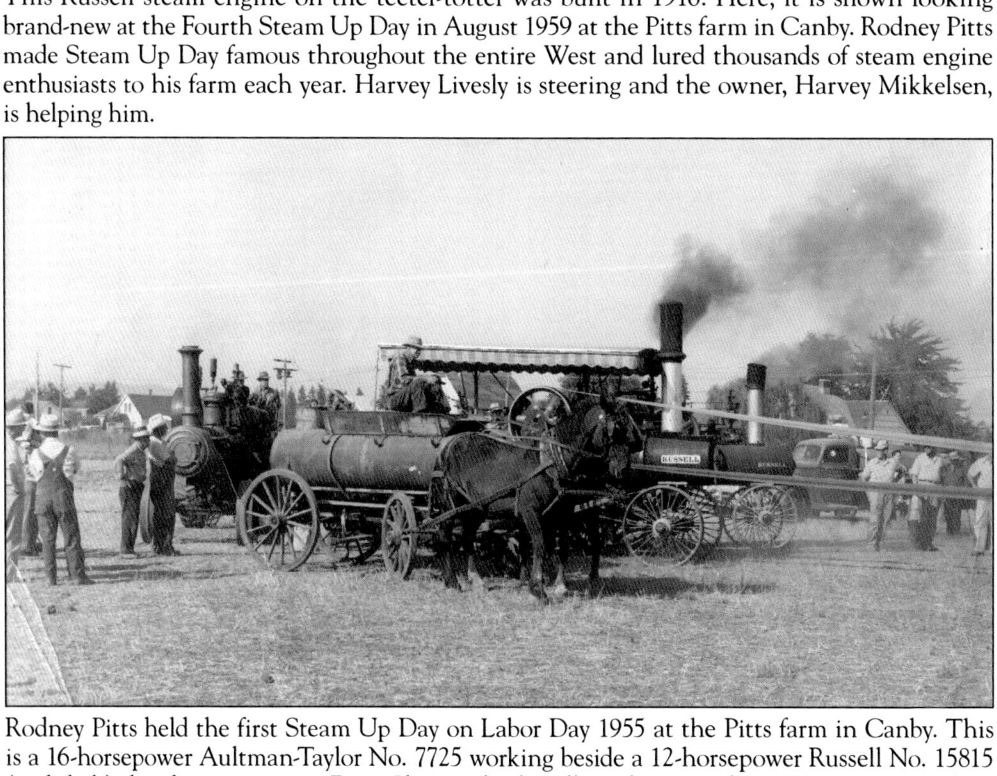

Rodney Pitts held the first Steam Up Day on Labor Day 1955 at the Pitts farm in Canby. This is a 16-horsepower Aultman-Taylor No. 7725 working beside a 12-horsepower Russell No. 15815 (with belt) threshing gray oats. Dave Sheppard is handling the team-drawn Case water tank in the foreground. The photograph was taken by Bill Wagner.

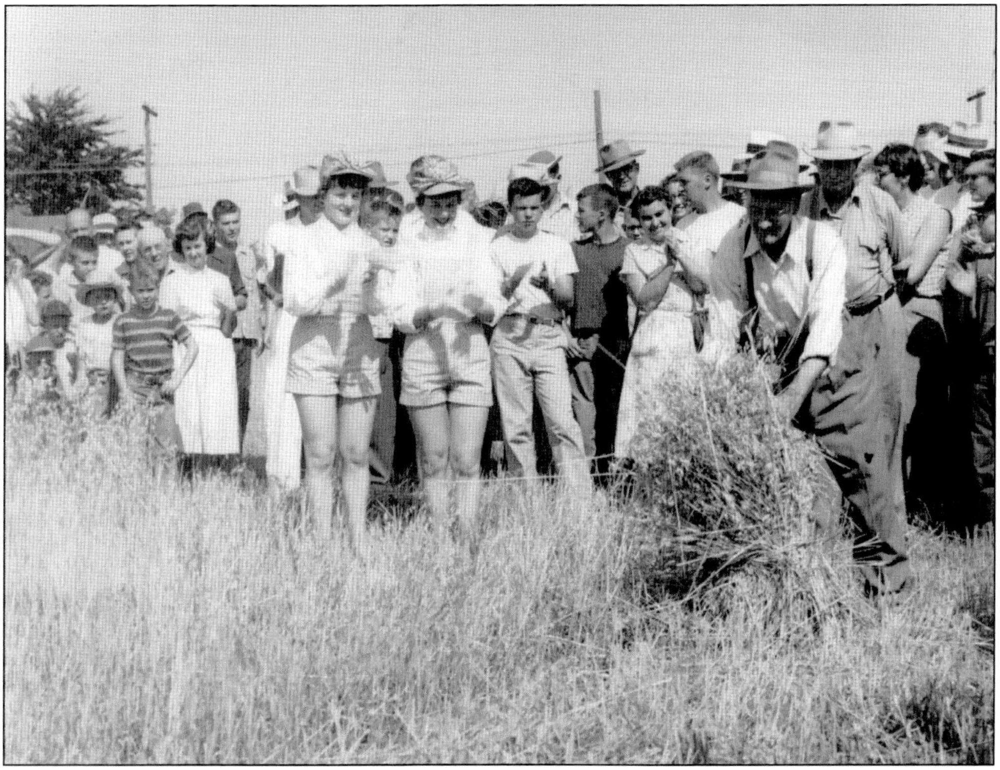

John Lowery holds out a bundle of oats after the cradle operation (harvesting is done chiefly by hand with a cradle) at Rodney Pitts's Steam Up Day in 1955. Two high school juniors, the Hulbert twins Rae (Hovland) and Kae (Edy), were cited as the honorary engineers for the day.

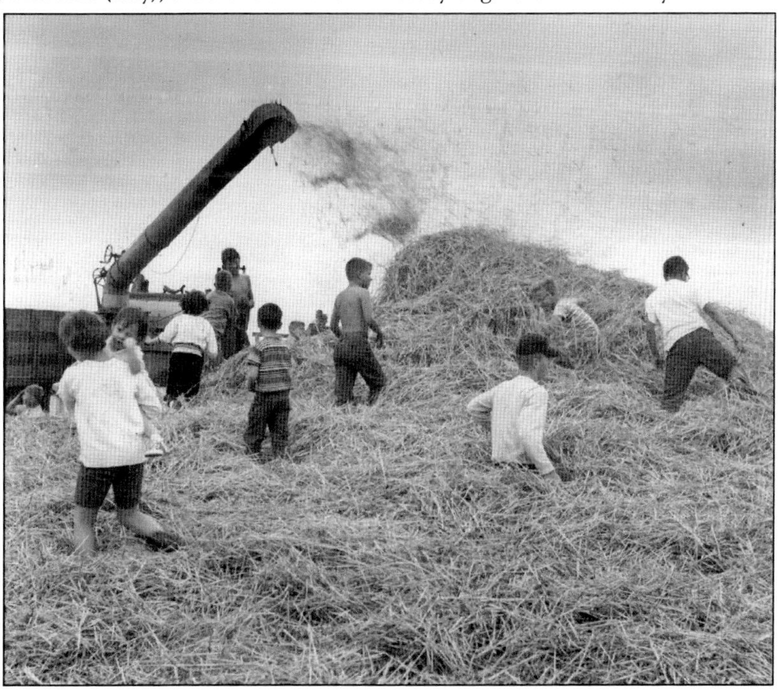

During the annual Steam Up Day, while parents are displaying their tractors and old farm machinery, children also have a fun day. It is a field day for youngsters, as they get to run, play, and interact with the farm gear. Here is a group of children digging and tossing the freshly piled hay from an old steam-powered thresher.

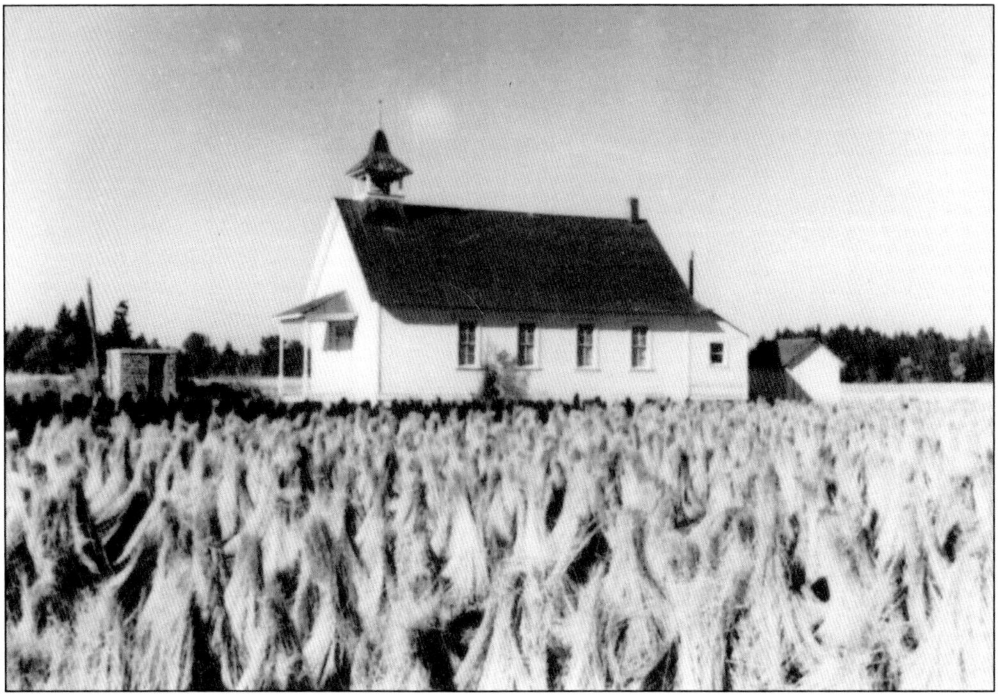

The fiber of flax, also called linseed, is used to make linen yarn for thread or fabrics. Oregon's weather is good for growing flax if the seed is planted early, as there is usually a lot of rain from March through early June. The dry weather in late June and July cures the flax to a golden yellow, creating a very strong fiber.

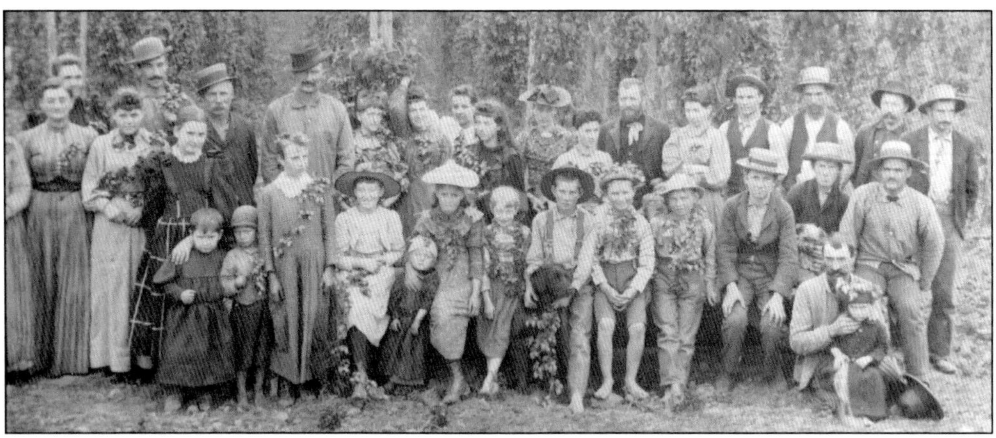

These hop pickers are wearing decorations after a long day of work. Before the days of farm machinery, hop picking was the only method of gathering the plants for harvest. It was a very labor-intensive process, needing a huge number of workers for each field. Entire families, including the children, would leave their homes and work endlessly until the task was finished.

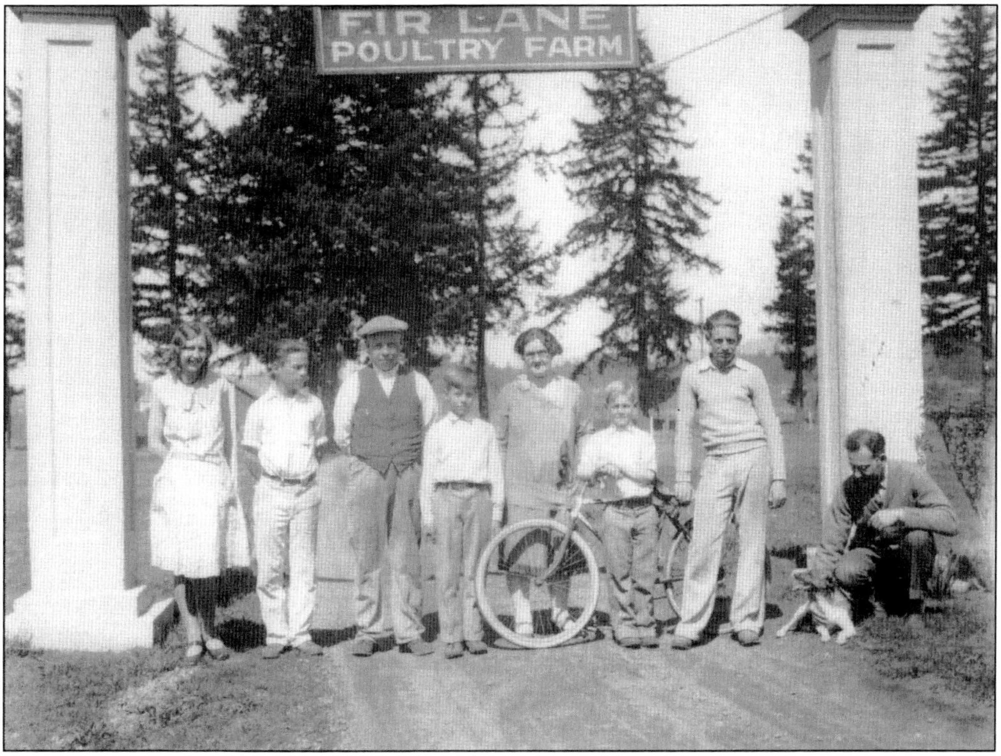

Wesley and Laura Thompson opened their business, the Fir Lane Poultry farm on NW Territorial Road, in the 1920s. They welcomed visitors from the Oregon State College to learn about farming. Fir Lane's two 40,000-egg incubators hatched 104,000 eggs in 1924. From left to right are Almeda, Kenneth, Wesley H., Allen, Laura, Donald, and Neal Thompson, their hired hand, William Eller, and the Thompsons' dog, Trixie.

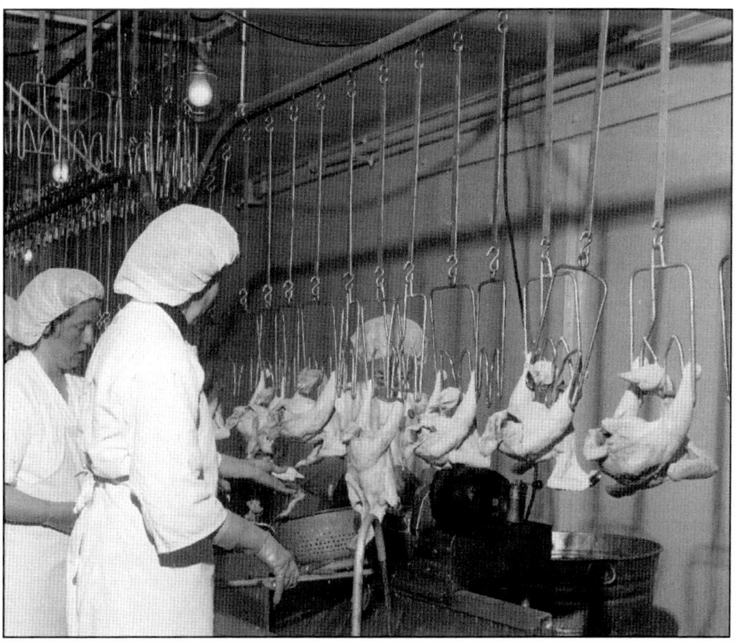

From farms to warehouse, processing turkeys was a profitable business. In 1928, plants opened in Roseburg, Salem, and Canby. Shown around 1940, these women are dressing birds for a market on SW First Avenue in Canby (Highway 99E) that dressed almost two million pounds of turkey through 1946. Oregon turkey growers supplied over a thousand pounds of meat to the public during World War II.

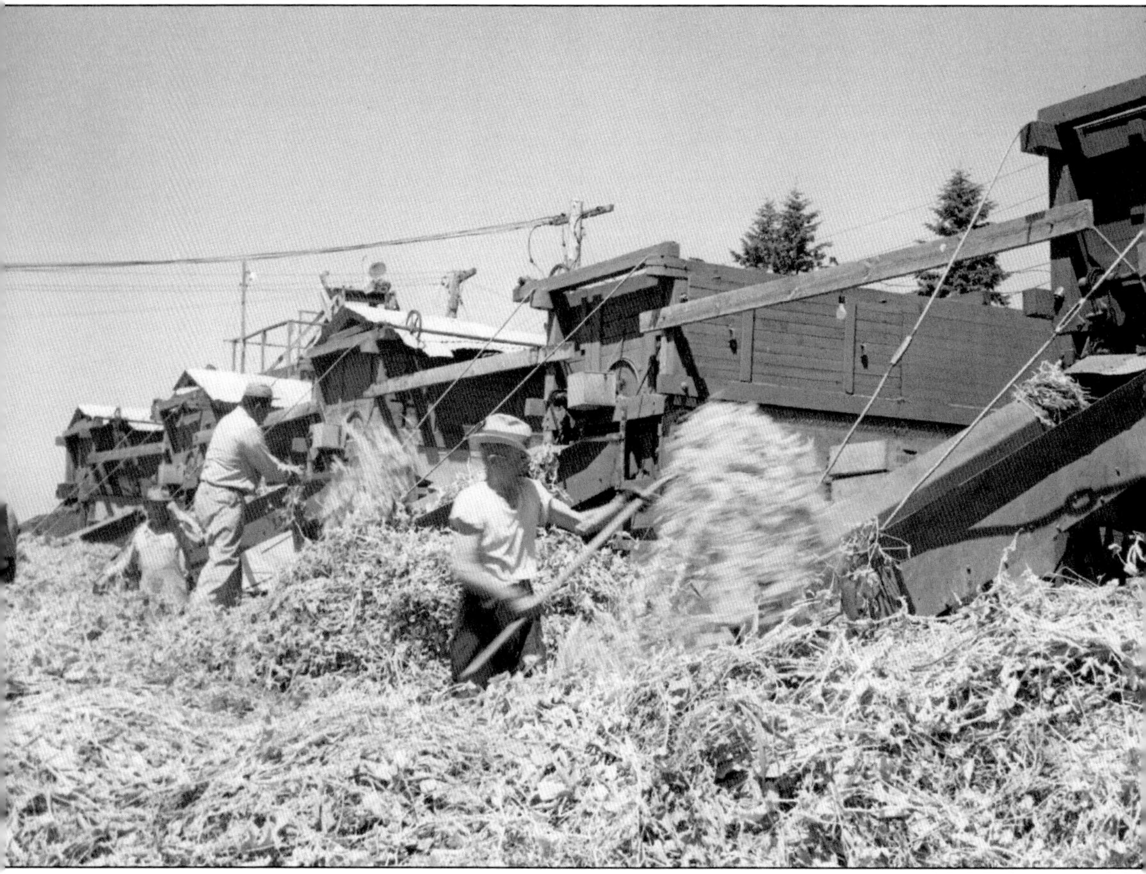

So much of the success of the Canby farmers relied on a good growing season for crops such as hay. When grazing was unavailable because of the rains or when the pastures were too dry from the summer sun, hay could be used as fodder for livestock. Hay was added to their feed during times when they were unable to access pasture or when they were kept in a stable or barn. The farmers had to grow it, bale it, rake it, and then market it near town. Hay not only kept the animals fed but was also used for bedding to keep them warm. It was used as a cover over the crops to protect them from weed overload. These men are baling hay at one of the largest farms in Canby.

Two

Canby
From Farms to the Road of a Thousand Wonders

Baker Prairie grew into the town of Canby. Once Canby joined in with the 15 other established cities in Oregon, the first problem its city council had to face was financial woes. Allotted only $100 to run the town on its first year, the mayor and recorder tried to keep all costs to a bare minimum.

By 1894, Canby had a jail, as well as taverns that paid $250 each for a six-month beer license. While the town paid $1 a month, keeping a police chief was difficult. In 1895, lighting new streetlamps and repairing the wooden sidewalks became part of the police chief's job, which also included a $3-a-month raise.

Large warehouses, such as the W.H. Bair and W.H. Lucke commission granaries, were built along the railroad tracks near the depot. The railroad carried the local companies' products to Oregon City. From the early settlers until the beginning of World War I, traveling to and from Canby was accomplished on worn-out dirt roads.

To reach Oregon City, one started on Main Street (now NW First Avenue), crossed over the railroad tracks at what is now Ivy Street, and proceeded up a steep rocky trail that led over many hills via South End Road. This trip took up to six hours with a loaded wagon. Canby had three hotels, and the Carlton & Rosenkrans department store opened in 1891; it would remain Canby's largest retailer for about 60 years. With the building of Highway 99E, also known as the Great Pacific Highway or the "Road of a Thousand Wonders," blasted through the basaltic rock along the Willamette River, travel became much easier. As more people came to settle in Canby, new companies and small family shops opened along its main streets.

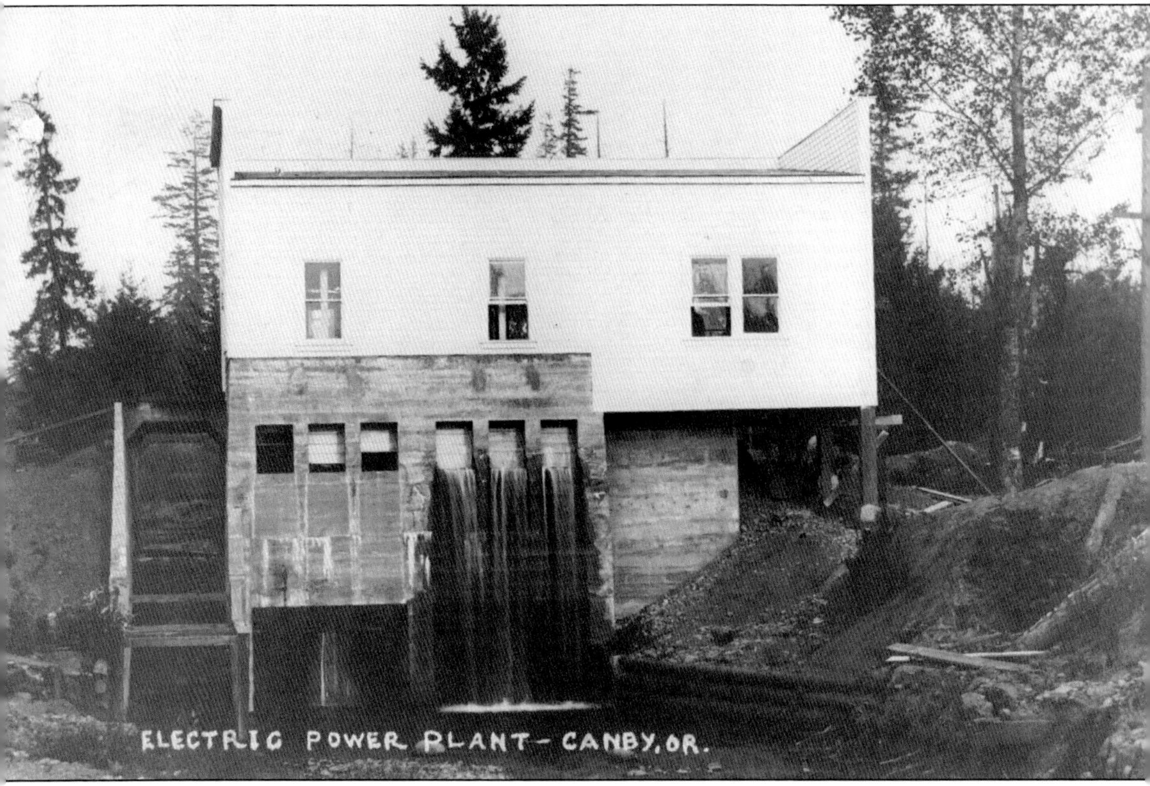

Electric power was active in Canby by 1902. Streetlamps lit by coal were used after 1894. Aurora Electric was the first supplier of power to Canby. William S. Hurst, who owned a warehouse in Aurora, built a flume from a pond made by damming Mill Creek. His power plant was driven with river water. A fire destroyed Hurst's business, so a steam plant was built. In 1903, this new plant supplied limited power to Canby. Around 1909, M.J. Lee, Canby-born grandson of Philander Lee, and others started the Canby Canal Company. A canal was dug to transport water from the Molalla River to a point below Good's Bridge to a power plant the company was building on the L.D. Cross Donation Land Claim, the former Joseph Knight sawmill site. A waterwheel produced electricity, but the output was small. The plant could meet only a small part of Canby's needs. It did not stay in business very long. Aurora Electric continued to be the chief supplier. This is the downstream face of the first power source.

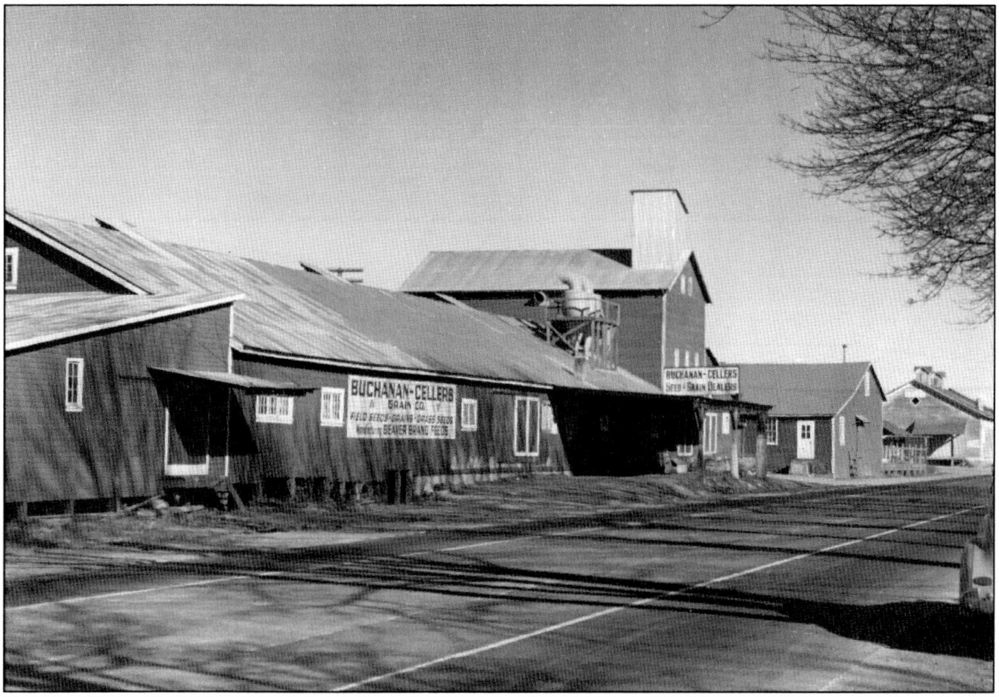

Highway 99E, also known as the Great Pacific Highway or the Road of a Thousand Wonders, was literally carved through the basaltic rock adjacent to the Willamette River. Similar to when the train had connected Canby to other communities, the opening of this new highway brought people into Canby, and they brought new and established industries. Buchanan-Cellers, a grain and feed company, built a shop along the railroad and the new thoroughfare.

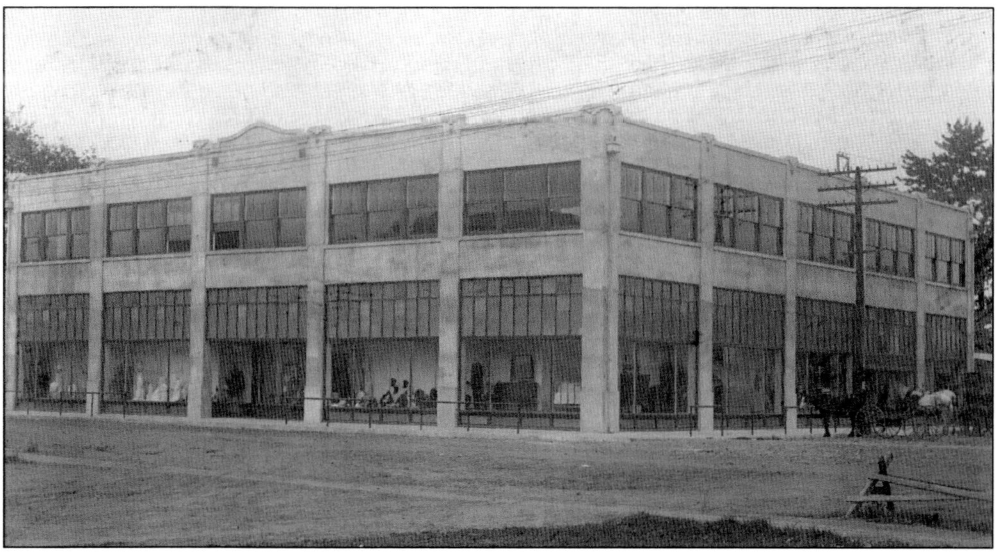

For several years, the Carlton & Rosenkrans Company was the biggest department store in Clackamas County. It opened in 1912 and sat on North Grant Street and Second Avenue. Hitching racks surrounded the exterior walls for customers' convenience. The C&R stocked everything from dry goods to groceries, livestock feed, fuel, building supplies, shoes, and much more. The building was destroyed by a fire in 1974.

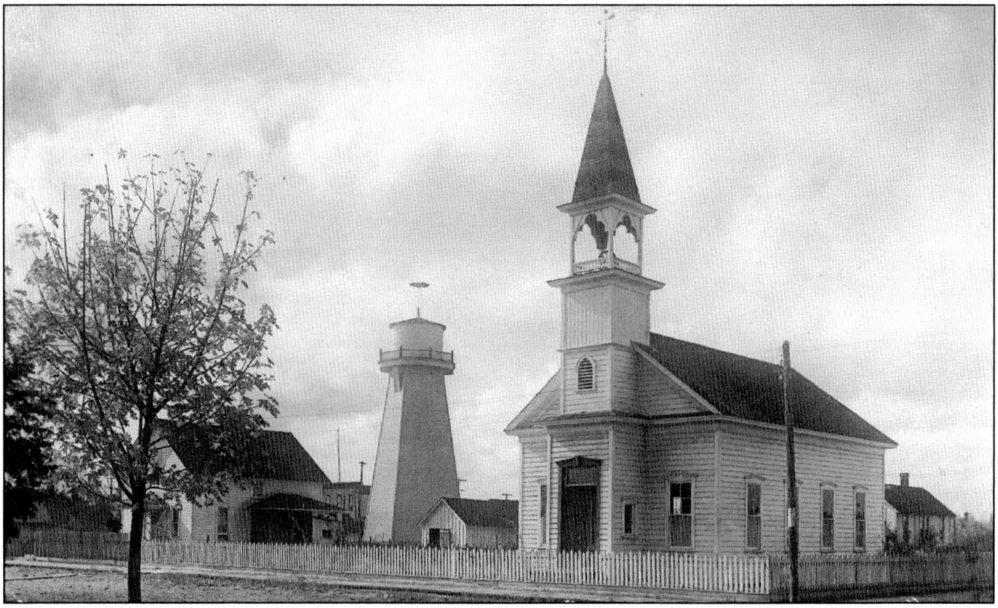

The Barlow Lutheran Church was built along the Road of a Thousand Wonders. This photograph was taken some time in 1910–1911. The church faces Maple Street and is still active. It has gone through many denominations and has been altered. The steeple was removed during the mid-1940s. The water tower is gone, but the parsonage still sits next to this church, which is now owned by the Barlow Community Church.

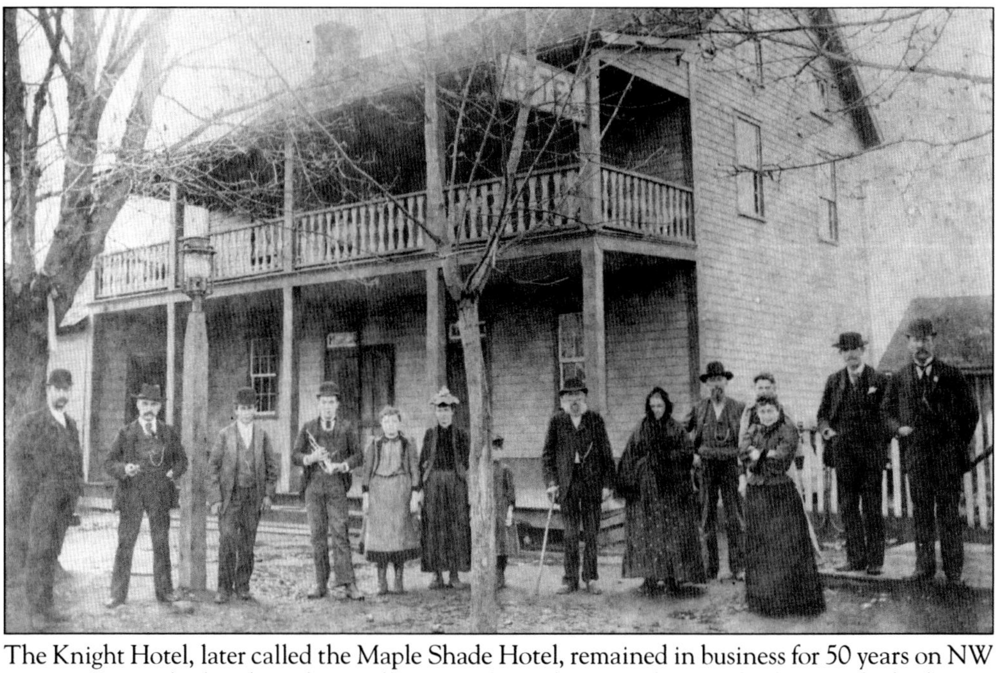

The Knight Hotel, later called the Maple Shade Hotel, remained in business for 50 years on NW First Avenue. The hotel sat diagonally across from the train depot. Charles Knight built it in 1871. Knight was an eager builder. He had already opened the first drugstore in town with his wife, Katie. Note the kerosene lamp on the left of NW First Avenue. It kept the street lit before electricity was active here.

Men were needed from Canby to work on the Willamette River log dump before and after World War II. This 1950 photograph shows Gerald Wires (in front) and Otto Hansen moving dumped logs onto rafts to take them downriver. Trucks brought small loads of logs from the Cascade forests over a road built in 1944. Crown Zellerbach ran the boom on the northeast edge of Canby through 1985.

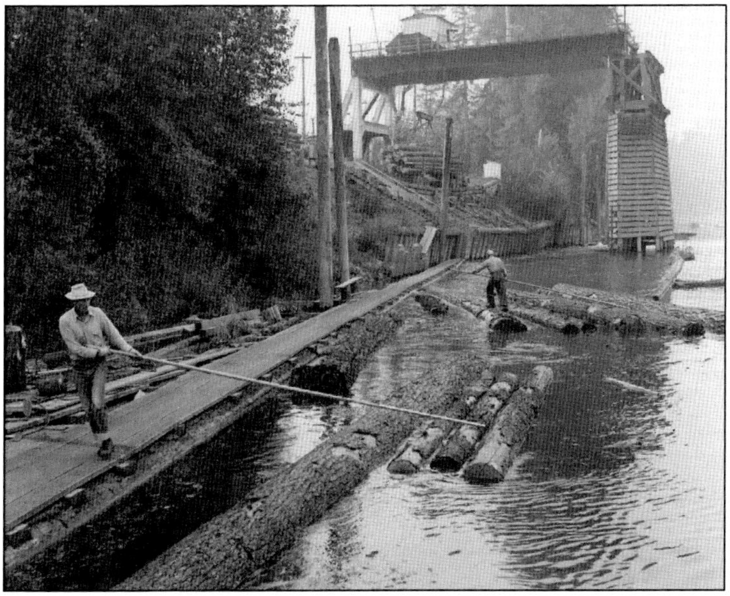

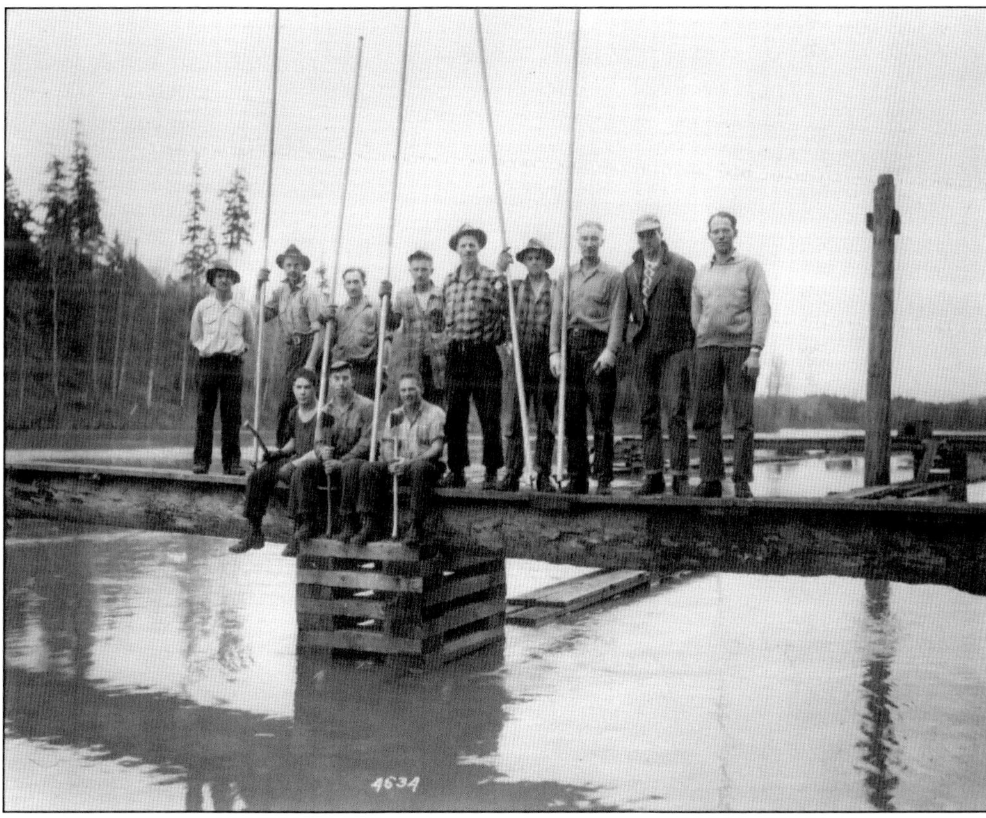

Men worked on rafters at the Canby log dump from 1946 until 1985. Cascade Mountain logs were transferred to Canby and unloaded into the Willamette River for hauling. The rafters in this 1950 photograph at the Canby log dump are waiting for the next load of logs.

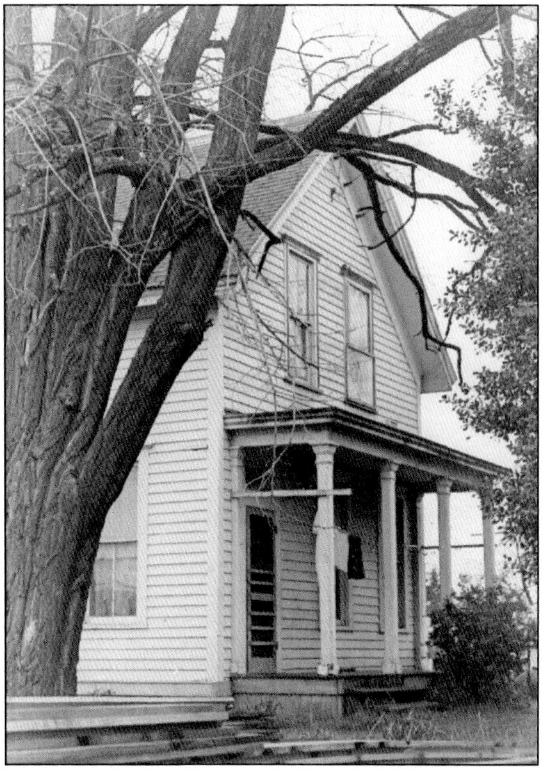

The Ben Holladay house was built in March 1870, the same year General Canby came to Oregon. It was set on Canby Builders Supply Company's land. The simple frame structure on NE First Avenue, just east of North Ivy Street, was demolished in the 1970s. Ben Holladay was a stagecoach and overland freight wagon operator between St. Joseph, Missouri, and Oregon and California. Holladay owned and ran the Pony Express and ox-wagon freight lines, controlling the St. Louis–to–Sacramento stage line, along with many more. He was quite the entrepreneur, investing $1 million towards the Oregon Central Railroad. He later worked at the Oregon & California Railroad (O&C) and built a rail line through Canby. He was president of the O&C from 1870 to 1881. Holladay also organized the Portland Street Railway Company by 1871.

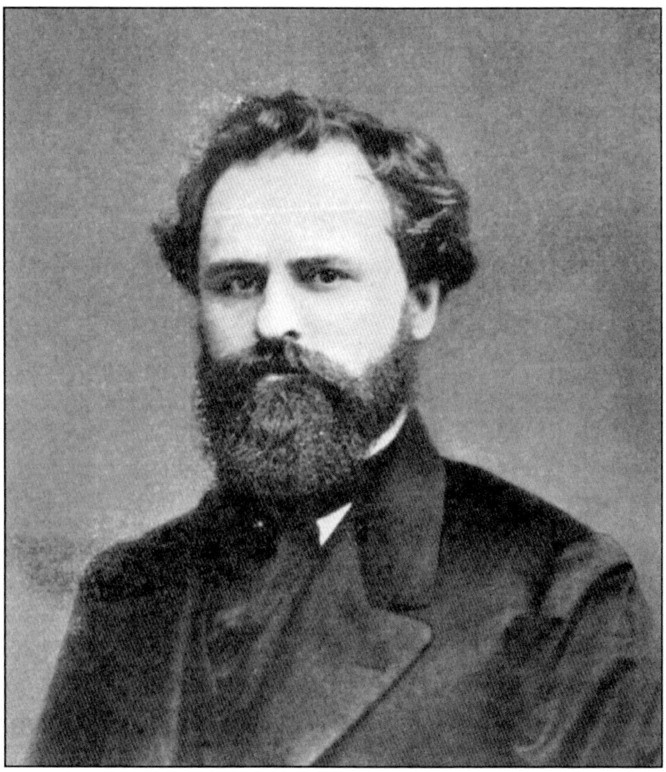

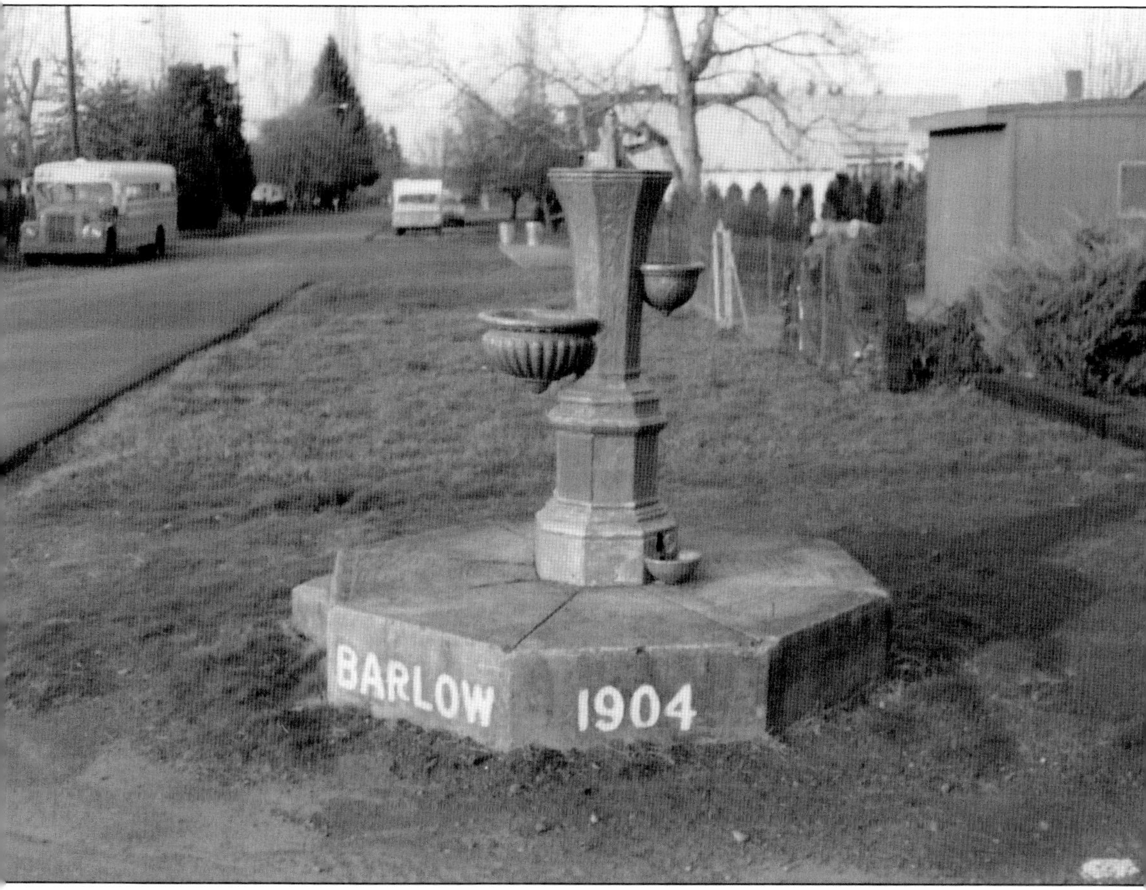

In 1845, the Barlow family came to Oregon along with Joel Palmer. The route that they trekked across heading towards Oregon later became known as the famous Barlow Road, built by Samuel Barlow. This roadway is considered the last section of the Oregon Trail. Samuel bought a donation land claim from Thomas McKay in 1850 and later sold the land to his son, William Barlow. As time moved on, this area became the town of Barlow. On February 7, 1871, the Town of Barlow opened a post office; it closed on January 3, 1975. In 1870, the railroad was built through Barlow. It became the main stop in this area until Canby expanded its farmlands. As Canby's economy grew, the train stop changed over to accommodate Canby's exported crops and cattle along the Southern Pacific Railroad route. To honor this industrious family, the Barlow Fountain was built. Mary Barlow, the daughter of Samuel and sister of William, who built the Barlow House on Highway 99E, dedicated the fountain in 1904. This photograph was taken by Diane Anderson.

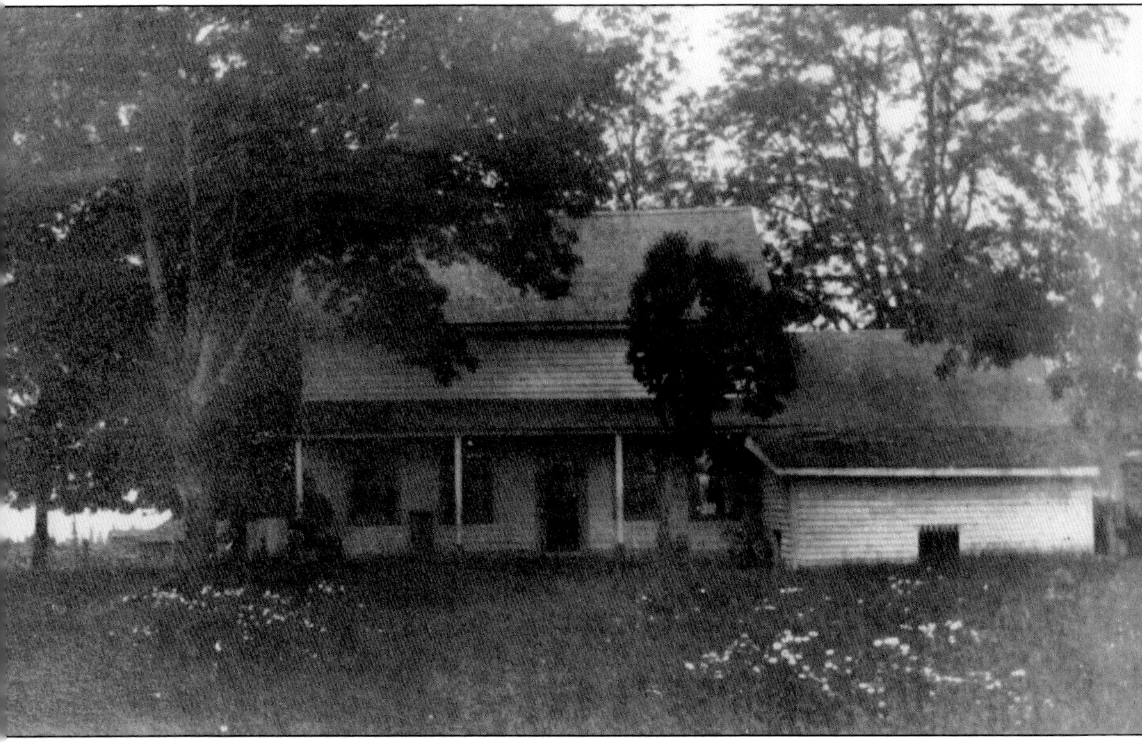

This is the home of George and Ora Melvina Lee Cattley, pictured in 1911. It sat in a filbert (hazelnut) orchard between the Clackamas County fairgrounds and the Southern Pacific Railroad right-of-way. It was the third house built on this land. When Mrs. Cattley's grandfather, Philander Lee, and his family arrived here in 1849, they built and lived in a log cabin. Philander had this home built on his donation land claim in 1868. Railroad carpenters who were laying rail lines through the Baker Prairie built it. Another home was built here and then moved to NE Third Avenue. Philander lived in this home until his death at the age of 84 in 1887. Here, Mrs. Cattley, who was a Canby librarian, stands on the lawn in front of her home.

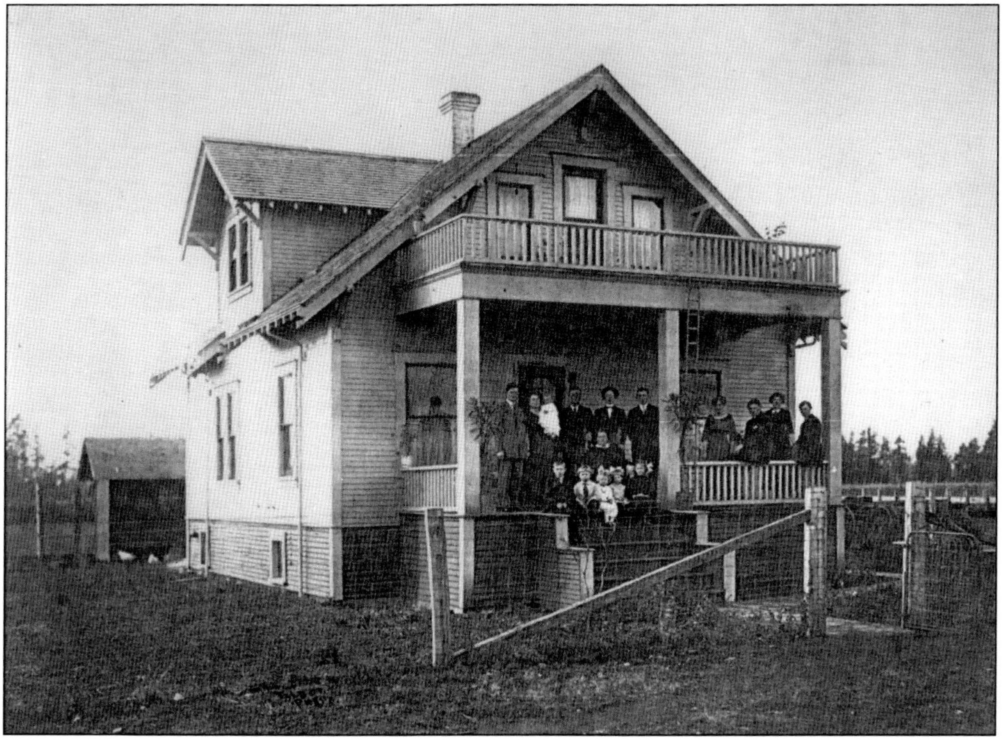

The wood-frame C.D. Sannes house was built on NE Third Avenue east of Holly Street in Canby. It was later moved to NW Fourth Avenue. The Sannes family came to Canby in 1901. Their son, Oscar L. Sannes, was born in Canby. He worked for G.W. White Motor Company.

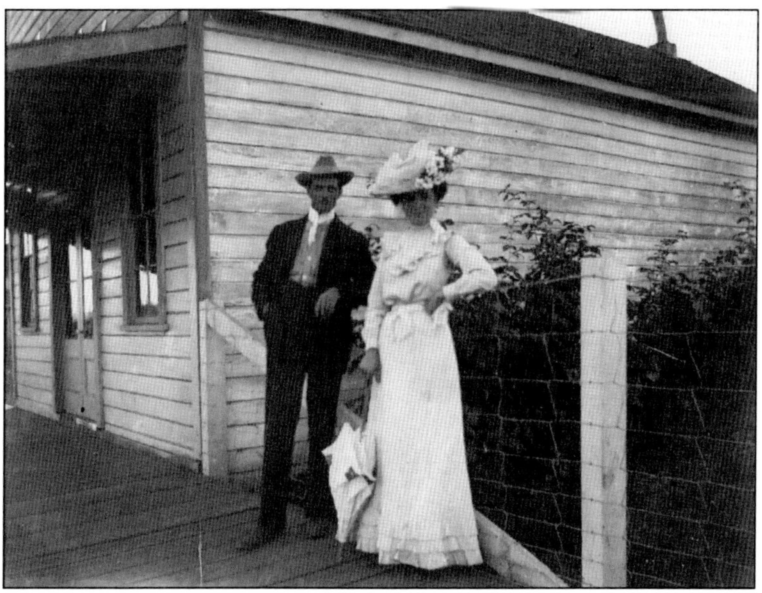

Just before their wedding on March 3, 1905, Lawrence Bair and Mabel Knight stop and pose for a photograph on the boardwalk. After their marriage, the couple had one son, Gerald Bair. Sadly, Lawrence died on May 1, 1913. Mabel remarried to Johannes "John" Eid. They stayed in Canby.

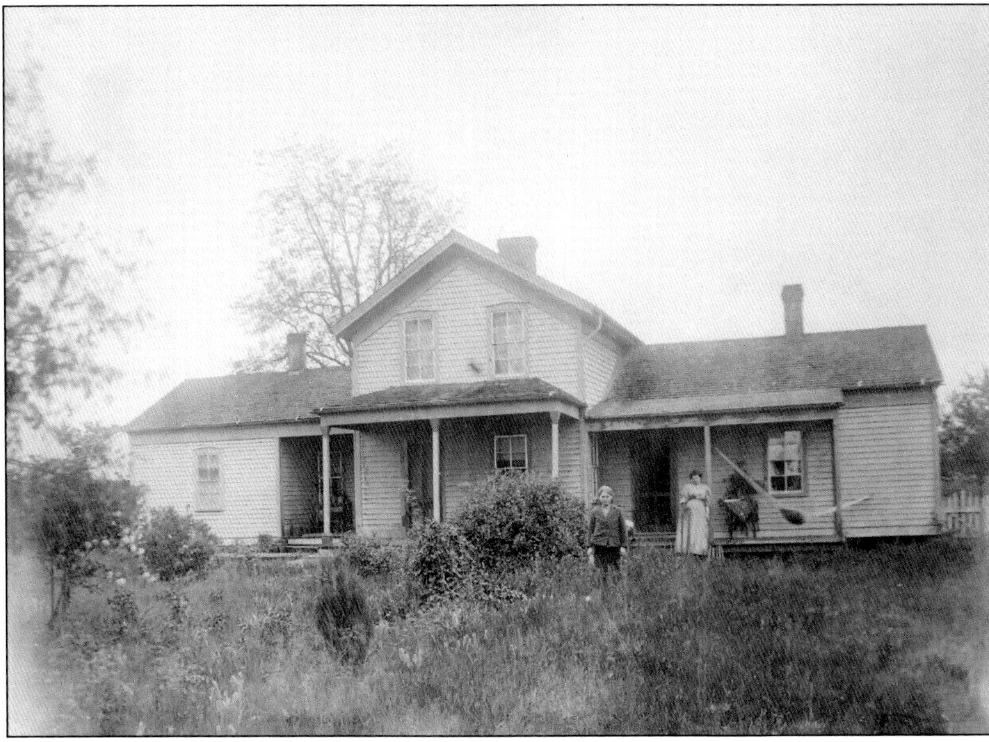

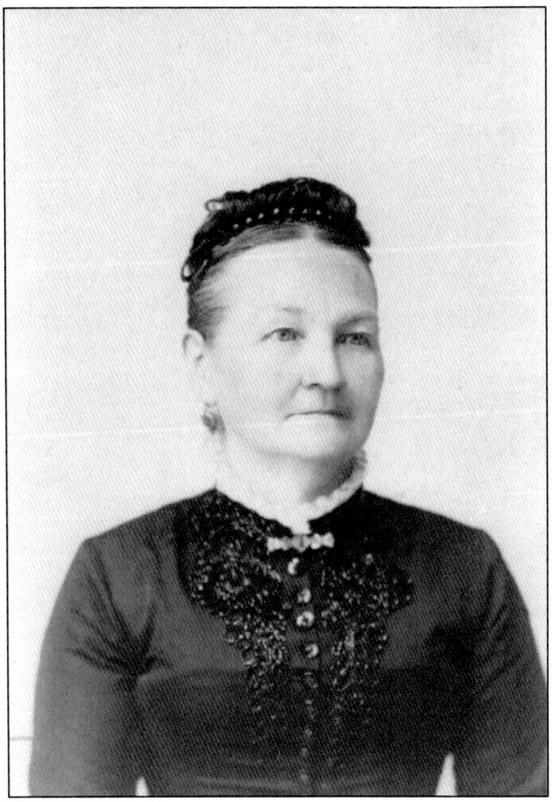

Built in 1879, the W.O. Mack home was located on South Ivy Street at the corner of SW Second Avenue. The Mack family had lived in Macksburg, a community named for them, up until 1897. O.R. "Rosco" Mack was the son of William O. and Louisa. This photograph was taken around 1904; a section of this original house still stands across the street on SW Second Avenue.

Estelle Mack Moshberger is pictured around 1904. Estelle was the wife of Charles Moshberger. She was also Darel Mack's great-grandmother. Her husband, Charles, worked in setting up telephone lines around the Canby area. The year 1908 was a very profitable one for him. A new one and a half miles of telephone line was ordered for Charles to install in the following year.

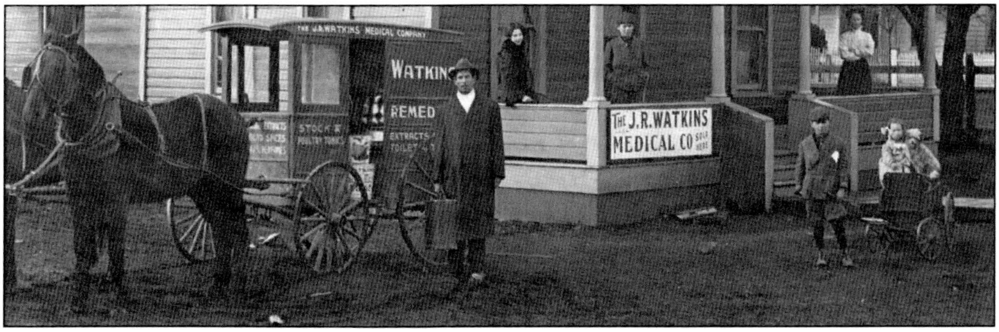

Joseph Ray Watkins created his own medical service in his home at Plainview, Minnesota. It was soon called the J.R. Watkins Medical Company. The business spiraled all around America and soon came to Canby. J.R. Watkins specialized in home remedies using extracts such as camphor (from the Asian evergreen tree), capsicum (from red peppers), oil of spruce, and other herbs and plant derivatives.

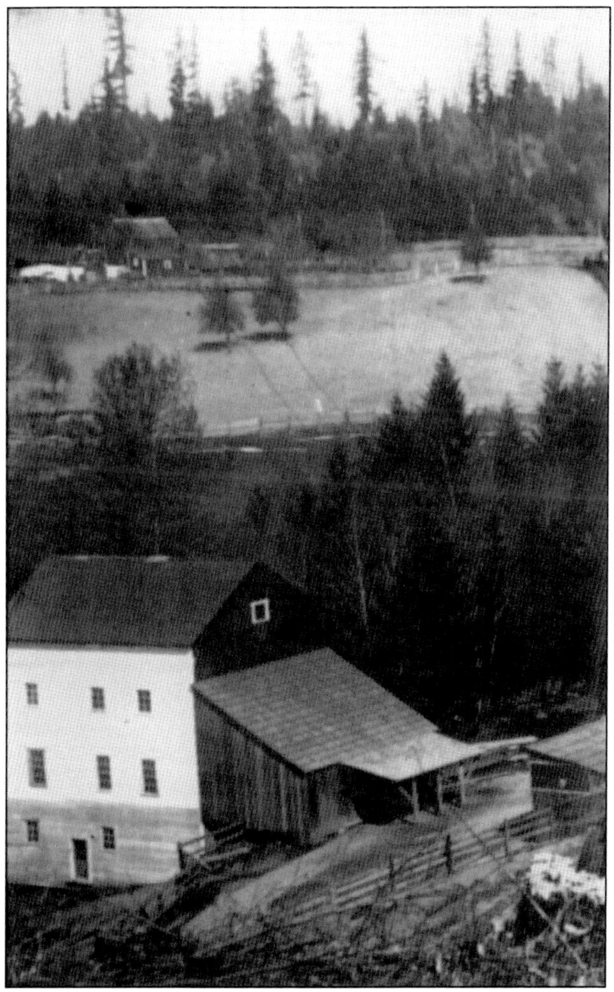

The New Era flour mill was established around 1890 on Parrott Creek. Vaclav Wesley Sevcik and his brother, Joseph, were the proprietors from 1891 until 1919. The men were both born in Bohemia and came to America with their parents. At the mill, they produced flour, and they later improved their mill by installing a wheat and vetch separator. They went on to add livestock and feed to their business.

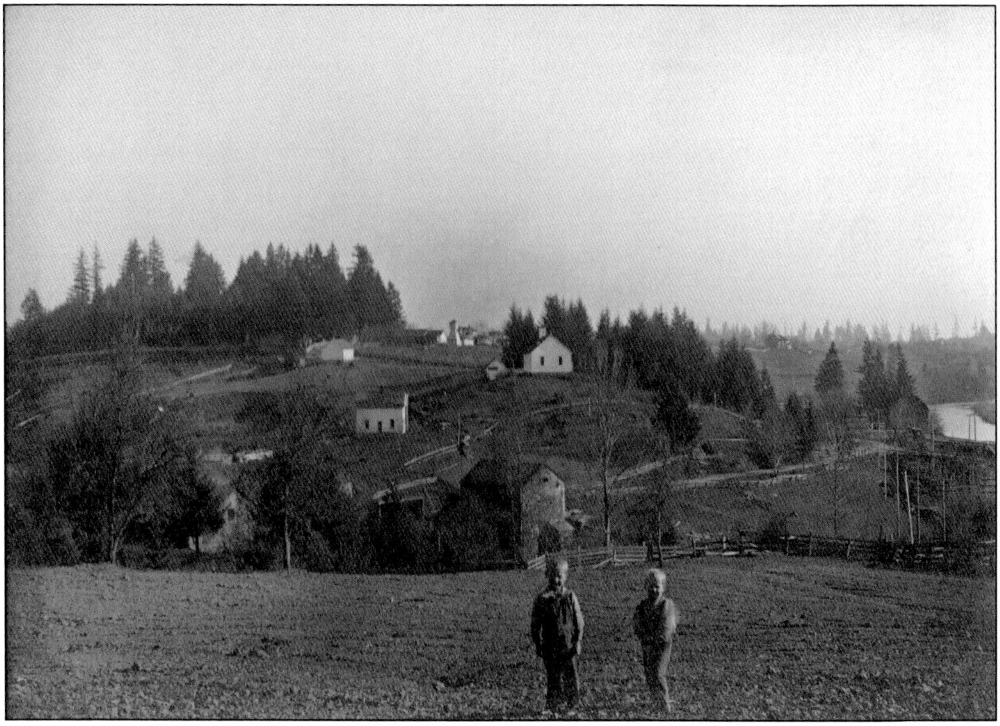

Here is the gristmill next to a pond where two boys are looking at the photographer, Elmer Veteto, around 1890. Behind the mill is the Sevcik family's home, next to the schoolhouse. The Woman's Christian Temperance Union/Grange Hall sits on the left slope. On top of the hill, with a tower and unique gate, is the home of Herman Anthony Sr., built between 1890 and 1891. This home is still a living space today.

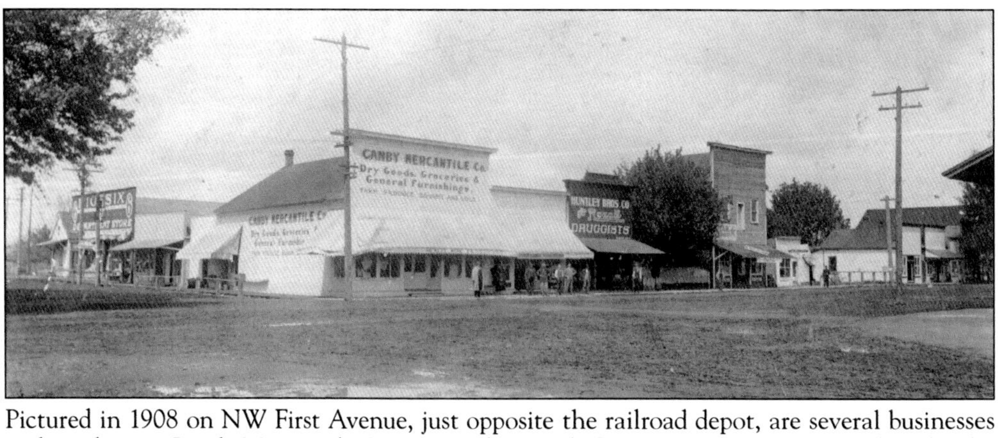

Pictured in 1908 on NW First Avenue, just opposite the railroad depot, are several businesses and one house. Candy Mercantile Co. sits on the North Grant Street corner. Next door (to the right) is a business with "Western Union" on its awning, then the Huntley Brothers Company, Druggists. The cherry tree stands in front of the George Knight home, built before 1870. There is also an ice-cream parlor, a jewelry store, and other trades.

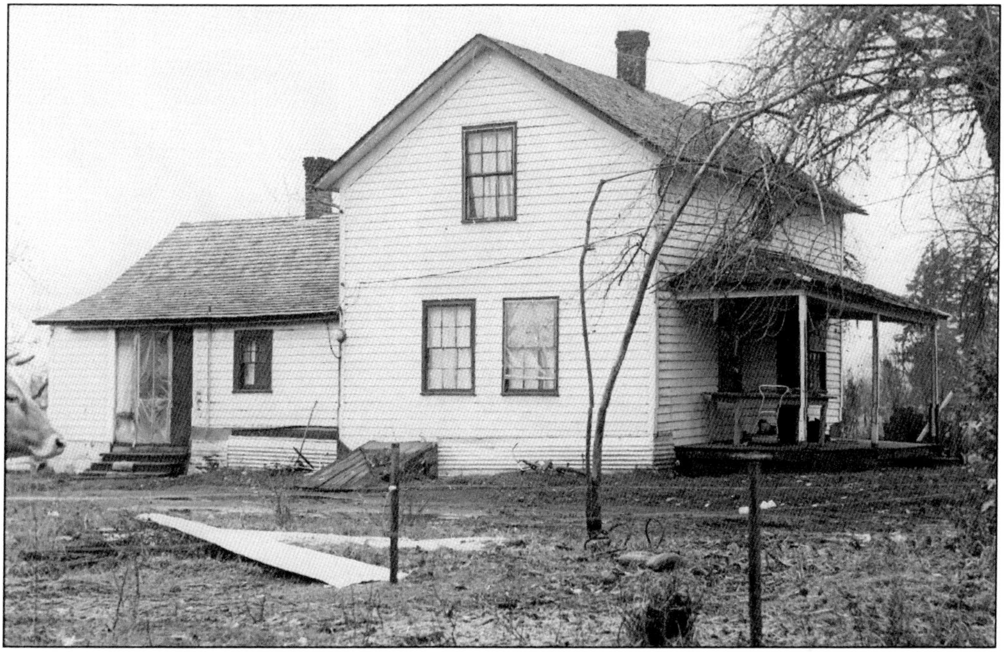

A blacksmith, Adam Knight (1832–1882), and his wife, Anna Burkholder Knight, built the house seen above around 1860. It sat above the Molalla River and overlooked an 1877 covered bridge that was constructed to replace the Joselyn Bridge, which crossed the Molalla River near Canby. The newer bridge was built by A.S. Miller & Sons between March and November 1877 and carried the Knight name. Knight's son, Adam H. Knight, was born on July 5, 1870. Shown below is Adam Knight Sr. working in his shop around the 1870s. Knight's shop was located on the corner of NW First Avenue and Fir Street. A fire destroyed this original Knight house in April 1967.

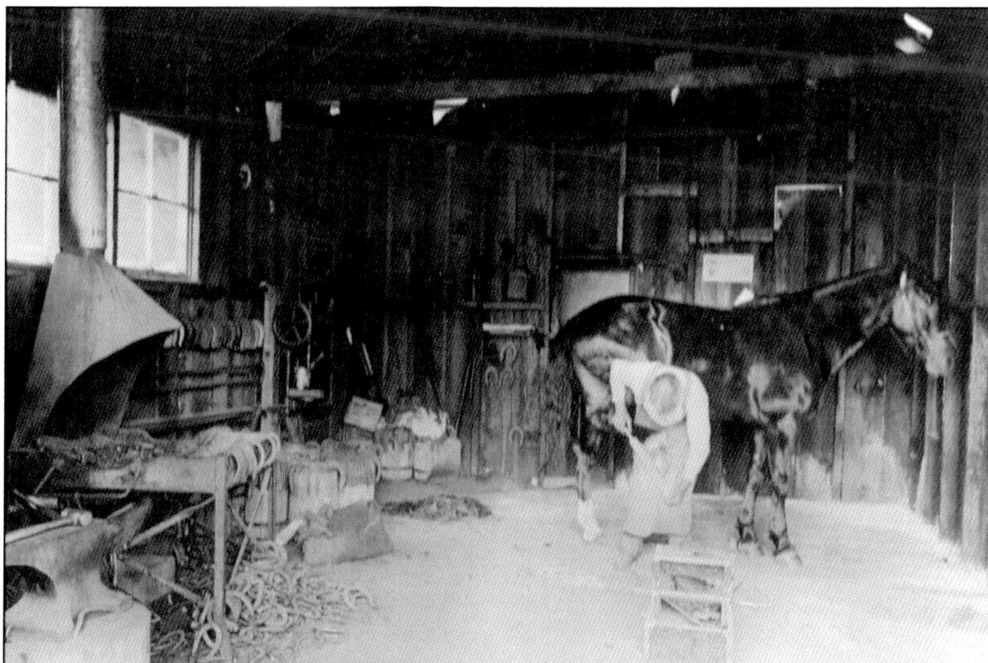

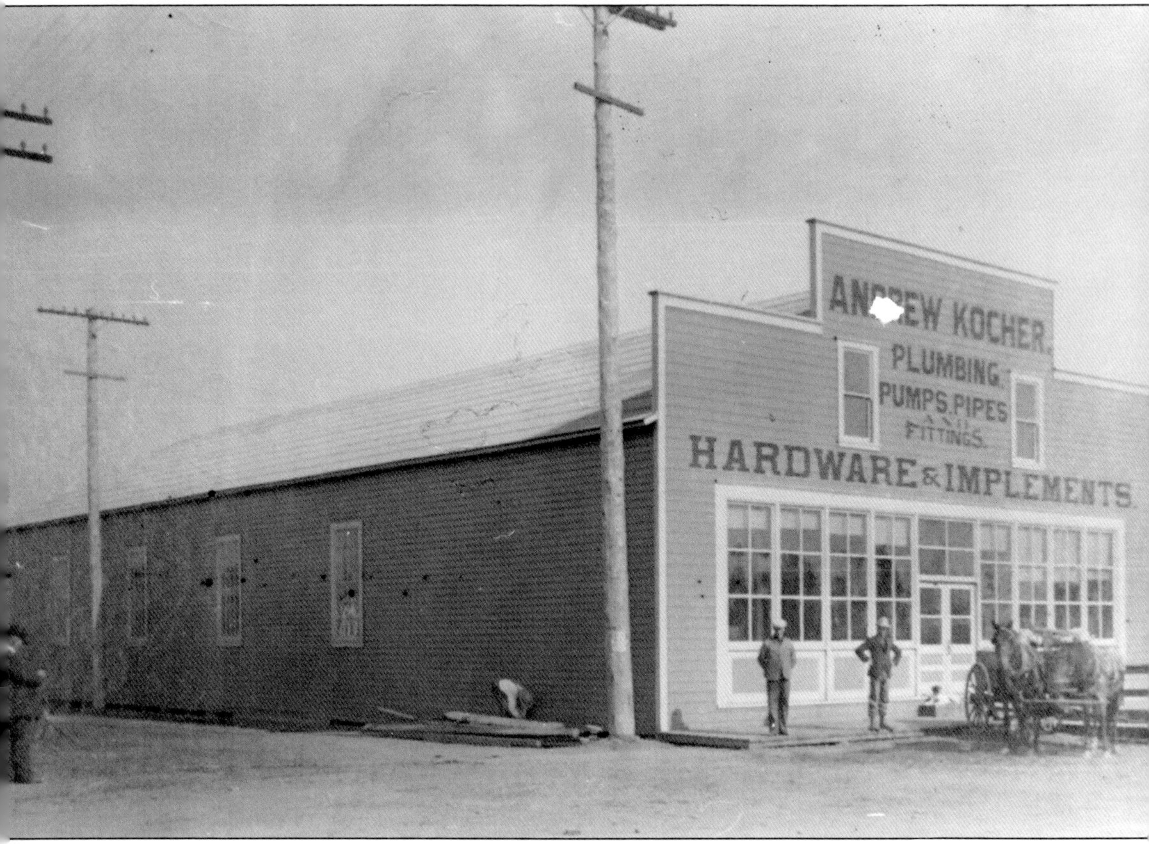

Andrew Kocher was one of the most prominent residents of Clackamas County. He opened a hardware store on NW First Avenue and Ivy Street. It sold everything: implements, separators, gasoline engines, machine oil, pumps, pipes, windmills, McCormick machines, and plumbing supplies. Kocher was born in Bethel, Missouri, on April 26, 1851. He came across the plains with his mother, Catherine Kocher, arriving in Oregon that same year. They made their home in Aurora (in neighboring Marion County and about four miles southwest of Canby) in one of the old colonies that settled there. After living there for quite some time, Kocher married Ella S. Carothers around 1880, and he later moved his family to Canby, where he lived the rest of his life. Kocher was always very active in the welfare of Canby, such as the Clackamas County Fairgrounds. He was a key player in developing a business trade in Canby. Here is his hardware store in 1905.

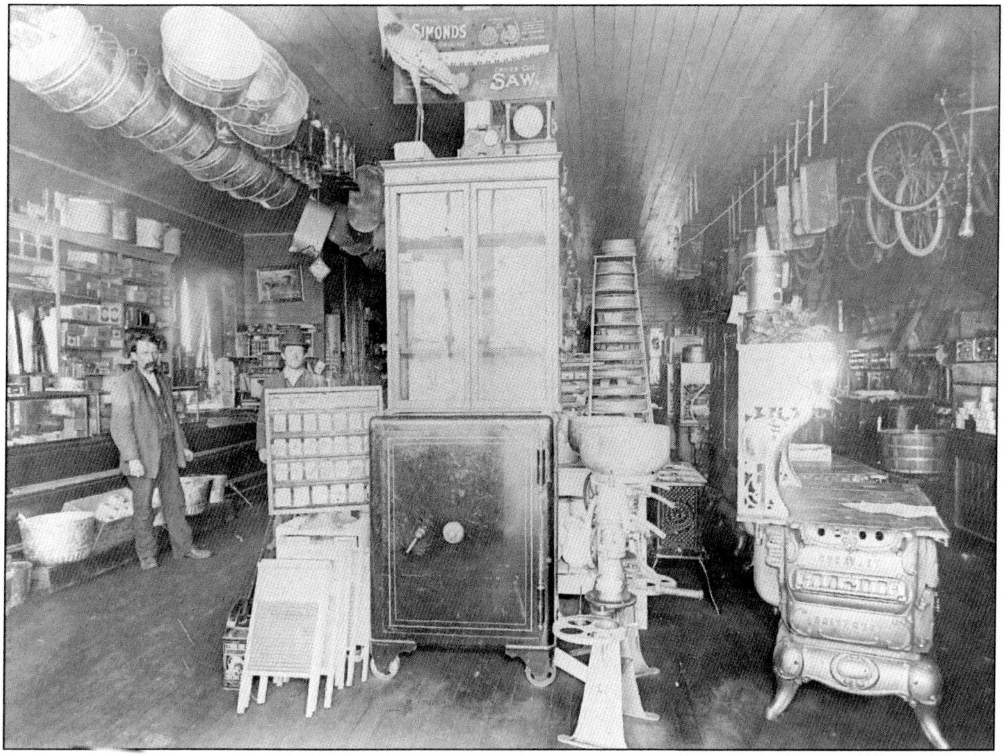

In the early 1900s, a new shop opened called Canby Hardware & Implement Store. J.J. Sandsness bought this store from its originator, Andrew Kocher, in 1907. By 1908, commodities were in demand, such as the washtubs and bicycles dangling from the ceiling. Also displayed here are washboards in front on the floor, cream separators on the right of the safe, and a then-modern wood-burning kitchen range.

The *Canby Herald* is a weekly newspaper that began in 1906. It primarily covers local news for the cities of Canby and Aurora. One of the Oregon's oldest newspapers, it started out as a biweekly newspaper delivered on Wednesdays and Saturdays; it is currently a weekly newspaper delivered on Wednesdays. Here is Bill Weston, publisher and owner (along with his wife, Myra) from 1947 to 1972.

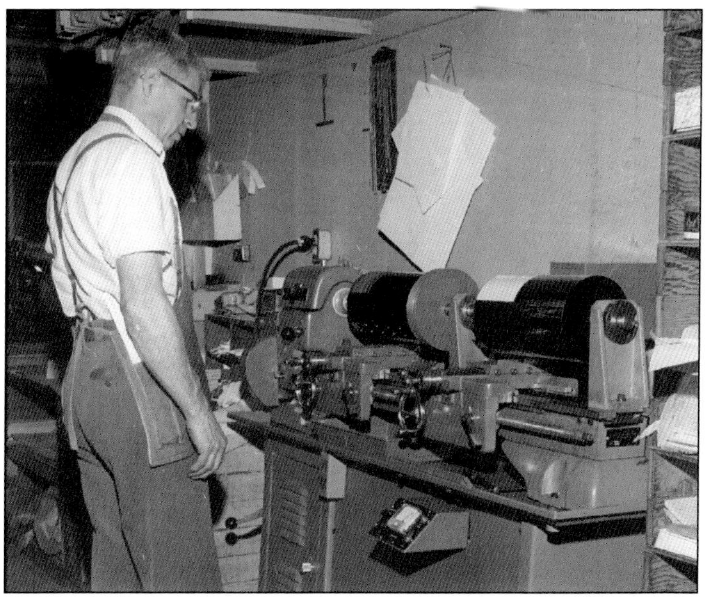

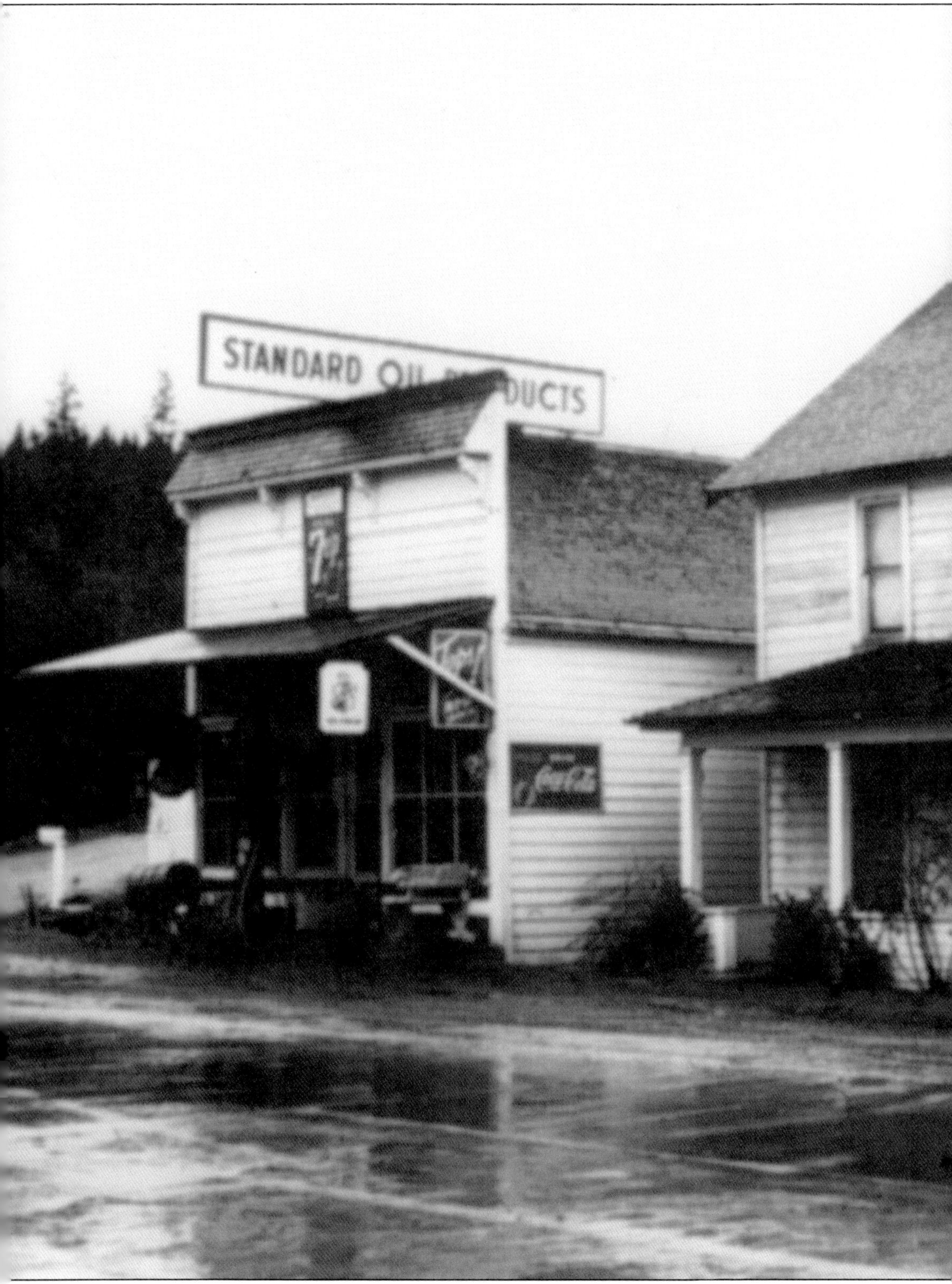
STANDARD OIL
UCTS

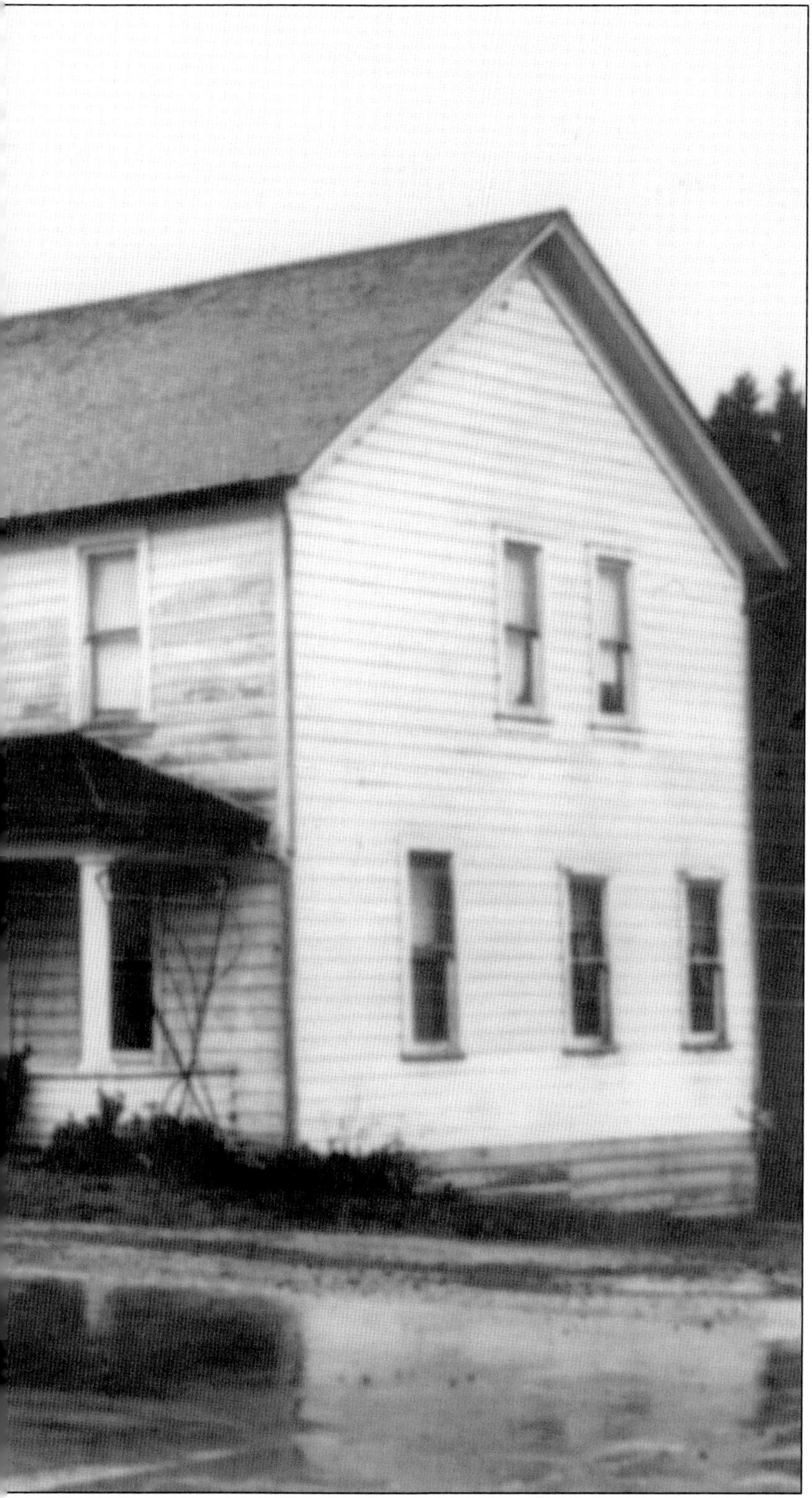

As more pioneers settled in the fertile area near Canby, a small community began to develop at the convergence of Beaver and Parrott Creeks. This village was called New Era. The New Era store and the Dustin House were in the Canby area. A post office opened in the store building in 1876. It closed in 1940, when it was merged with the Canby Post Office. The postmaster and storekeeper's home was next door. J.C. Castro was the postmaster from 1876 to 1906. Jennie Newbury Dustin followed him until the post office closed. In 1868, the New Era Rolling Mill started its business. It stayed open until 1935.

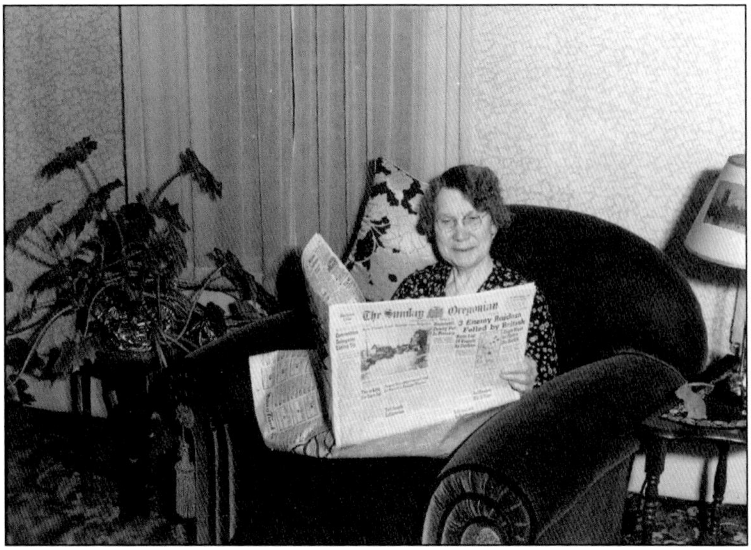

From their arrival in New Era, near Canby, in 1890, Jennie Newbury Dustin helped her husband with their new home. She became the postmaster of the New Era Post Office in 1906 and retired when she turned 74 years old. She died in 1952, shortly after the New Era store closed.

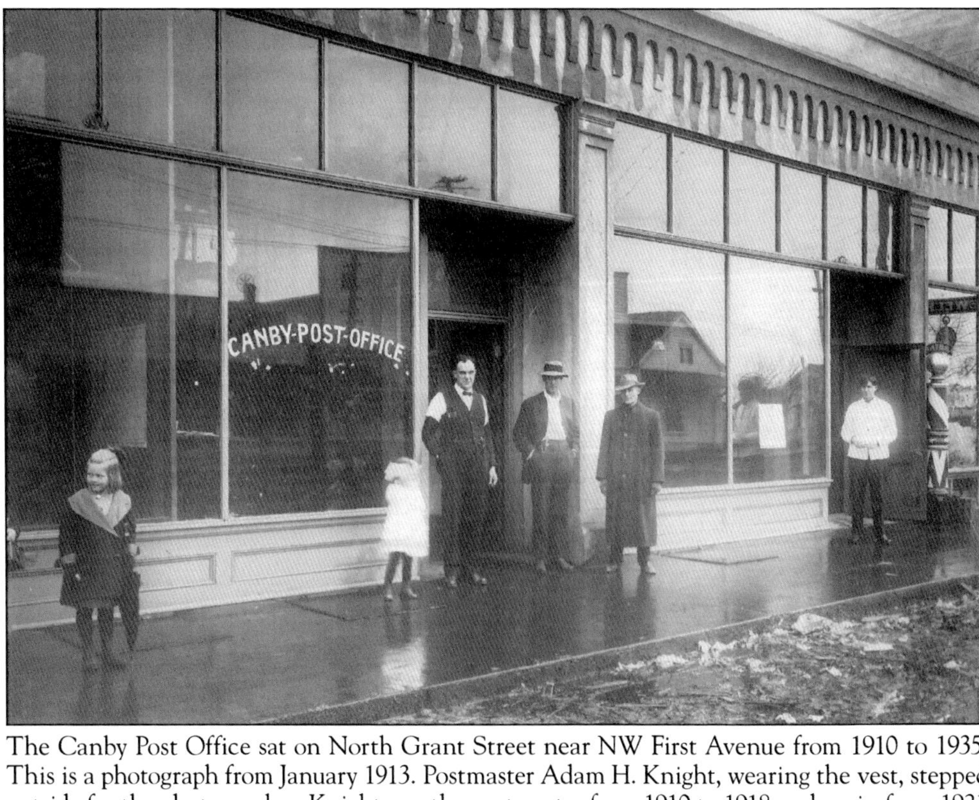

The Canby Post Office sat on North Grant Street near NW First Avenue from 1910 to 1935. This is a photograph from January 1913. Postmaster Adam H. Knight, wearing the vest, stepped outside for the photographer. Knight was the postmaster from 1910 to 1918 and again from 1923 to 1935. Others gathered with Knight for this picture.

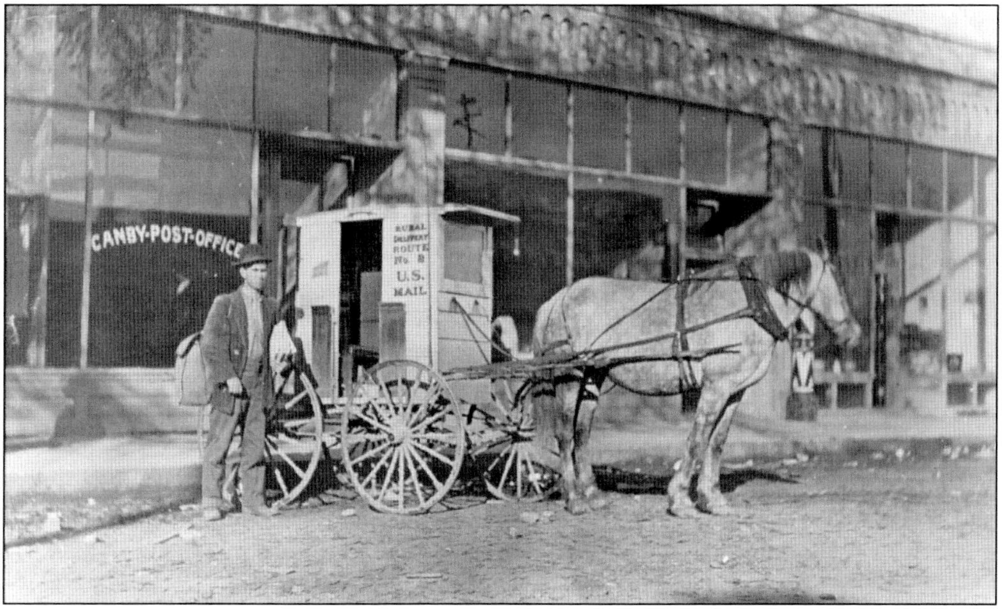

The mail carrier on Canby's Rural Route 2 from 1910 through 1936 was Warren P. Lee, the son of Heman and Ida Lee. Warren was a lifelong resident of Canby (1882–1956). He was the second regular rural mail carrier for Canby. He is standing in front of the post office on North Grant Street in 1914. Canby's first rural mail service began on May 15, 1905.

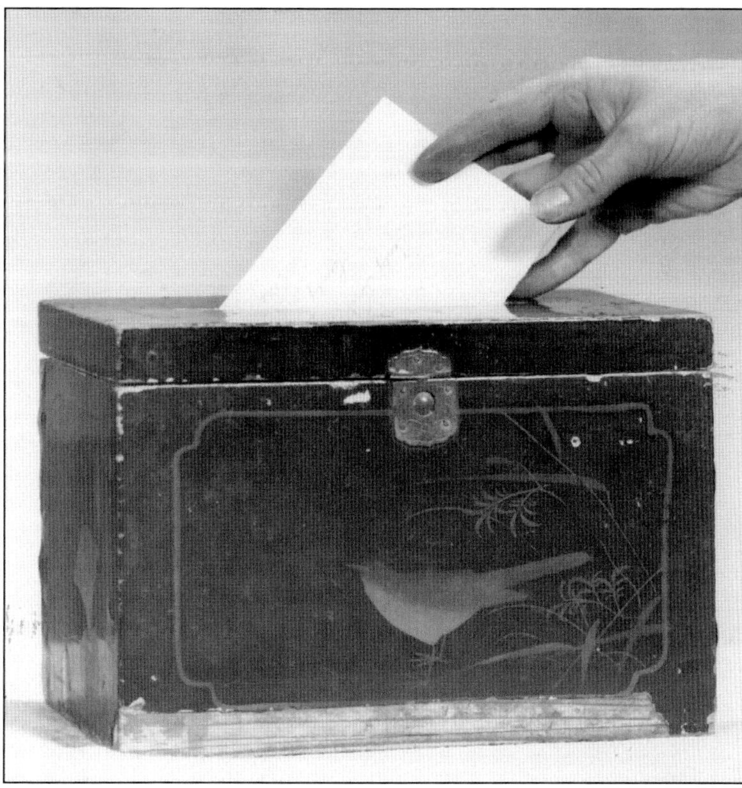

By 1871, the Canby community included stores, warehouses, and a post office. Even though it had delivery service, mail was not picked up from private homes. This decorative lacquer box functioned as the town's postal drop box for letters. The box was stationed in the Canby general store. Charles "Doc" Knight was Canby's first postmaster.

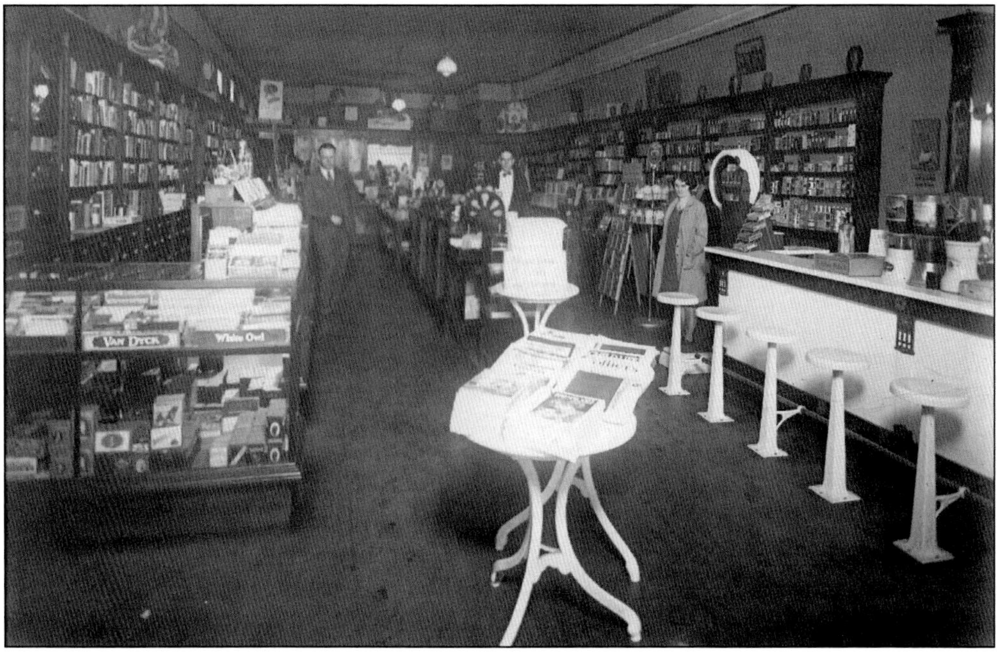

The Graham Drug Company opened in 1925 in the newly built Koehler Building on the corner of NW First Avenue and Grant Street. This business replaced the old Knight Drug Store and Confectionery. Three years later, the name was changed to Dedman Drug. Shown here are Craig Dedman, Carroll Meeks, and Mirabel Bates.

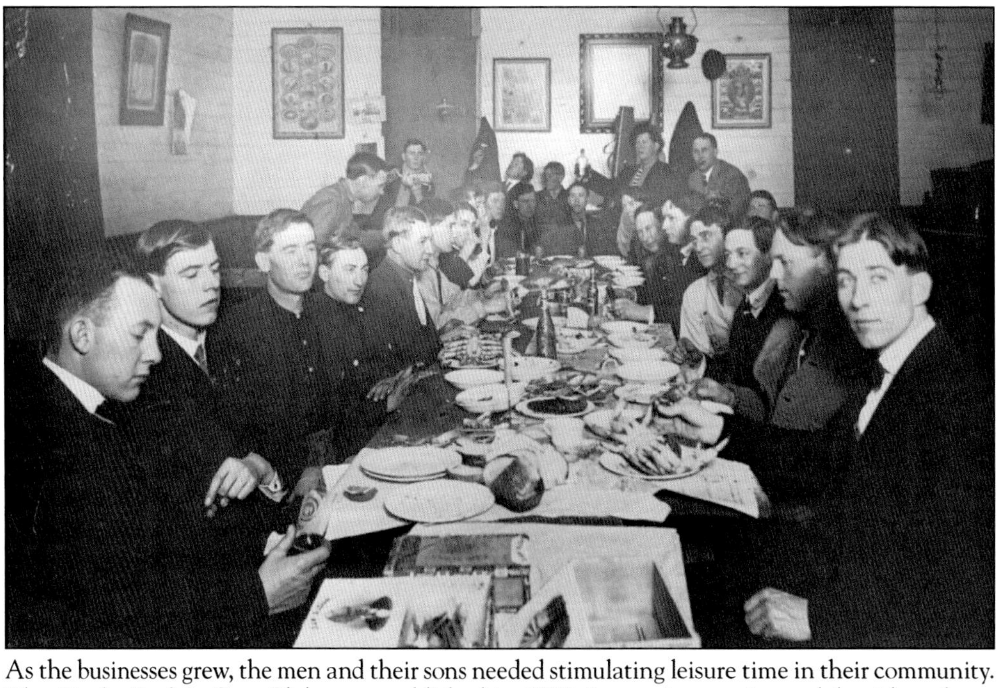

As the businesses grew, the men and their sons needed stimulating leisure time in their community. The Canby Rod & Gun Club was established in 1888. It remains a private club with archery, pistol, rifle, and trap shooting. These members of the Canby Rod & Gun Club are gathered at Knight's Hall in January 1914 to celebrate a wonderful year of sportsmanship and comradery.

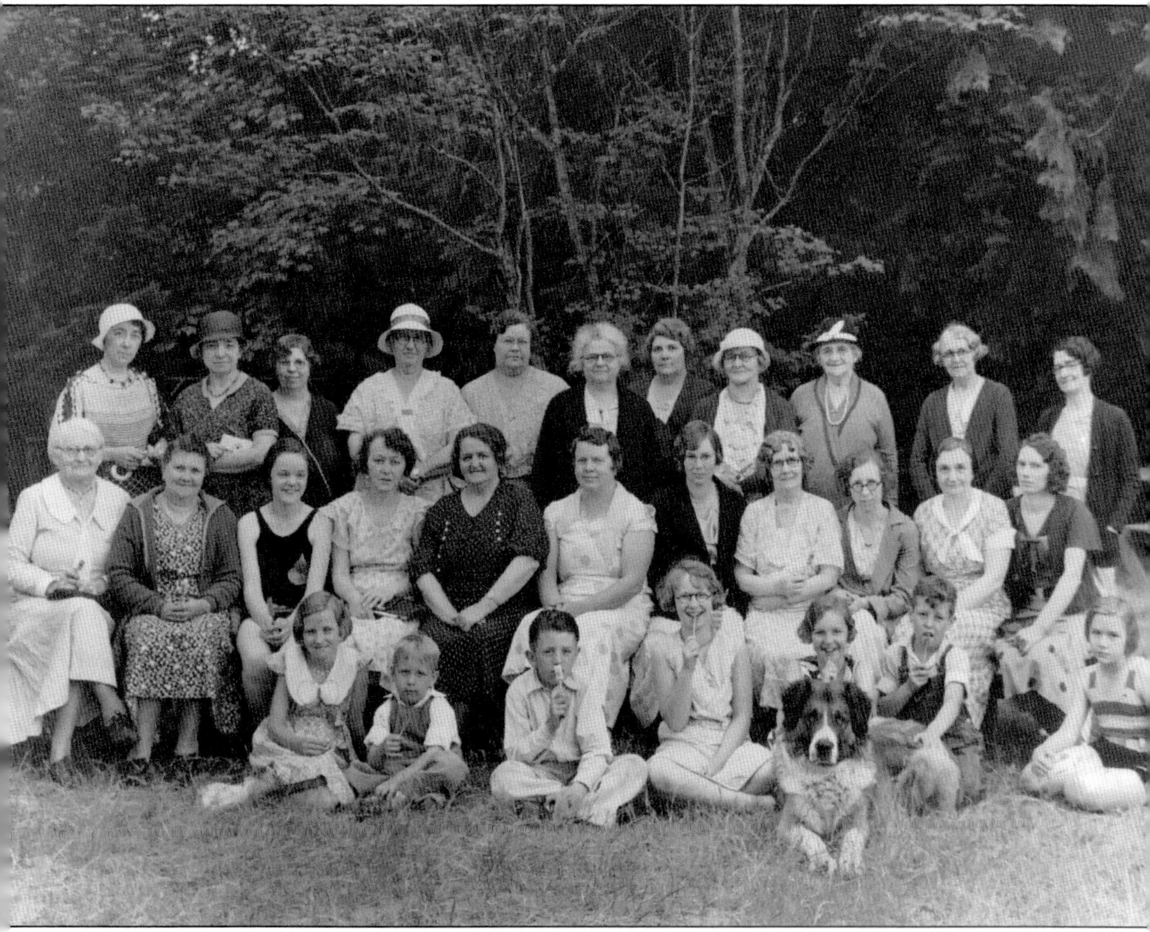

Women also developed clubs and charities for their social lives. The Canby Women's Civic Club began in 1924 and continued through the mid-1960s. Its first project was planting big-leaf maple trees along NW First Avenue. The club held an annual picnic at Island Park on the Molalla River. This photograph was taken at the June 29, 1933, picnic. Pictured are, from left to right, (first row) Elizabeth Eid, Ervin Collins, a son of the unidentified woman sitting behind him, Ida Widdows, Vivian Leffingwell, Dale Collins, and Betty Krueger; (second row) Mrs. J.H. Graham, Mrs. Henry E. Browne, Doris Cattley, Mildred Brown, Mrs. Grant W. White, unidentified, Mabel Widdows, Mrs. Elmer Gribble, Mrs. R.J. Collins, Mrs. George Cattley, and Mrs. Edward Krueger; (third row) Mrs. Delbert Clark, Mrs. John Eid, Mrs. Howard H. Eccles, Mrs. J.C. Kaupisch, Mrs. B.M. Randall, Mrs. Hoyt N. Brown, Mrs. Louis Lent, Caroline Wang, Mrs. Homer McCutchin, Tillie Phillips, and Katherine Prahl. The dog, named Pardner, belonged to the photographer, Hal Cooley.

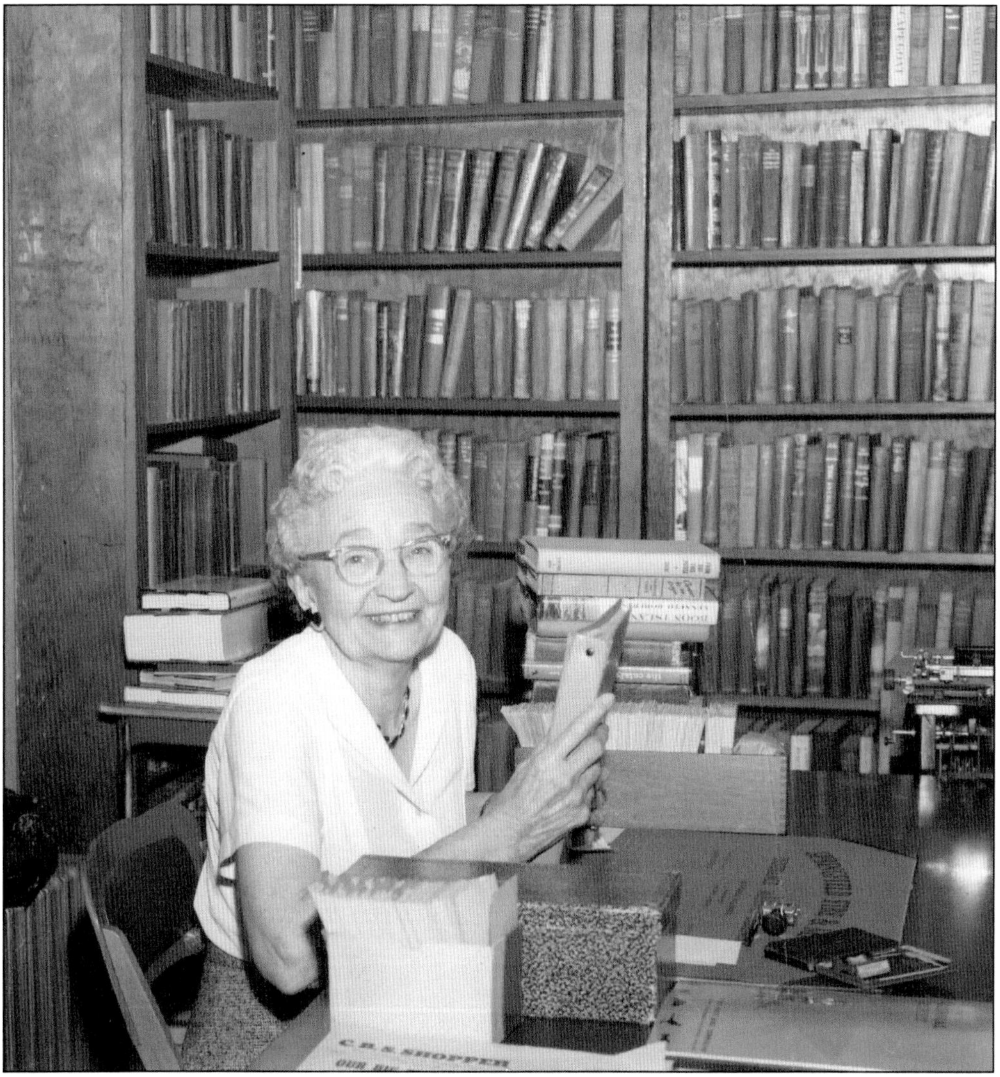

A library was much needed in Canby. From 1896 through 1916, many local retailers held tiny libraries in their shops, but they were short-lived. By World War I, the city created a traveling library using materials from the Oregon State Library. When the Canby Women's Civic Club took on the project, an area for a simple library run by volunteers was created in 1925. In 1935, this group sponsored building a true library for Canby. In 1937, Portia Shewey, Mabel Gabriel, and Edna Johnson went to each door in their community to ask for money, donations, and books to create a public library. That same year, in June, the city council voted to supply a room in the new city hall as a library. Doris Wilbourn was hired as the first librarian. On September 16, 1937, the new library opened in what is now Canby's city hall meeting room. Over the years, Canby's library has moved to several other downtown locations as its need for space has grown. Here is Ora Lee Cattley, one of Canby's early librarians.

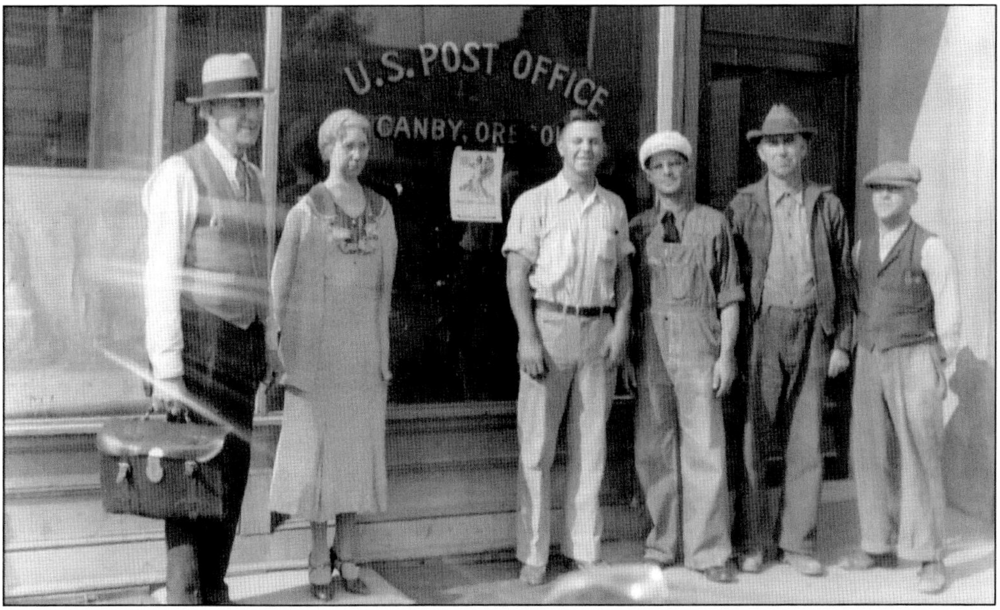

Some of the staff at the Canby Post Office on September 30, 1935 includes, from left to right, postmaster Adam H. Knight and his wife, Ida B. Knight (her husband's assistant clerk for the 25 years he was the postmaster), John R. Hans Nieland (clerk), Carl L. Ellingson, Warren P. Lee, and William E. Flick. The latter three men were rural carriers. The post office was located on North Grant Street.

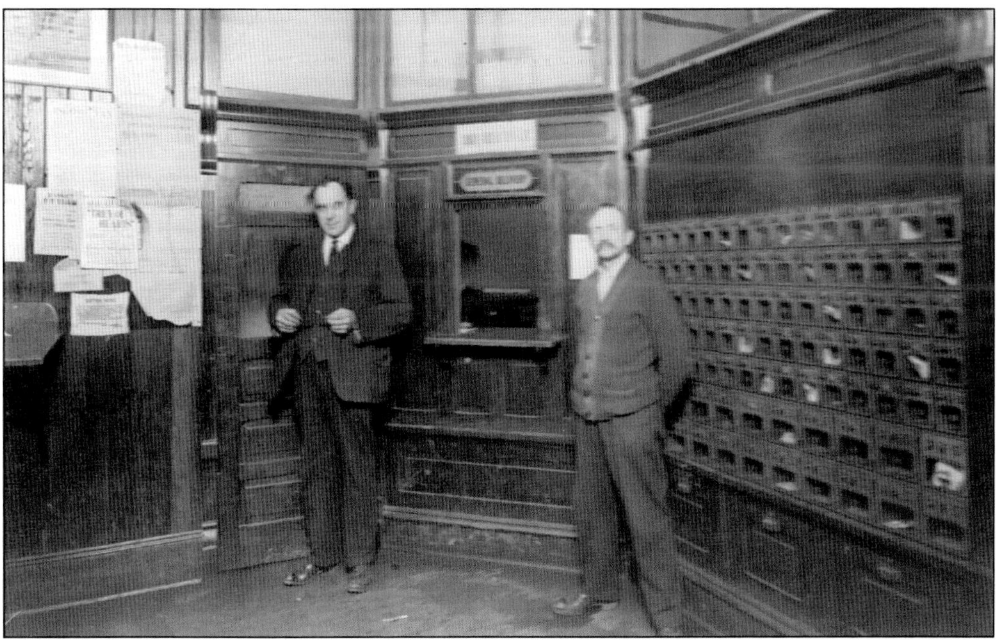

Canby's post office originated in 1871. In 1914, postmaster Charles N. Wait (on the right) and Adam H. Knight managed the local postal service. Knight followed his family's trade; three of his uncles had been postmasters in the 1870s and 1880s. Knight was the postmaster from 1910 to 1918 and 1923 to 1935. Wait Park, located in downtown Canby, was named after Charles Wait's father, Aaron E. Wait, a chief justice of the Oregon Supreme Court.

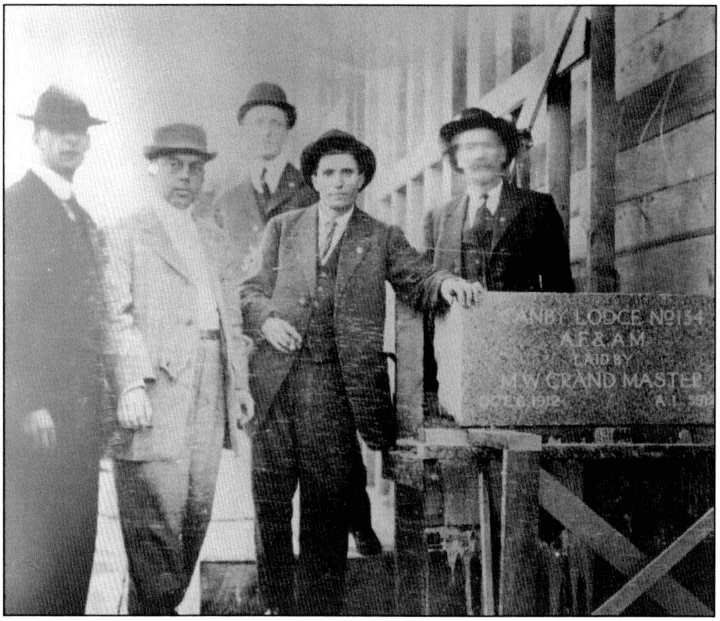

The Canby Masonic lodge became very active in the early 1900s. It was established on October 6, 1912. The Masonic organization in Canby was named Champoeg Lodge No. 27; the building is still on First Avenue. Here, from left to right, are Arthur Graham, Fred Roth, Ross Coppock, Ora Slyter, and Harry Graham standing by their Masonic sign with the initials AF&AM (Ancient Free & Accepted Masons).

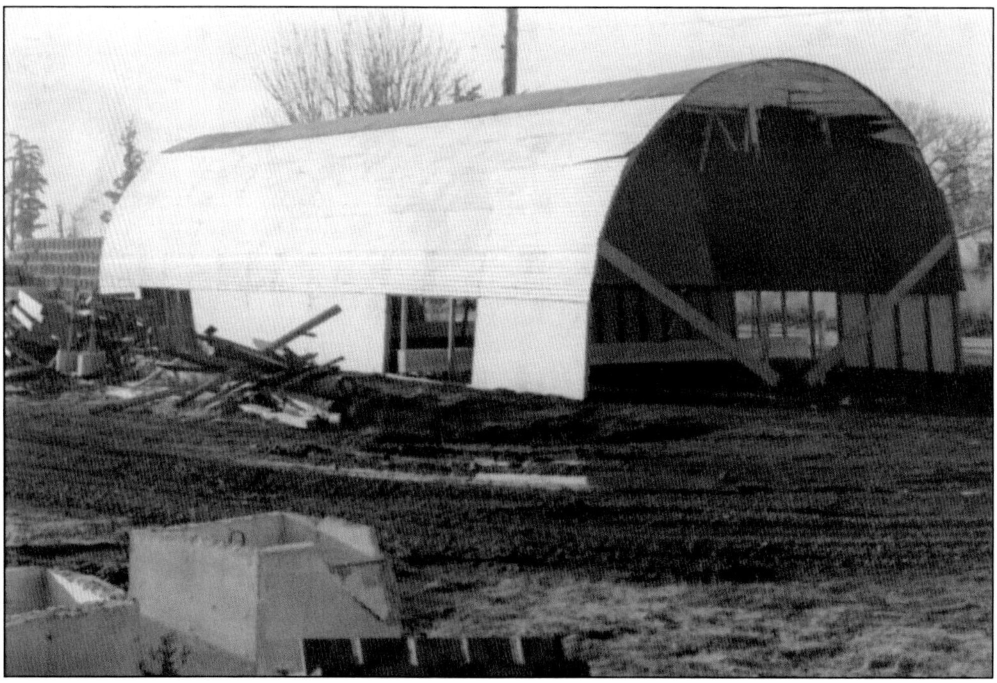

This Quonset hut was placed in Canby in 1947. It was Army surplus, but it was much needed after the war. The hut sat at NW Fourth Avenue and Grant Street, in one corner of Wait Park. It was used as a youth center, then later by Boy Scout Troop No. 258. The Kiwanis endowed the Canby Recreation Commission the needed funds to move it to NW Third Avenue.

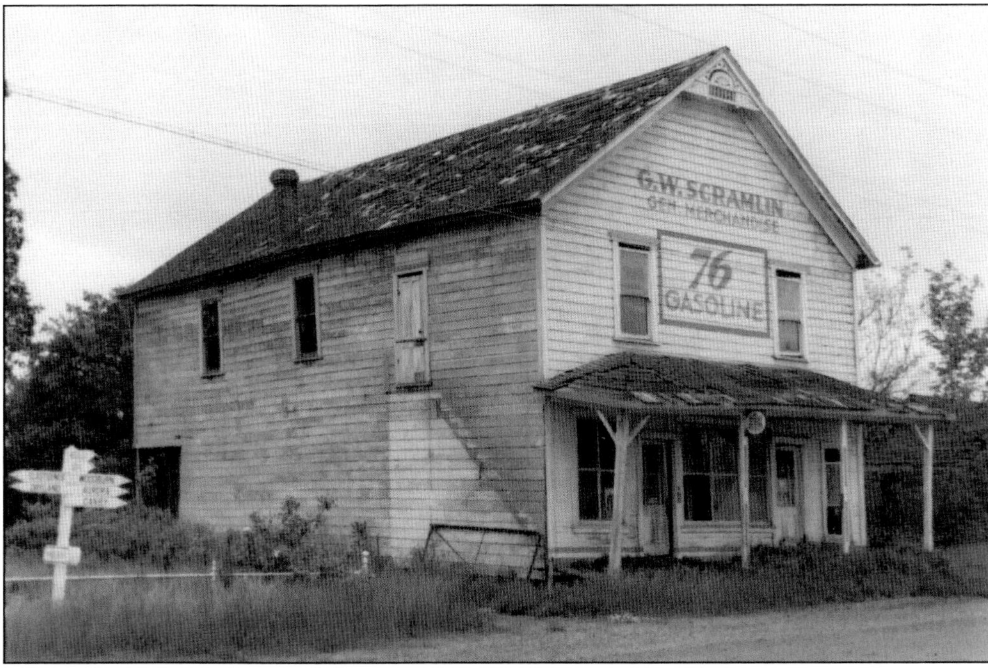

George Washington Scramlin was born in Detroit, Michigan, on July 4, 1853. He married his wife, Odessa, on August 7, 1885. They had two children, Russell and Cora. The family moved to Macksburg, near Canby, where Scramlin built a house and opened a general merchandising store. His shop and home were just five miles east of Canby. The store was used for social gatherings. Many dances and festivities took place on the second floor of the shop. Scramlin was the postmaster of Macksburg, a farmer, and a storeowner and was responsible for getting a telephone system set up. This telephone line took in Barlow, Canby, Macksburg, Aurora, Hubbard, Woodburn, Needy, and Baker Prairie. The cost per month for the use of the phone was the small sum of 75¢. The picture below was taken in 1959 by Lela Carr.

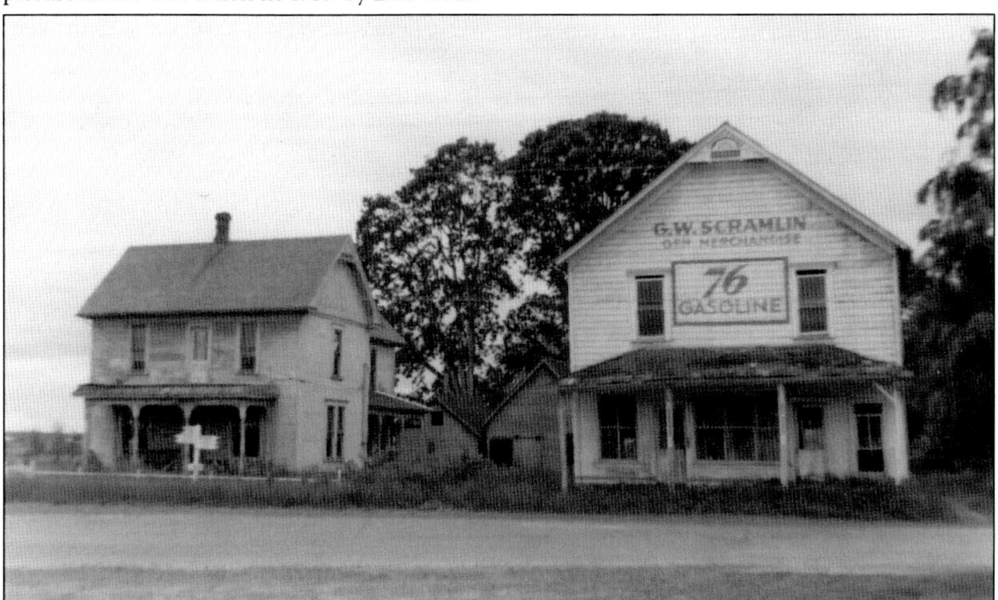

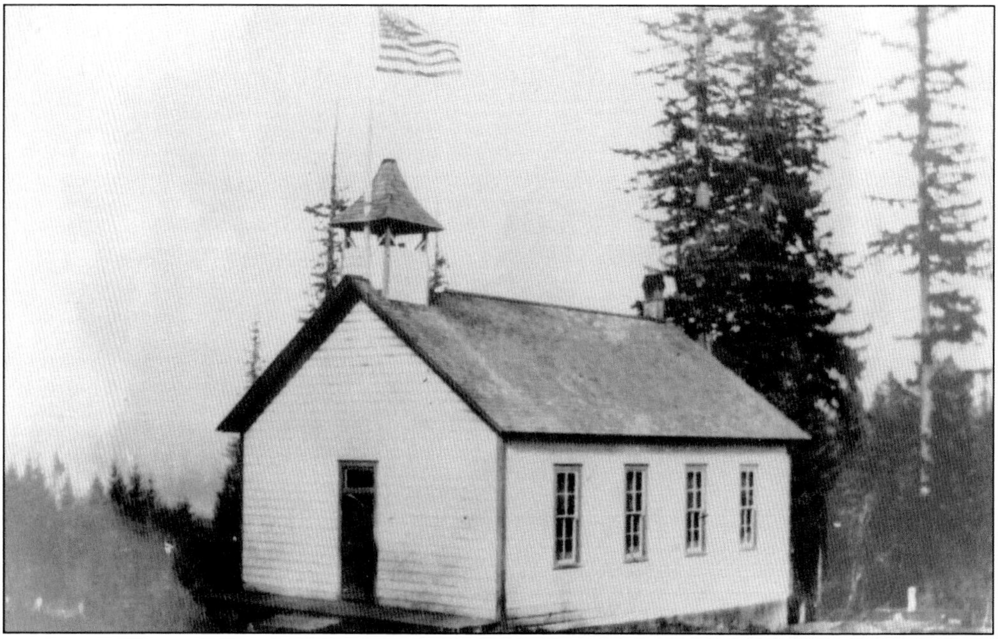

Canby School District No. 86 was established on July 9, 1887, to provide public education. The district wanted to provide every child with opportunities to achieve his or her maximum potential. At the core of the curriculum was basic reading, writing, and mathematics. One teacher was hired to instruct all of the children in a one-room school. There was no central transportation; the children either walked or were driven to school by horse and buggy. Often, a child was only able to attend school when he or she was not needed to work at home. When it was planting or harvesting time, the child might stay home to help. The people of Canby knew how important educating their children was, so new schools—like Leland Elementary, shown above in 1890, and the Brown School, shown below in 1917—were of the very best quality.

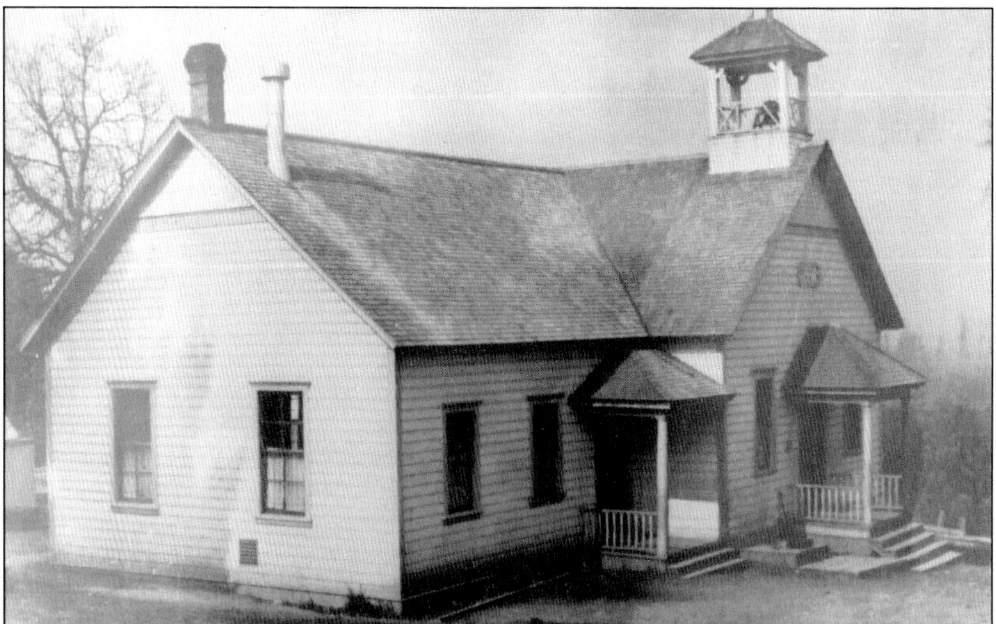

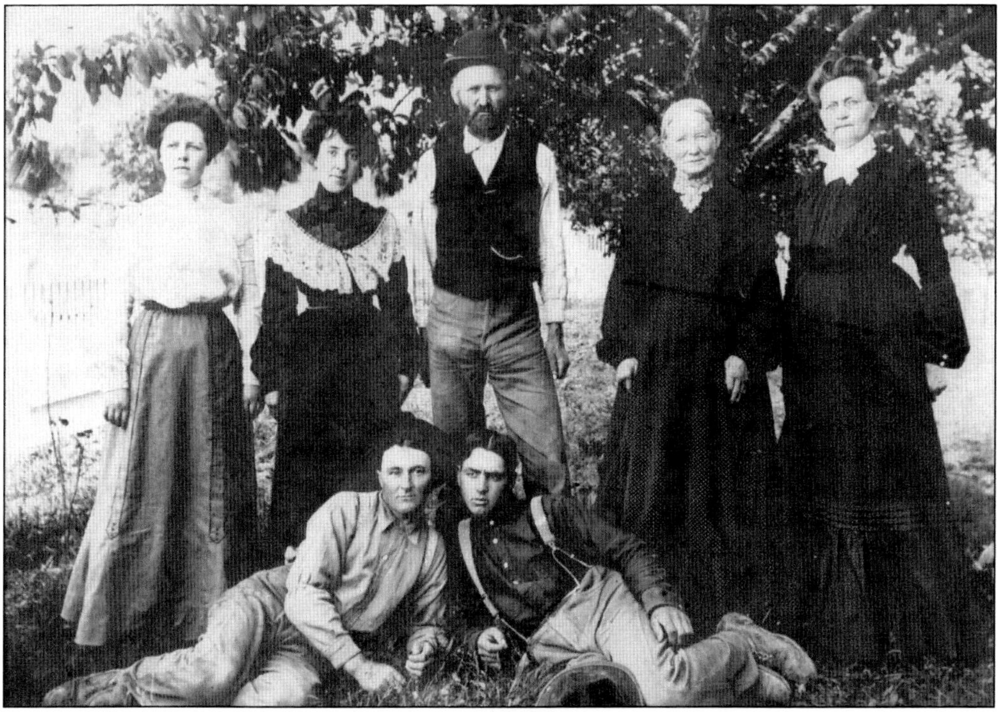

Samuel and Hanna Ellis Brown bought land to make a farm in 1869. It later became the Staehely Dairy farm. The Browns created a public school, the Brown School No. 63, where as many as 54 students were taught, all in one room, in the 1890s. In 1900, it expanded to a two-room schoolhouse. The Brown School merged into Canby School District No. 86 in 1948. That year, Canby's school district census counted 720 children. The photograph above was taken in 1900. Lying on the ground are William Weismandel, left, and Elmer Lucas. Standing are, from left to right, Charlotte (Blanchard) Dundas, Helen Gleason (a teacher at the Brown School), Robert James Brown (the son of Samuel and Hanna), Hanna Brown, and an unidentified nurse for Hanna's care. The photograph at right shows the Brown School. (Above, courtesy of Harley Blanchard.)

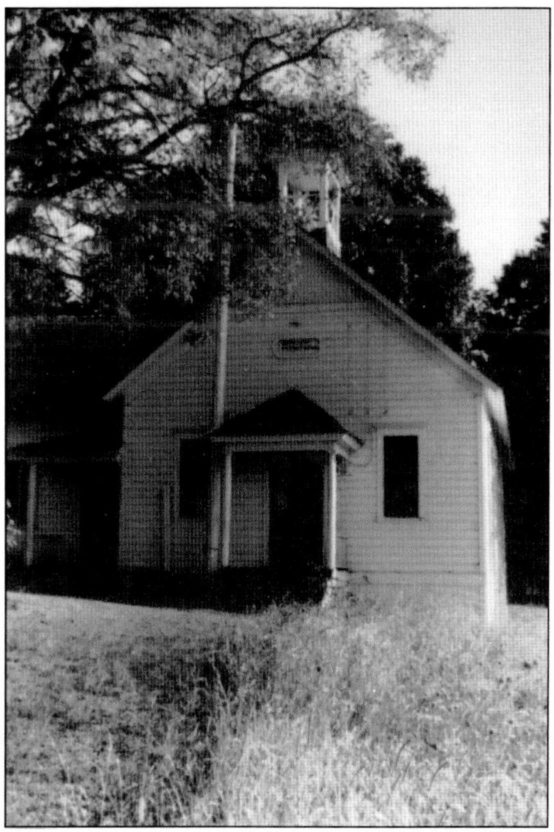

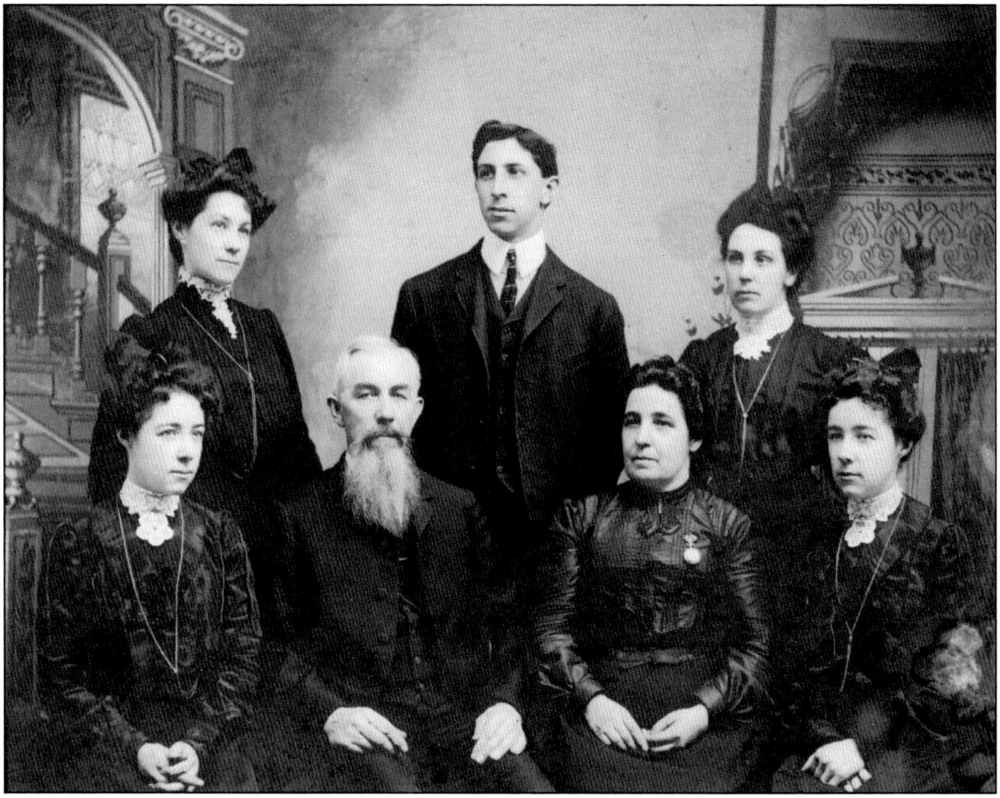

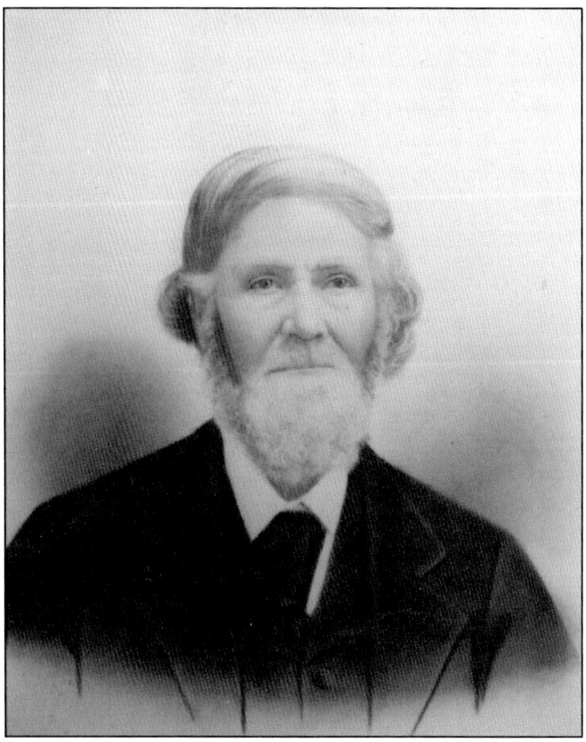

The William Knight Elementary School in Canby is named after William Knight, who served 43 years as school clerk. He and his wife, Martha E. Birtchet, built a home the same year they were married, 1875. They also built the first frame schoolhouse in Canby. Here they are with their children. On the left is Veva; her twin sister, Vesta, is on the right. Behind them are, from left to right, Bertha, Arthur, and Vinnie.

Philander Lee moved to the Canby area in 1847. His talent and knowledge helped bring the rail line to Canby. In 1870, Philander plotted a piece of his Baker Prairie apple orchard into sections for development. The railroad company bought 300 acres from Lee and the Knight brothers. Because of Lee's ingenuity and success in Canby, the Philander Lee Elementary School was named in his honor.

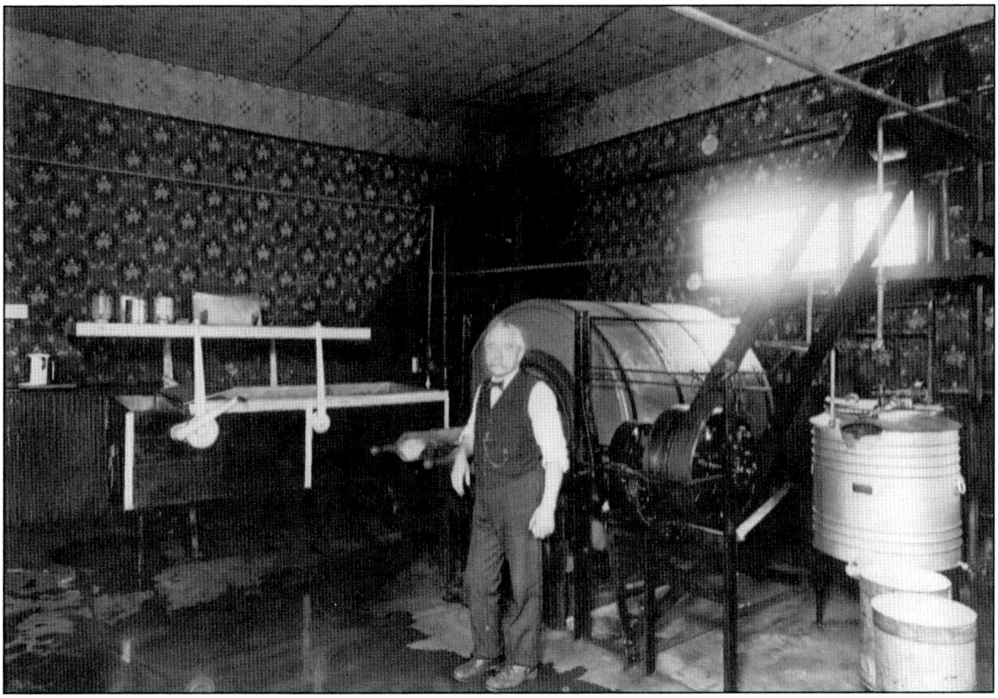

Before the First World War, the Canby Creamery ran on NW First Avenue next door to a blacksmith shop on North Ivy Street. Journalist J.C. Kaupisch from the *Canby Herald*, the local newspaper, reported in November 1918 that the Canby Creamery had made its largest one-day churning—400 pounds of butter. This creamery had an active market all around the Willamette Valley.

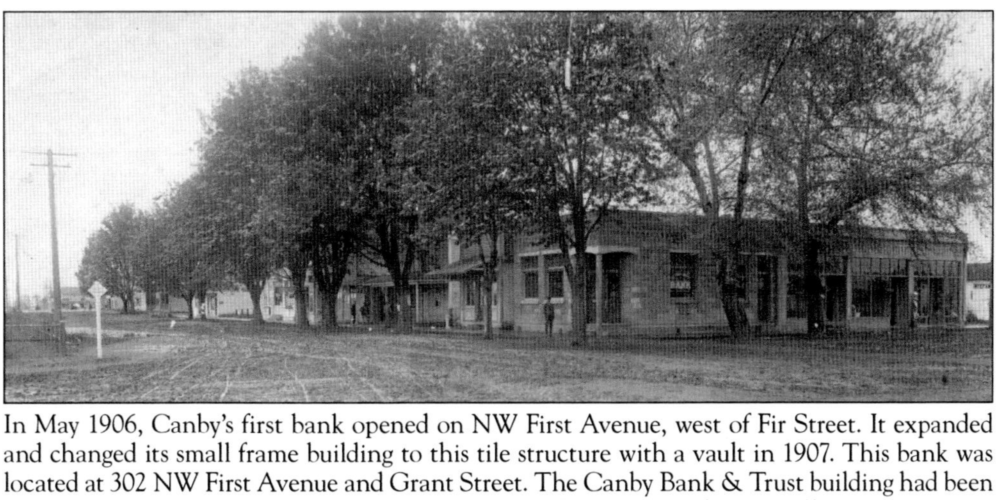

In May 1906, Canby's first bank opened on NW First Avenue, west of Fir Street. It expanded and changed its small frame building to this tile structure with a vault in 1907. This bank was located at 302 NW First Avenue and Grant Street. The Canby Bank & Trust building had been the location of Canby's first drugstore. Next door to the bank was the post office.

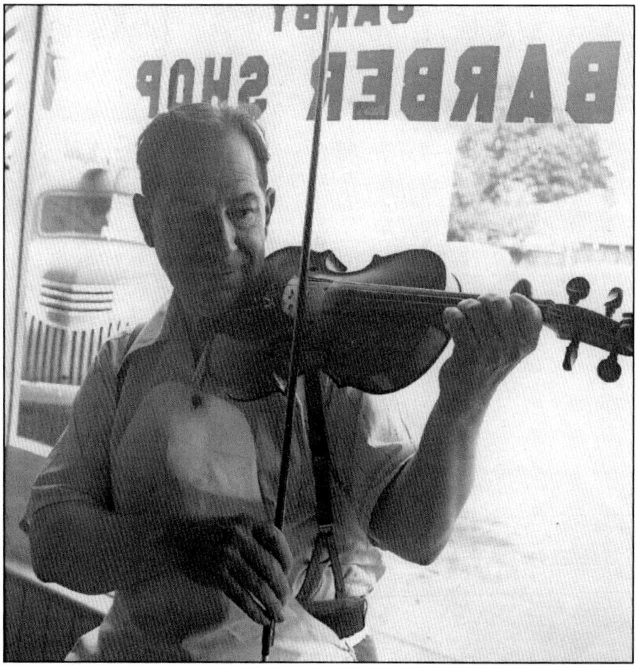

John Edward Kabourek (son of John Kabourek and Gertrude Margaret Reis) was born on December 27, 1891, in Manitowoc, Wisconsin; he died on October 4, 1973. He was buried at Zion Memorial Park Cemetery in Canby. He never married. All during his life, he enjoyed playing his fiddle as much as he enjoyed cutting the townsfolk's hair. He was as good as a musician as he was a barber. Kabourek was Canby's oldest businessman, retiring in December 1971, when he was 80 years old. He spent 52 years as a barber. In the photograph below, Kabourek is cutting Clayton Yoder's hair.

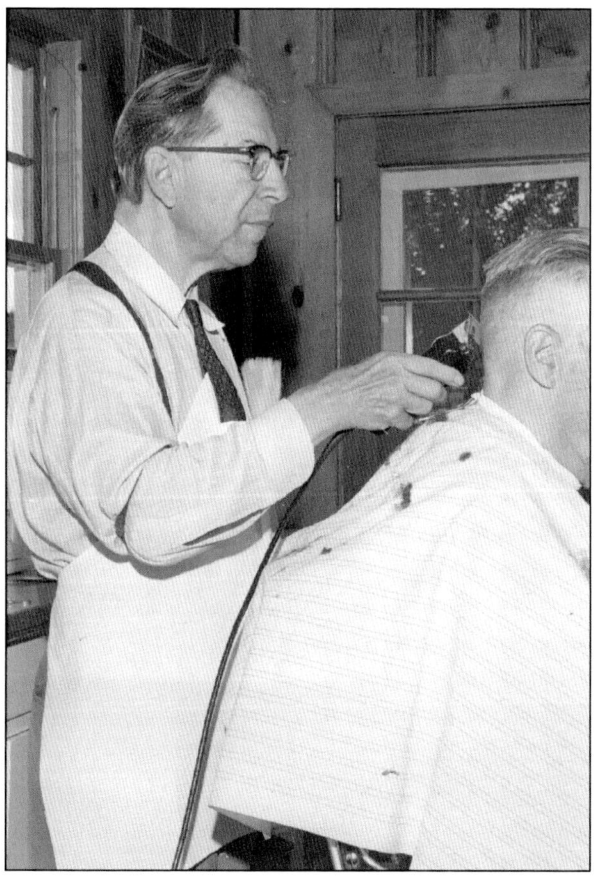

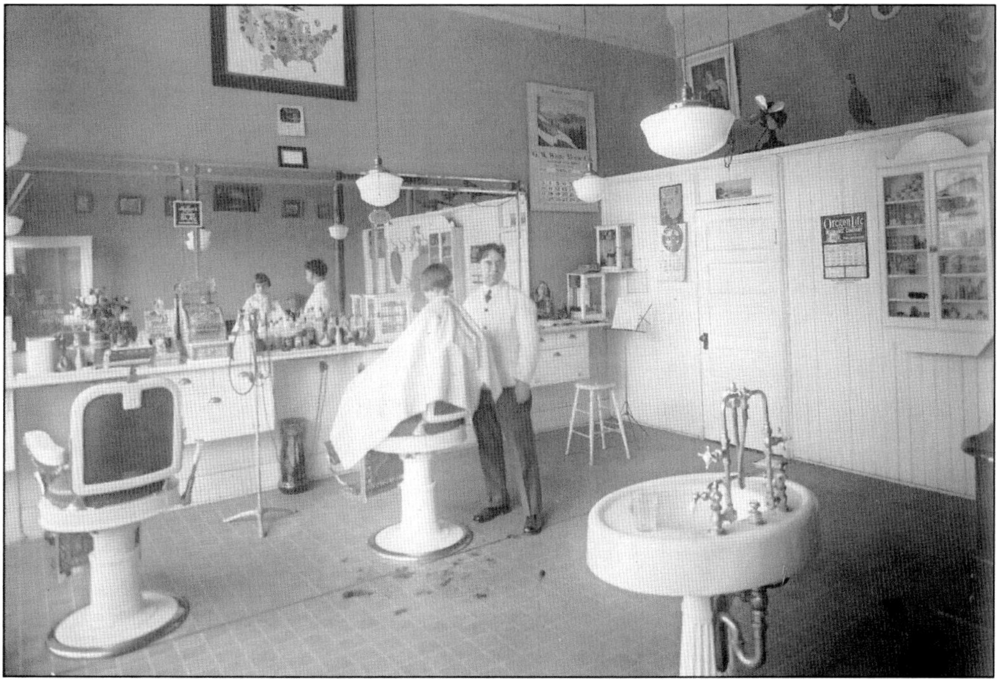

John Edward Kabourek's barbershop was on North Grant Street; this photograph was taken around 1929. After he had served as a private in the US Army during World War I, John studied to become a barber's apprentice. Aside from his career and playing the violin, John was also devoted to his family, including his brother, Joseph.

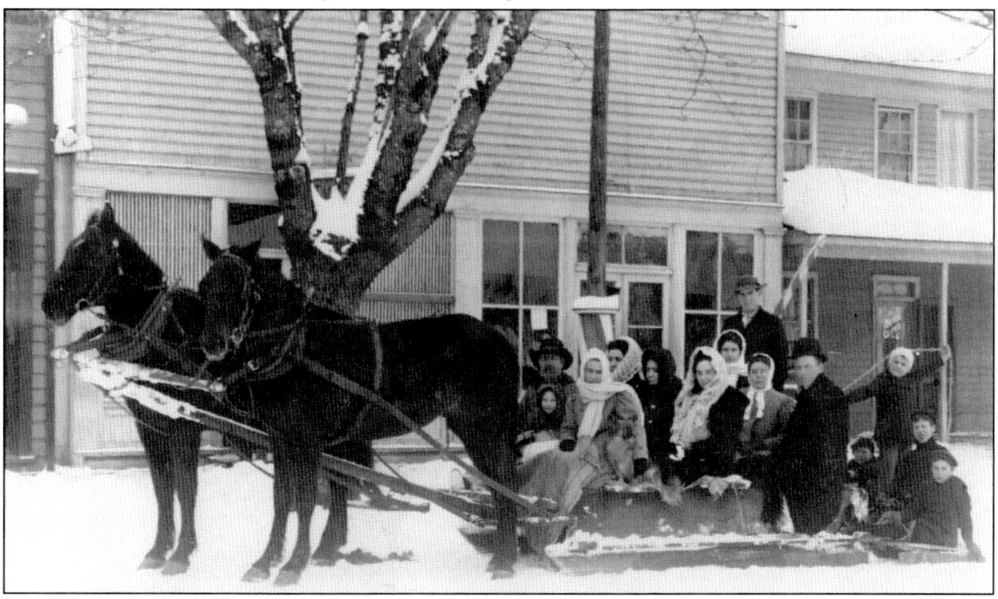

Some folks are all bundled up to go on a horse-drawn sled ride along NW First Avenue, west of Grant Street. An early steamboat captain, James Evans, built the Evans Building behind them. In 1885, the upper level of this building was rented by the city council at $1 a night. Dr. H.A. Dedman used the Evans Building, and later, the local Kiwanis used it for their thrift shop; it was demolished in 1961.

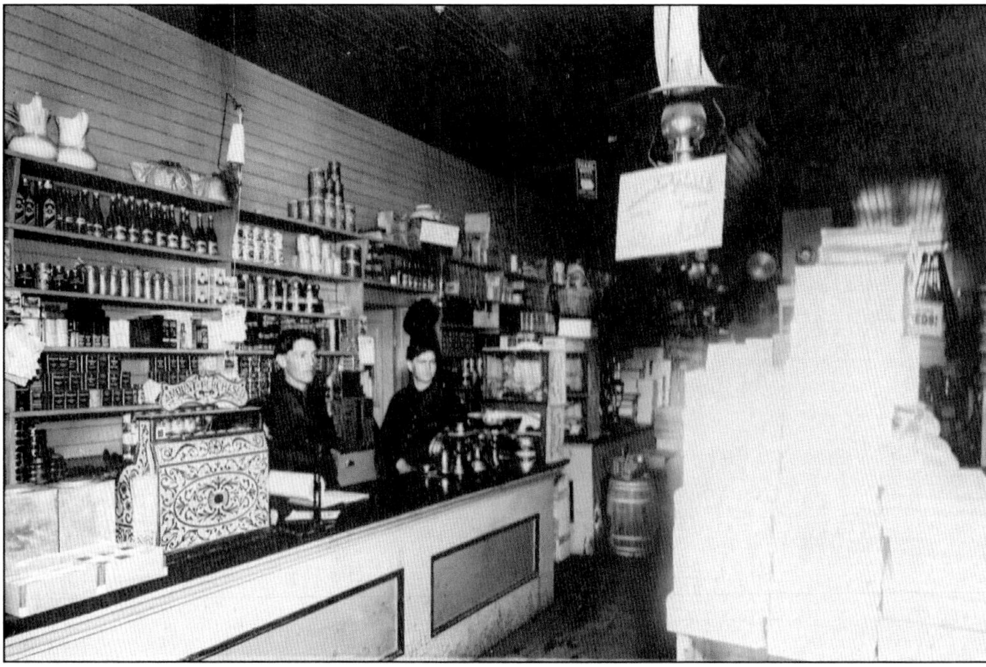

Louis H. Wang bought land and a building from a hobbyist photographer, Frank Zollner, who also owned a bicycle shop. Wang opened his general store, naming it on behalf of his wife, Caroline (C. Wang & Co.). It was located on the southwest corner of NW First Avenue and Holly Street. This store offered not only goods but also employment for young workers. Long before he was the Canby mayor from 1933 until 1946, a young James Raymond Vinyard was hired in 1904 to work in Wang's store. He is pictured above in 1907 with Ralph E. May to his left. Vinyard collaborated with Louis Wang in operating the store in 1917. By 1919, he bought Wang's store and changed the name to J.R. Vinyard General Merchandise; he retired his business in 1950. A fire burned the building down in 1990.

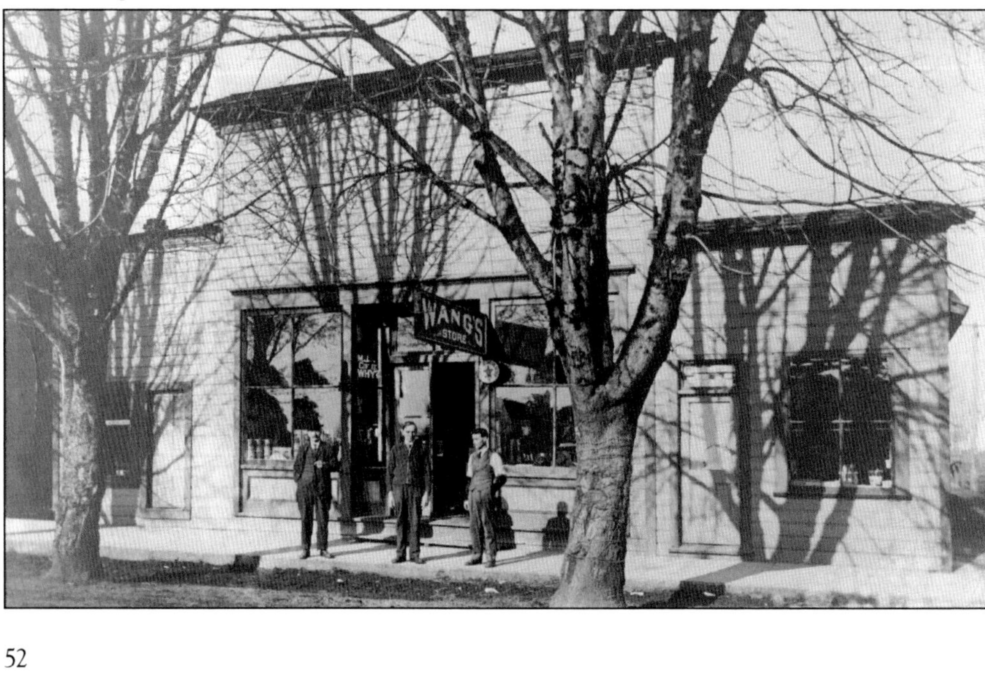

D.M. Osborne Co. was an agricultural equipment retailer in Auburn, New York. By 1903, it became the third-largest operation of its kind in the country. It sold binders, mowers, and rakes and manufactured its own line of gear, including the Osborne No. 8 reaper. The store also sold Studebaker wagons and buggies. The company created direct trade with dealers in California, Southern Oregon, and one in Canby around 1901.

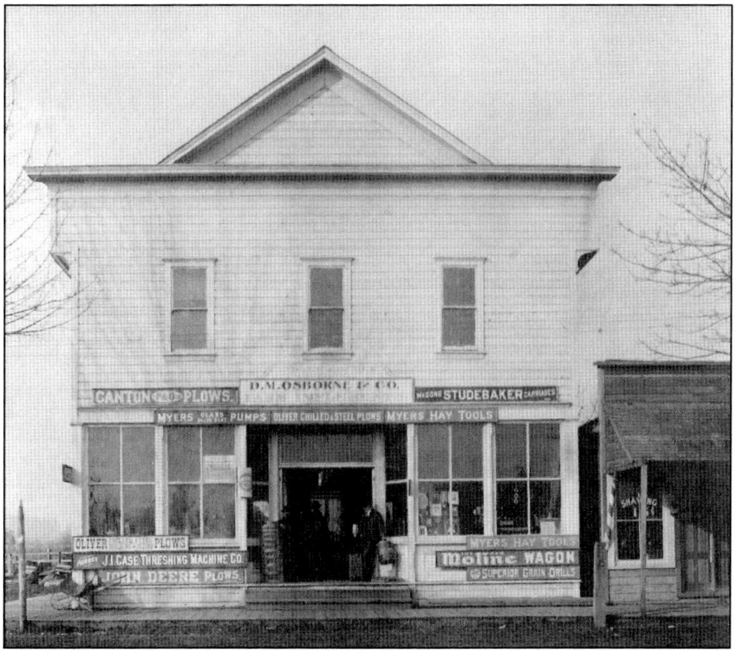

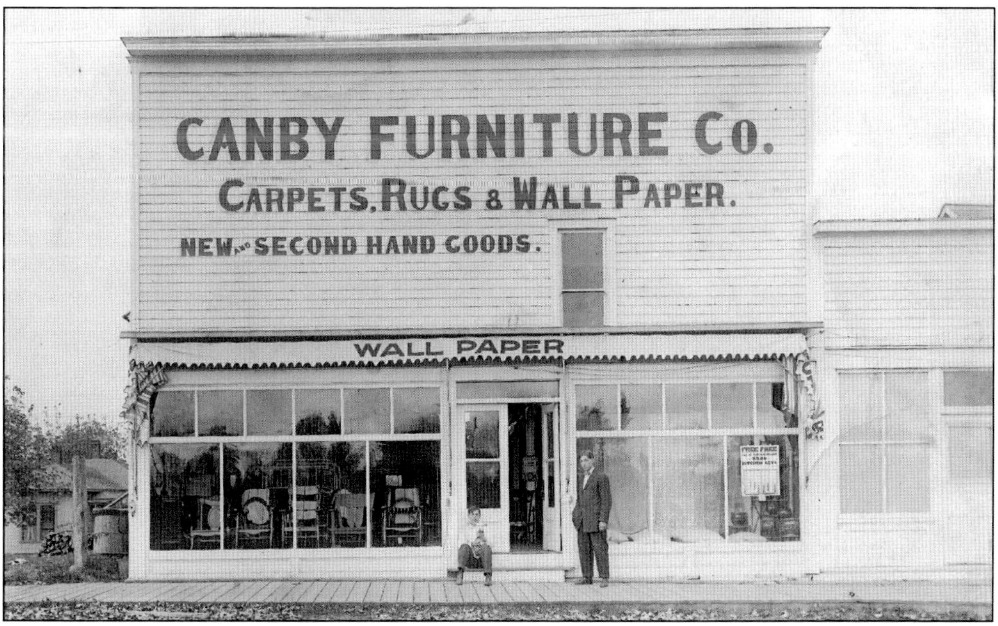

Canby's new furniture house, called the Canby Furniture Co., advertised in the Oregon City newspaper the *Enterprise* on August 25, 1911. It was on NW First Avenue and was owned by Ed Krueger. The shop carried a full line of furniture, carpets, rugs, and wallpaper. It advertised: "Prices right, give us a call and see for yourselves. Look over our stock of rugs the most popular priced rugs ever carried in town."

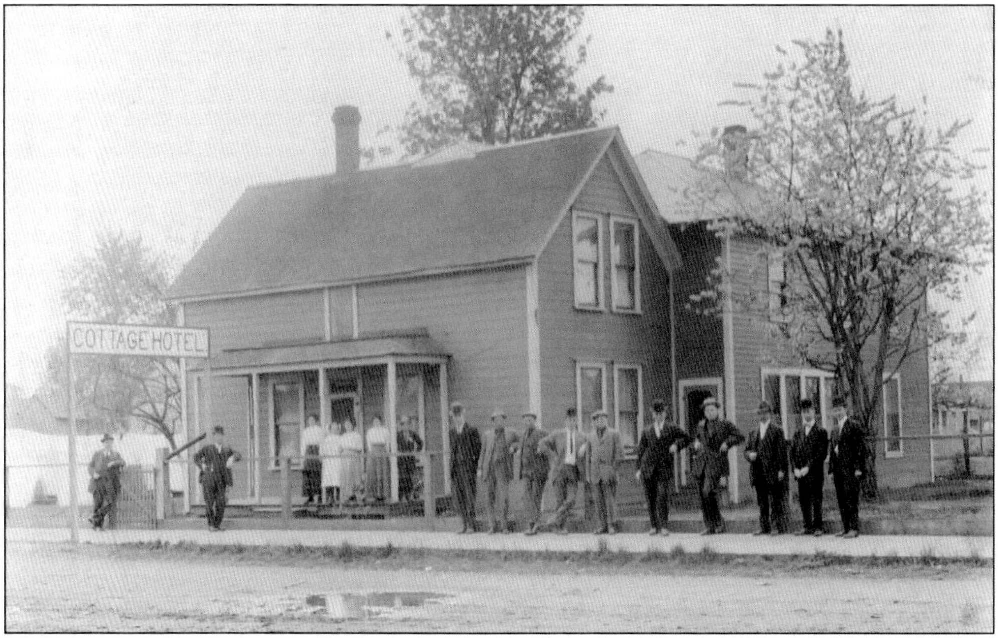

Cassie Fuller ran the Cottage Hotel from 1894 to 1940. It was located on North Grant Street, near Third Avenue. It kept busy just before World War I. The building was a residential house after the war until the Kiwanis Club bought it to use as a thrift store in the 1950s. It was torn down in 1975.

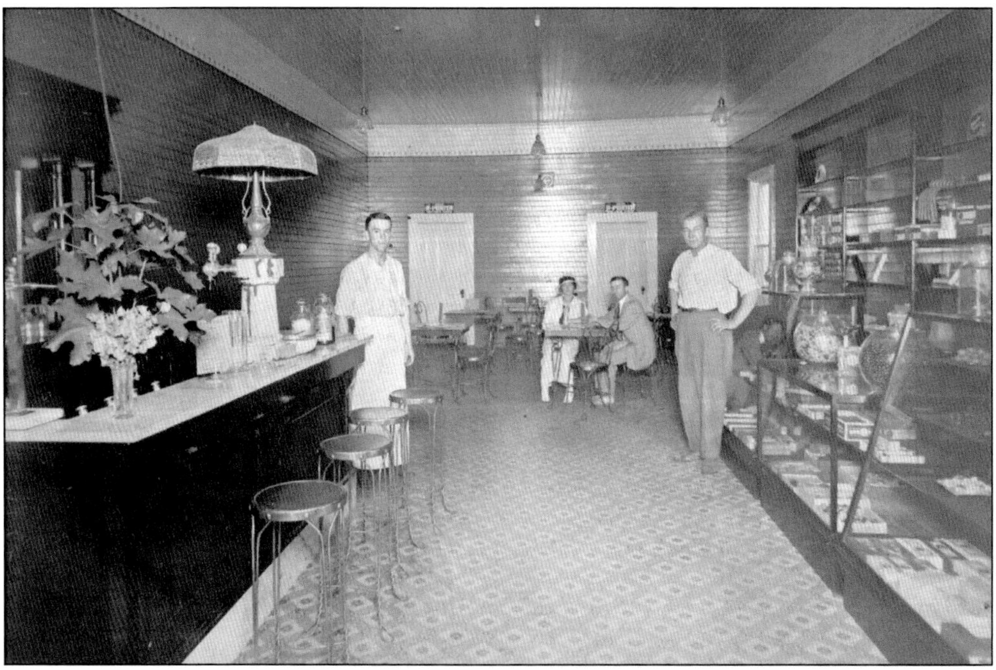

The Oathes and Anderson ice-cream parlor was a very popular place to go in 1911. The owners were Clifford Anderson, standing on the left, and Clarence Oathes. The parlor was one of the first family gathering places aside from the local churches for parents to take their children for a family activity.

As the *Canby Herald* expanded its coverage, it needed to enlarge its printing equipment and delivery for best service, so the print shop ordered an additional press. Here, *Herald* printers Bob West (left) and assistant Warren Lindsay help Art Reed, the Hi-Way Lumber forklift driver, move the press into their shop. *Herald* publisher Tom Dillion was very pleased with this new piece of equipment.

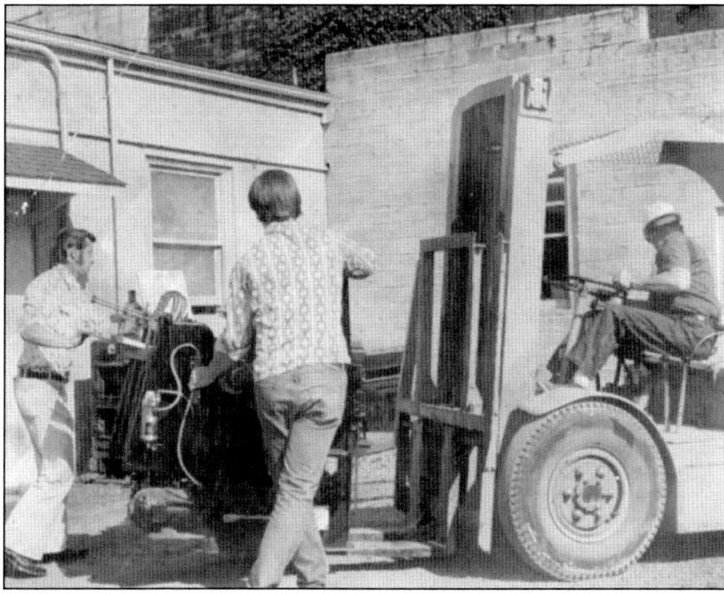

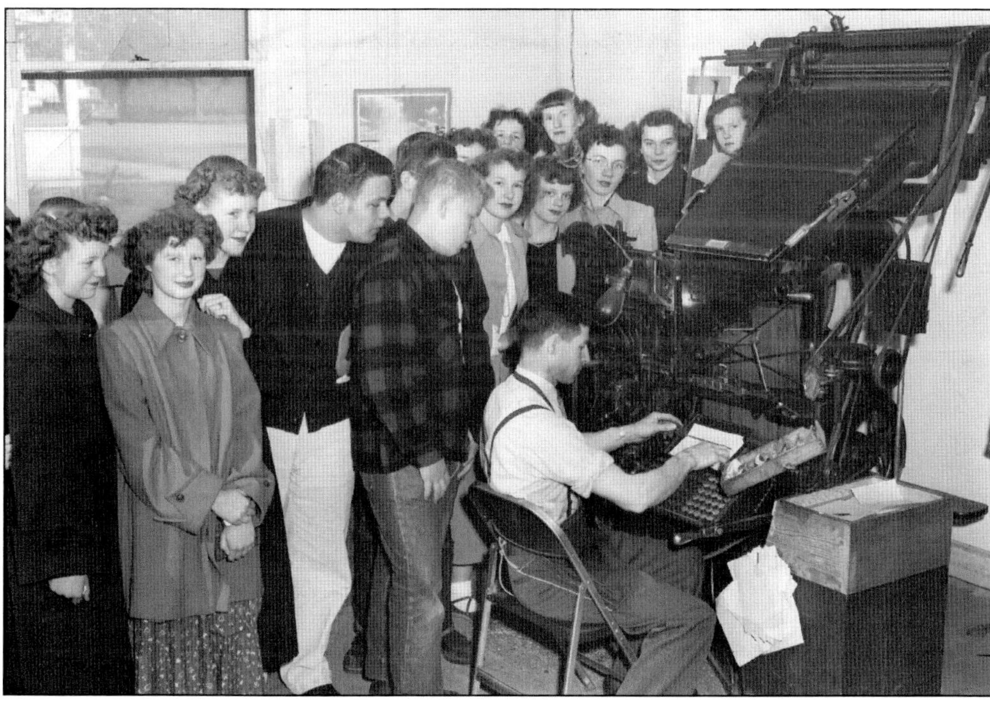

William G. Weston is shown on the linotype at the *Canby Herald.* He and his wife, Myra Weston, owned the *Canby Herald* from 1947 to 1972. After selling the paper, both Westons still stayed in touch with their newspaper. Myra would chronicle births, deaths, weddings, and local activities. In 1994, the Westons were honored in the General Canby Day festivities and led the annual parade as king and queen.

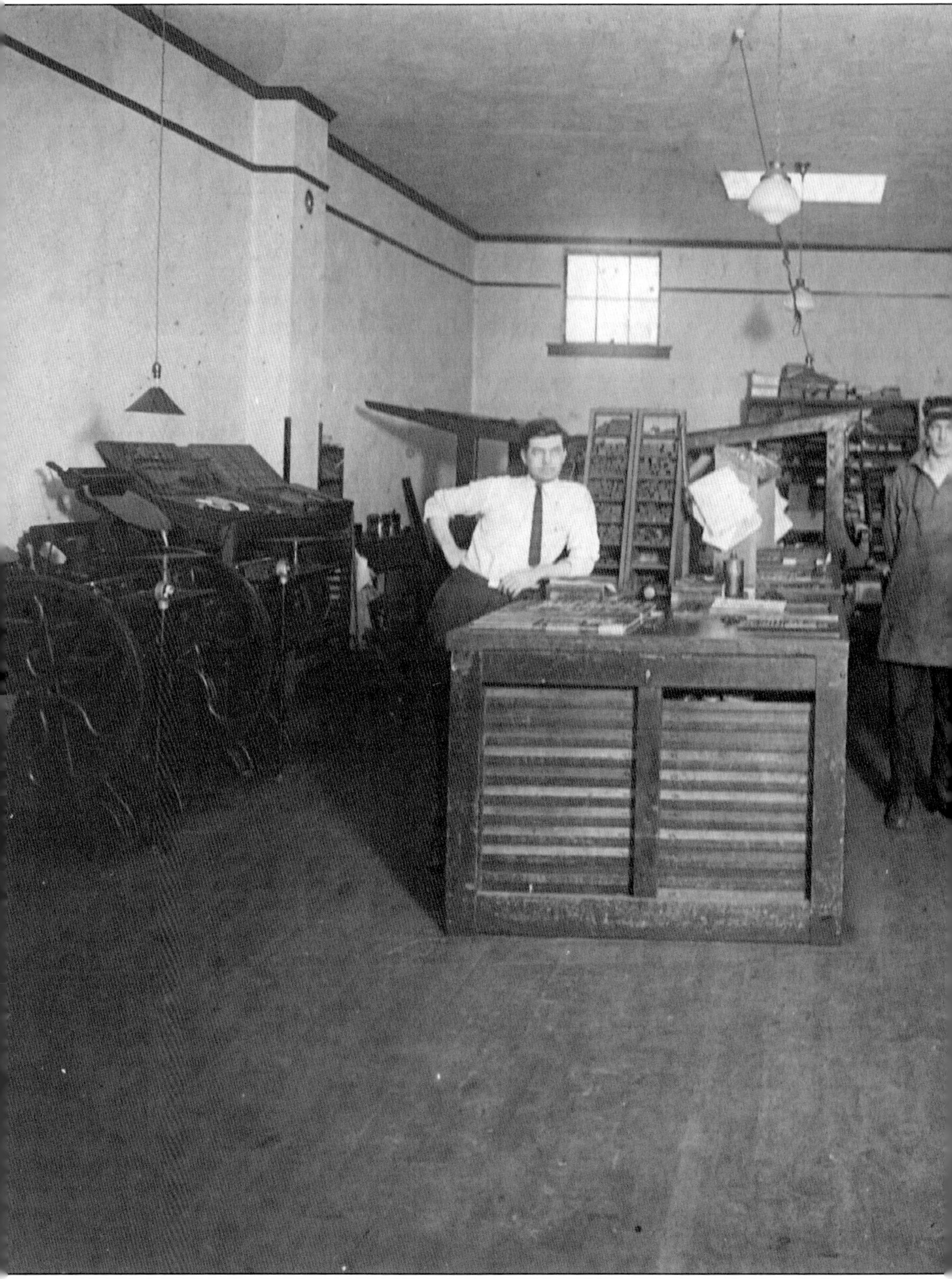

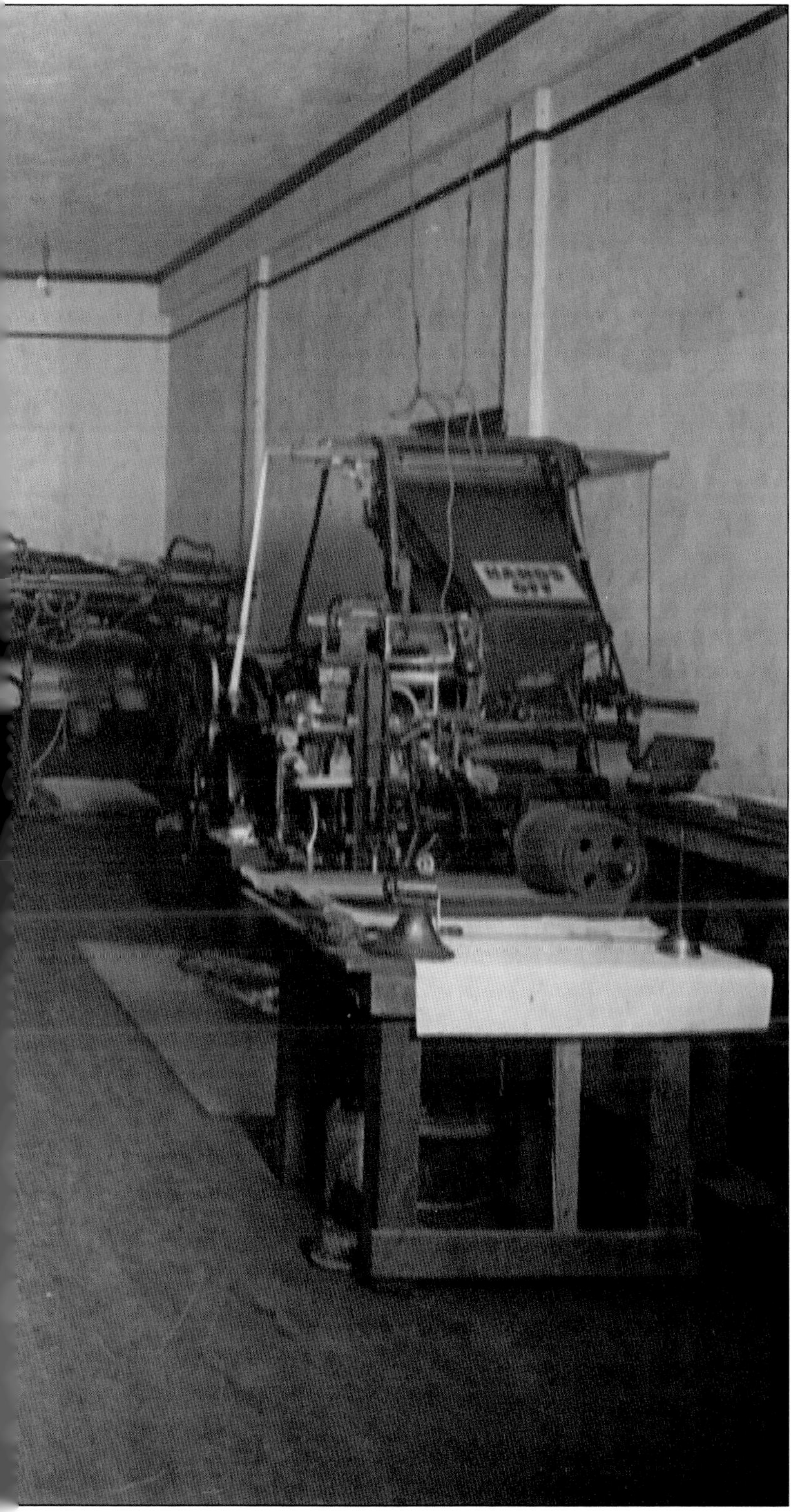

Located on NW Second Avenue and Grant Street in the 1914-built Canby State Bank (today the Direct Line) was the *Canby Herald* office. The newspaper used this building from 1922 into the 1940s. The man in the apron, to the left of an unidentified man, is Edward Satter. He was in charge of the printing. Satter was later the *Canby Herald*'s editor and publisher. When he was just 12, Satter worked under George W. Dixon at the *Canby Tribune*, founded in 1906. At right is the Model X Intertype that came into Canby in 1922. This machine was used in the *Canby Herald* office for more than 50 years. In 1925, after 40 years of work in Canby, Satter went to Salem, Oregon, and became a typesetter for the *Oregon Statesman* newspaper.

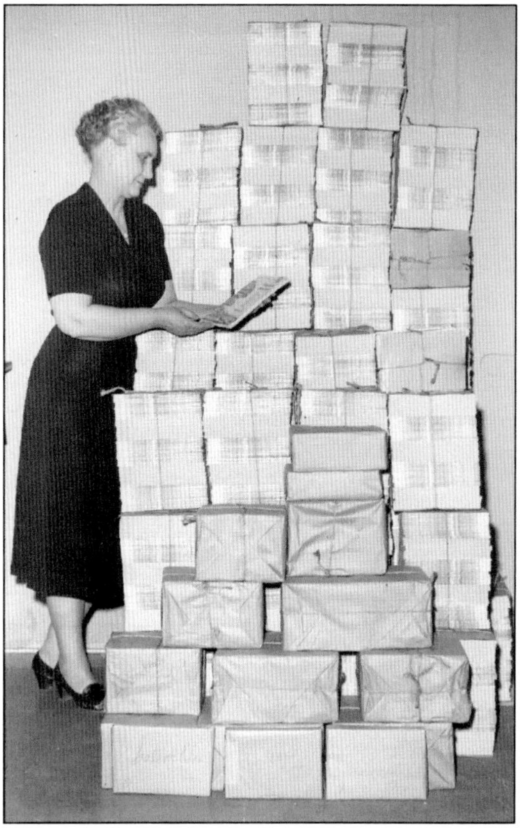

The *Canby Herald* was not only the local newspaper in Canby, but published other items as well. Myra Weston stands next to a huge stack of phone books in 1959. These books were all set and ready for delivery to Canby households. The *Canby Herald* printed the books and distributed them.

The Kozy Corner confectionery was owned in 1925 by George and Ora Lee Cattley (center). Behind them are their nephew and niece, Earl and Hazel Lee Jenkins. The Kozy Corner was also the town's bus depot at Ivy Street and Highway 99E (First Avenue). Later, George and Ora's daughter, Doris Cattley, worked there as well.

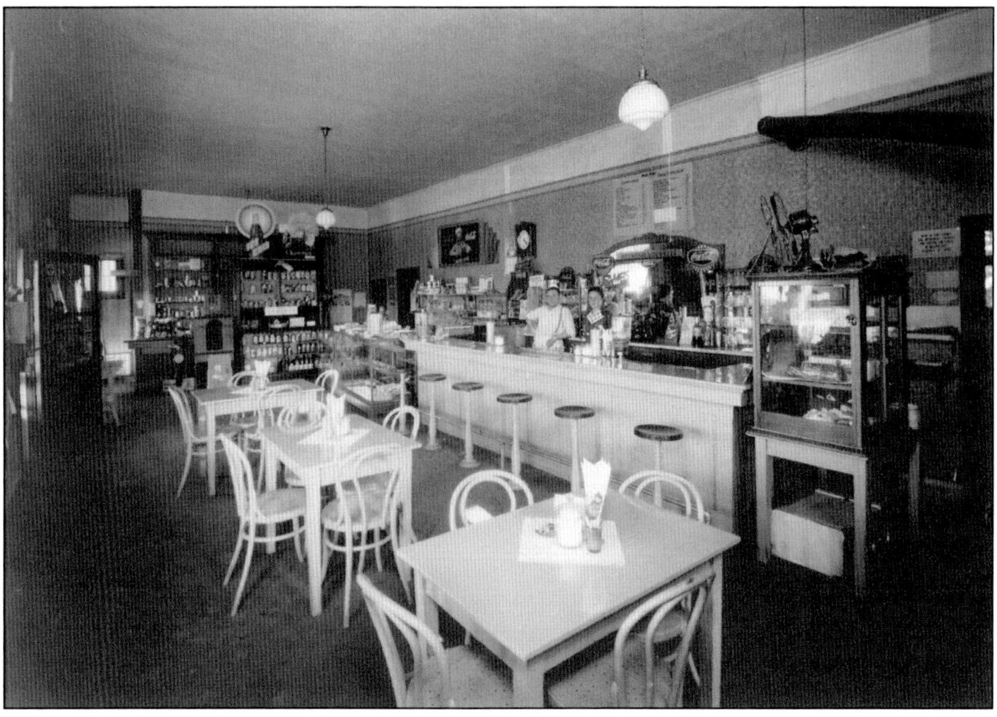

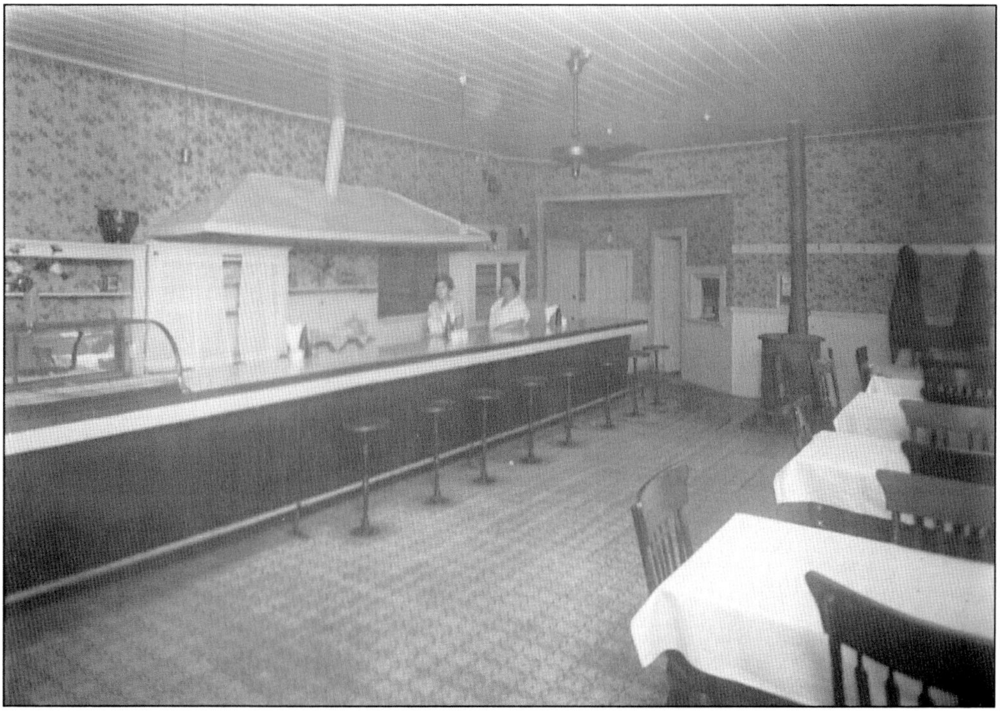

Here is the Maple Corner Restaurant in 1929. It was located at NW First Avenue and Fir Street. Shown are May Nieland and her mother, Anna Nieland. Anna was born in Wisconsin in 1878. Her father had emigrated from Germany and had given her a love for cooking fine food.

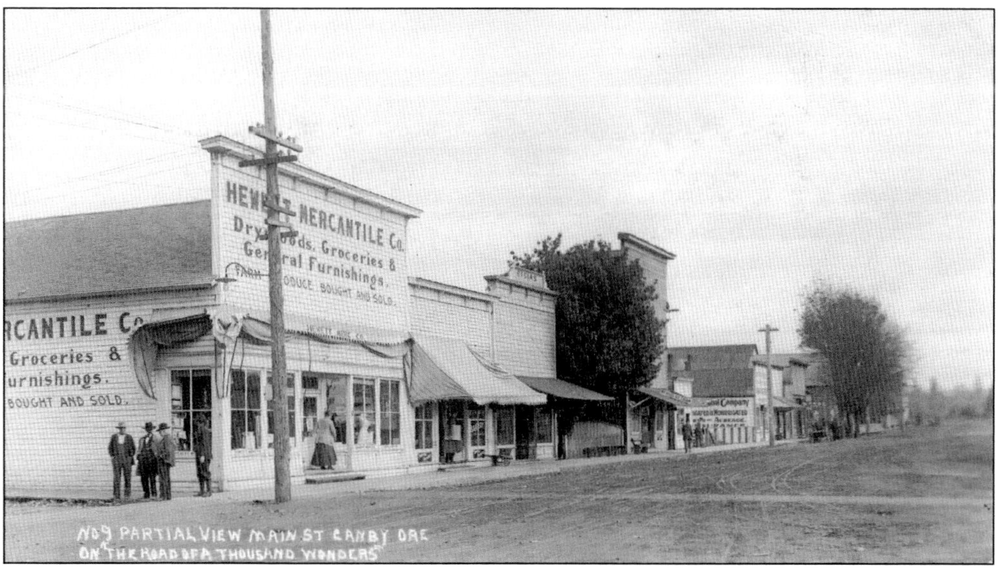

Here, in 1910, are some of the businesses sitting on Main Street in Canby: Hewett Mercantile Company; behind it, M.J. Lee's Canby Canal Company; and the Wang store on the North Holly Street corner. The Knight brothers store of the 1870s had become the Hewett Mercantile Company; it was later moved to make way for the Masonic Building's construction. This photograph is from the Ralph E. May Collection.

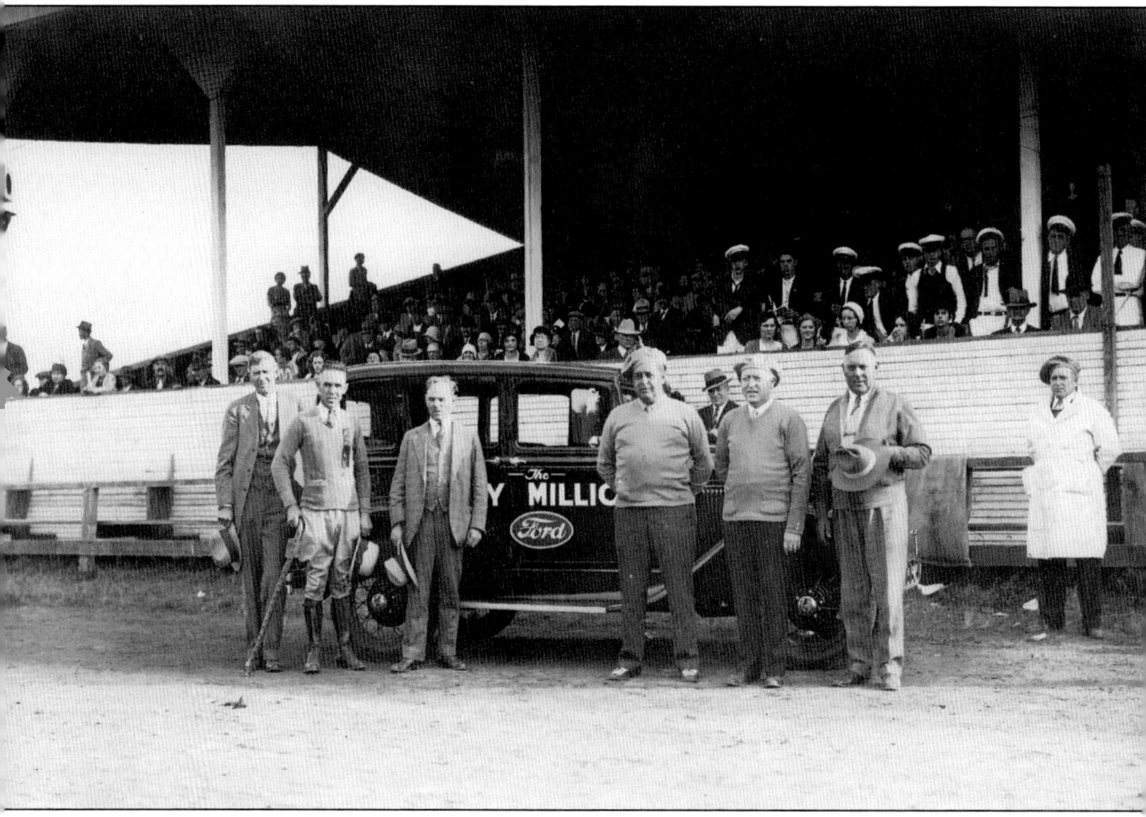

Dr. Henry Alvin Dedman was quite active in helping Canby develop. Born in Missouri in 1863, Henry came with his parents, Dr. E.C. and Sarah E. Paddock Dedman, to Clackamas in 1878. His father was a physician but retired soon after his relocation to Oregon. Dr. Henry Dedman, a general practitioner, opened his medical office in Canby in 1897. In 1906, he was influential in forming the Canby Bank & Trust Company, which established the first banking institution in this area. In 1914, the name was changed to the Canby State Bank. Later, the same stockholders organized the First National Bank of Canby; Dr. Dedman was president of both banks. In 1898, Henry married Anna B. Armstrong, and they had two children, Craig and Mildred. Here, Henry is pictured with the 20-millionth Ford in front of the Canby Fairgrounds grandstand in 1927. From left to right are Louis Lent, Herman H. Chindgren, Henry, two unidentified men from Ford, and Grant White; in back is Carl Bethke, another Ford employee.

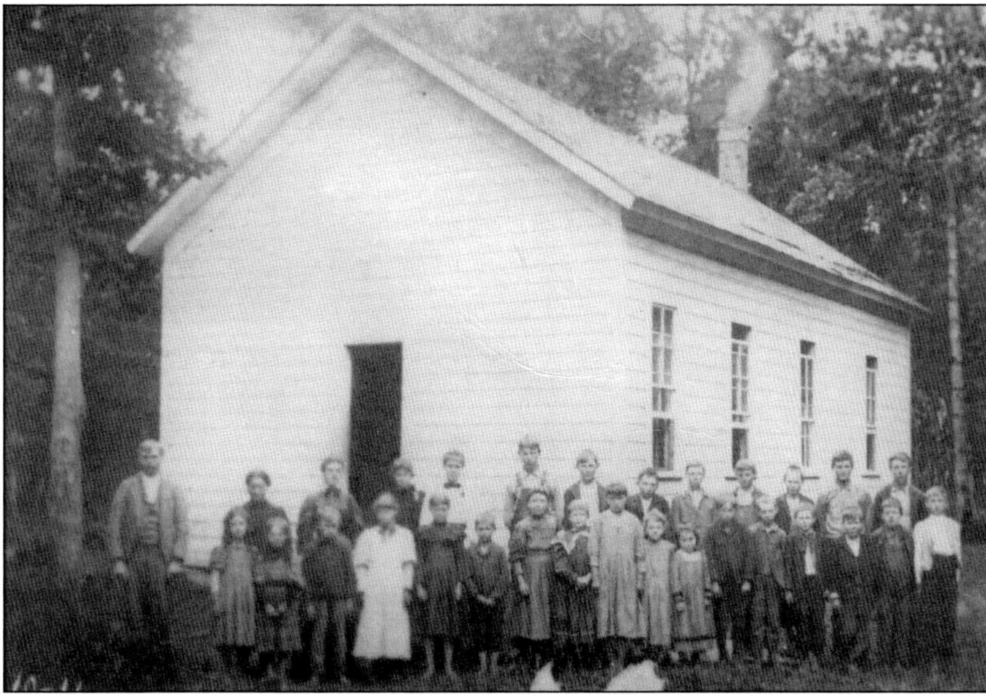

The South Oak Grove School District No. 93 was established in the 1890s. This schoolhouse was built around 1887 in the nearby neighborhood known then as the Latourette Woods. This area was close enough to the growing families of Canby that many parents loaded their children in wagons and took them to study here. This is a portrait of the 1910–1911 class; one teacher in one room taught every grade.

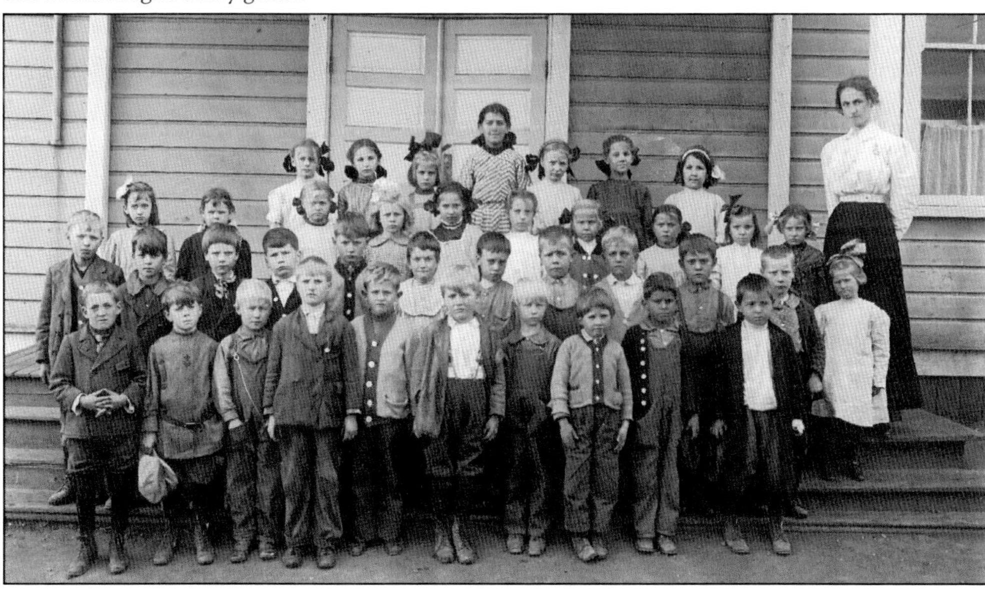

As soon as these grade schools were built, teachers were hired and the classrooms filled with eager young minds. These students worked on their reading, writing, and mathematics, and after walking home, they worked just as hard with their families on the farms—feeding the animals, picking the fruits, keeping the house tidy, and watching over their younger siblings.

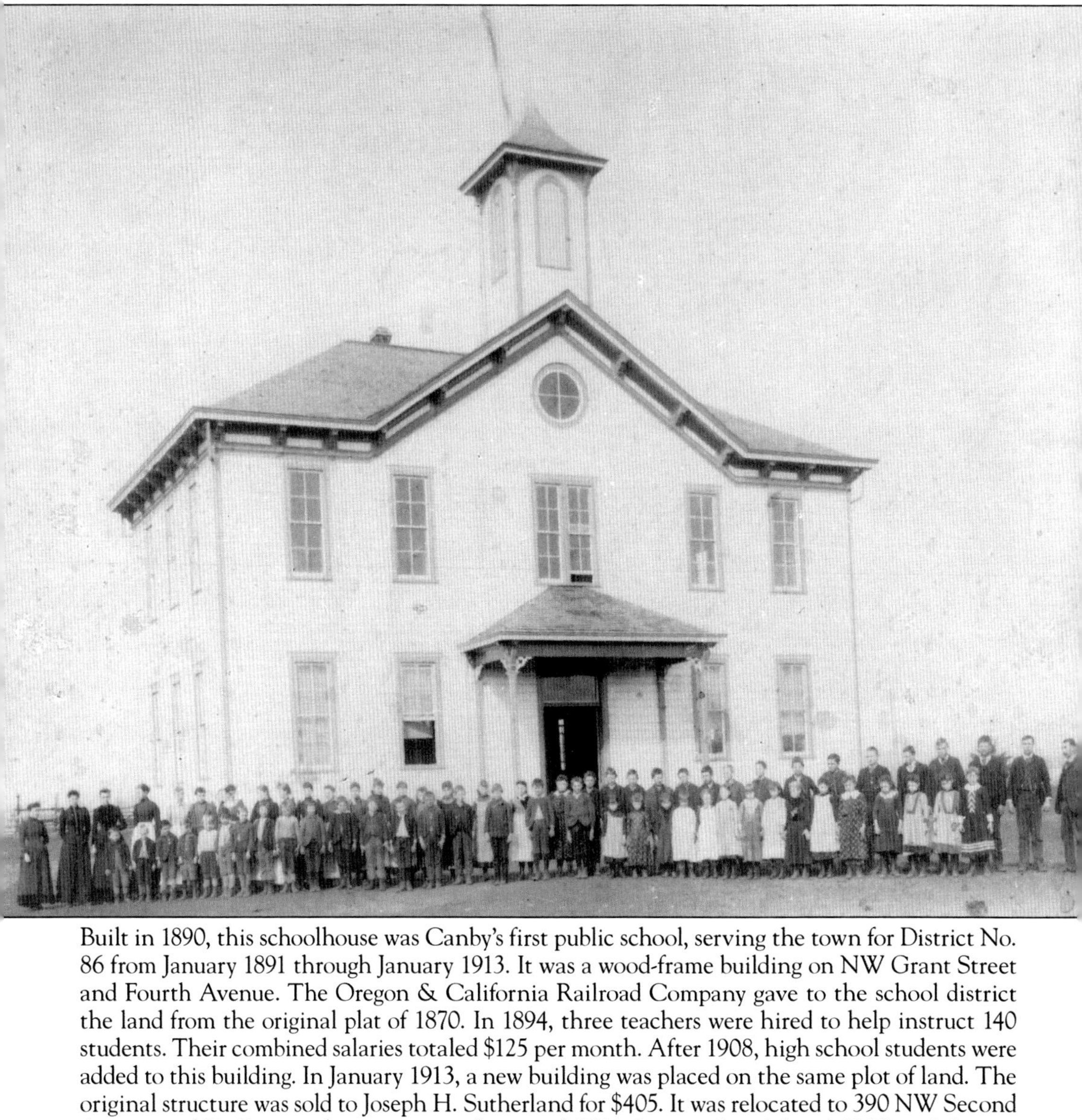

Built in 1890, this schoolhouse was Canby's first public school, serving the town for District No. 86 from January 1891 through January 1913. It was a wood-frame building on NW Grant Street and Fourth Avenue. The Oregon & California Railroad Company gave to the school district the land from the original plat of 1870. In 1894, three teachers were hired to help instruct 140 students. Their combined salaries totaled $125 per month. After 1908, high school students were added to this building. In January 1913, a new building was placed on the same plot of land. The original structure was sold to Joseph H. Sutherland for $405. It was relocated to 390 NW Second Avenue and Fir Street, where it was used up until 1974, first as a hotel (until 1961) and then as a nursing home.

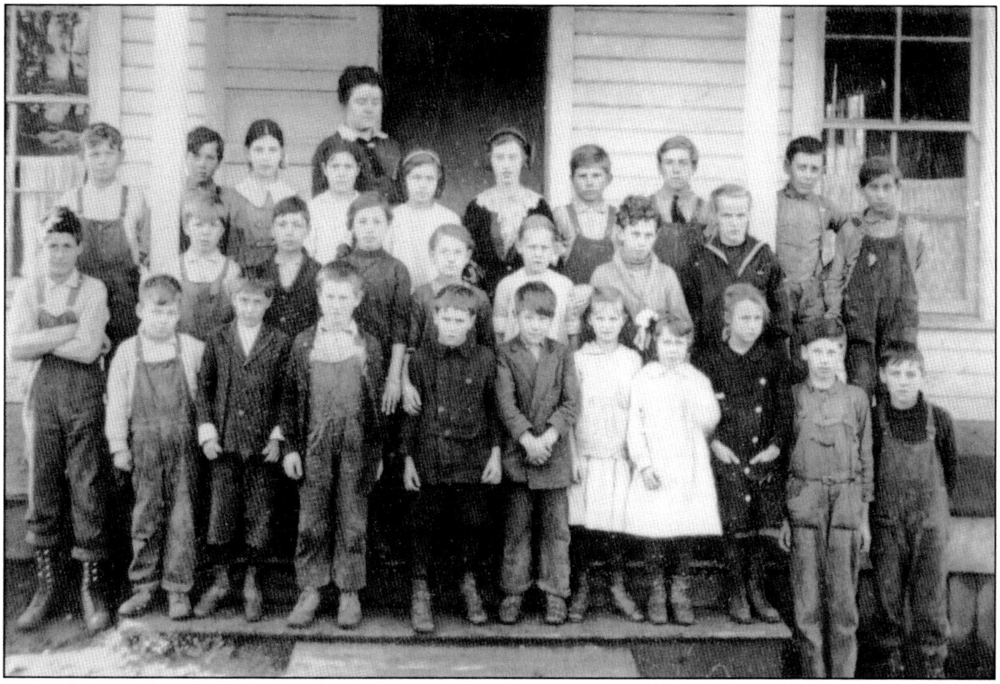

The Union Hall School, also known as the Phelps School, had just one teacher to instruct all eight grades of the elementary level. The schoolhouse faced toward Union Hall (now Central Point) Road. This former School District No. 81 merged into Canby's District No. 86. This building no longer exists.

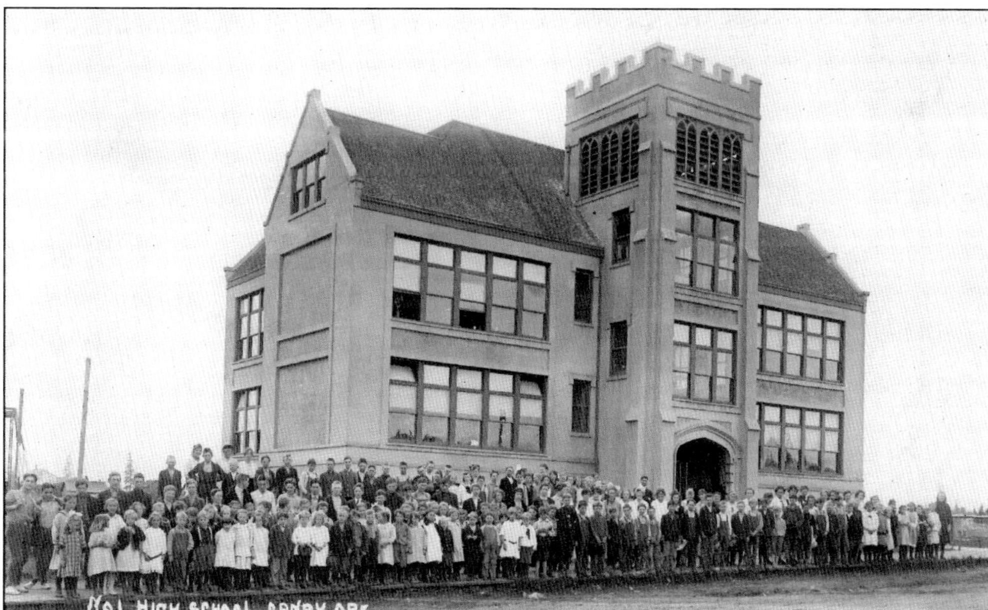

In 1912, a new massive structure was erected to hold Canby's growing School District No. 86 and house grades 1 through 12. It was active from 1913 until 1928. This school was called the "Canby Castle" before its bell tower was removed several years after it was built. The school was still used for the elementary grades until it caught fire on February 19, 1974, and was destroyed.

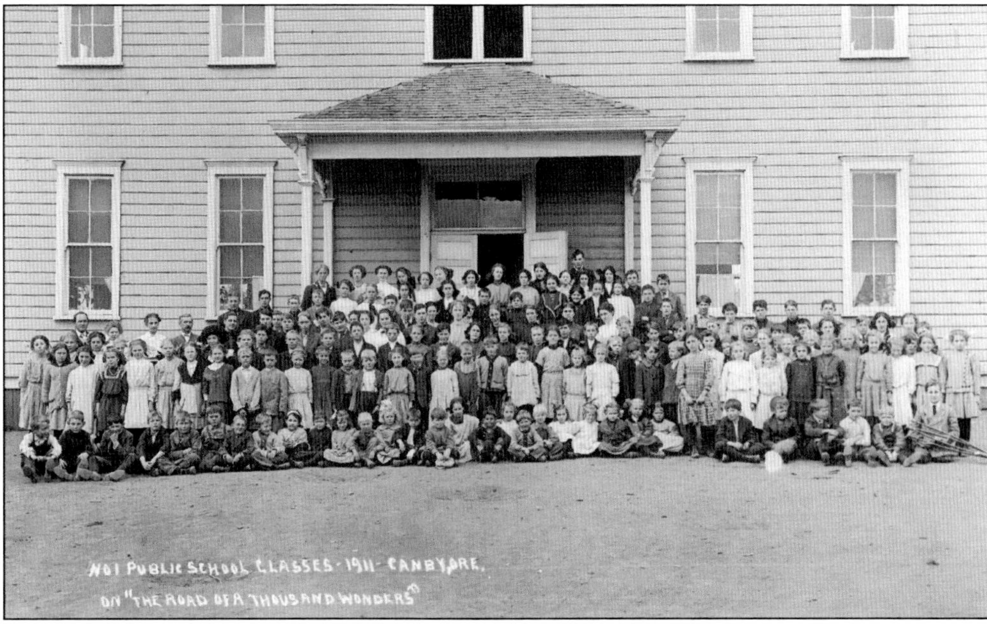

As Canby grew and its schools expanded, the teaching jobs increased as well. Canby became an attractive place to work and live. Mr. and Mrs. Ashton moved from Oregon City and rented the Will Kendall residence. Professor Ashton taught at the Macksburg School, while his wife, an accomplished instrumentalist, taught music. Here is the Canby public school student body of 1911.

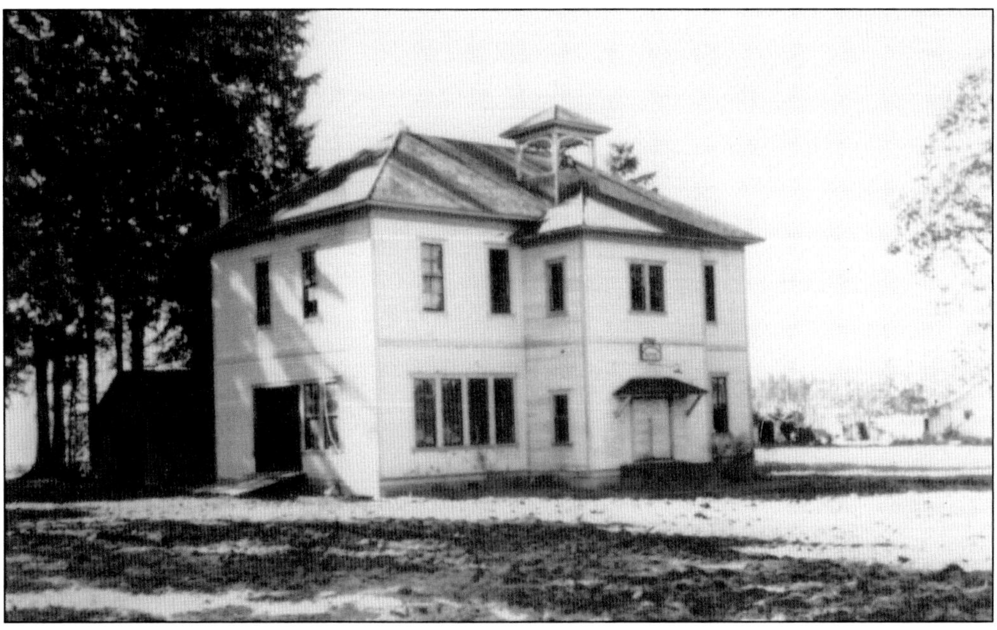

The Macksburg School District No. 20 was set on two acres donated by Jacob and Rachael Roop. It merged with Canby School District No. 86 on July 7, 1945. This building replaced a smaller one-room school and was one of the larger schoolhouses in Clackamas County. It faced Macksburg Road between Dryland and Elisha Roads. Classes at Macksburg schools were discontinued after voters approved the 1945 merger with Canby.

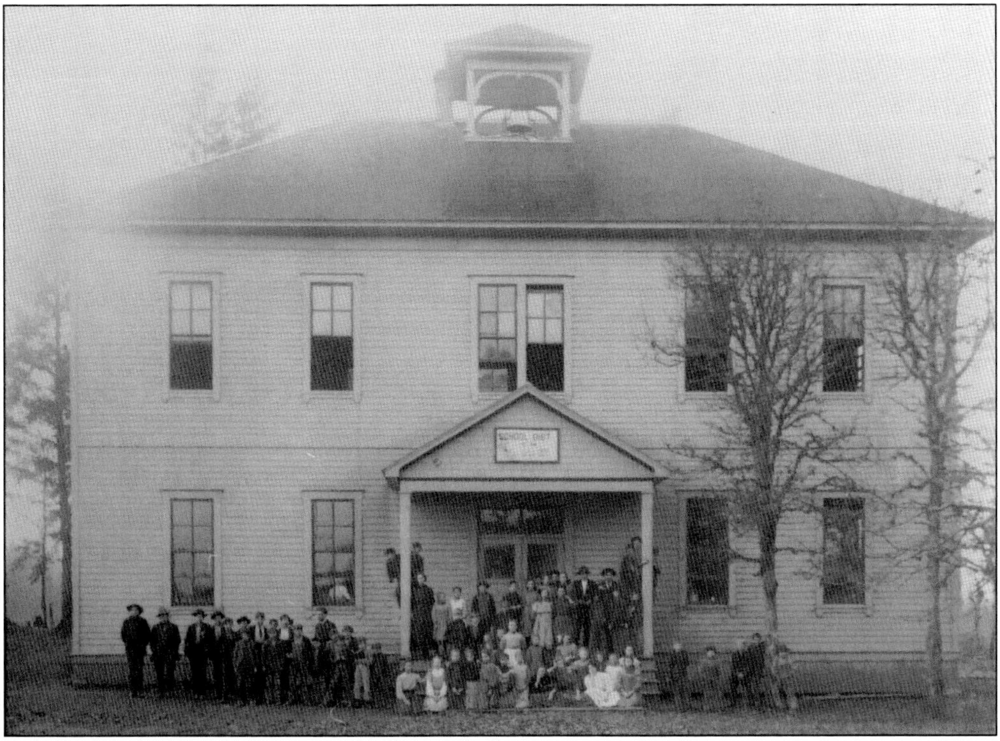

By 1915, Macksburg, an unincorporated community four miles southeast of Canby, had a population of 200, a public school, two Lutheran churches, a Grange Hall, and a number of stores. Here is the Macksburg Schoolhouse, built in 1905, which became part of School District No. 20. This photograph shows the schoolchildren with their teachers.

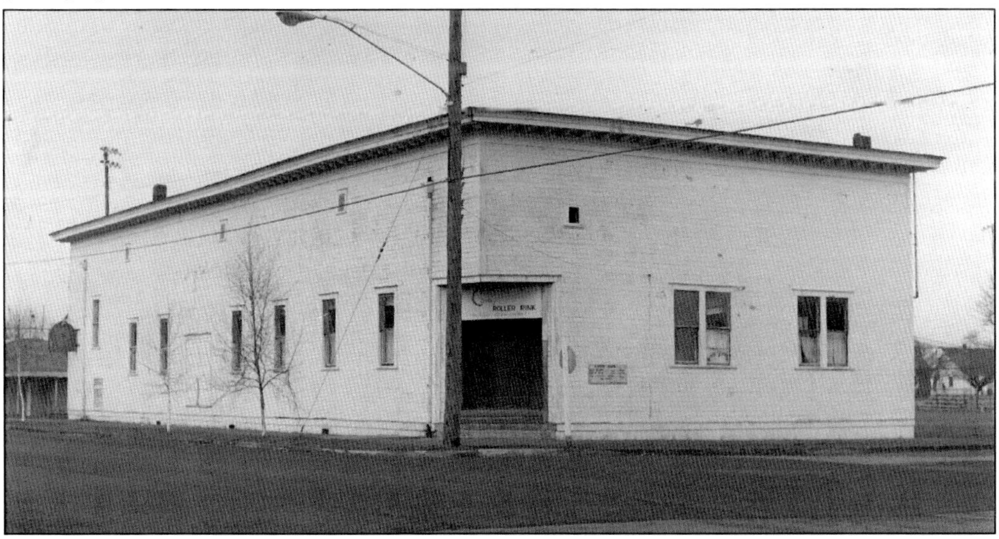

The Band Hall was built in 1912. It was located at the southwest corner of what is now Wait Park. The Canby School District No. 86 owned this hall from 1913 to 1935. It was used for graduations, basketball, and gymnasium classes, while the American Legion Post 122 used the back half of the building. In 1967, Canby purchased the site for $8,000 to use for improving the facilities at Wait Park.

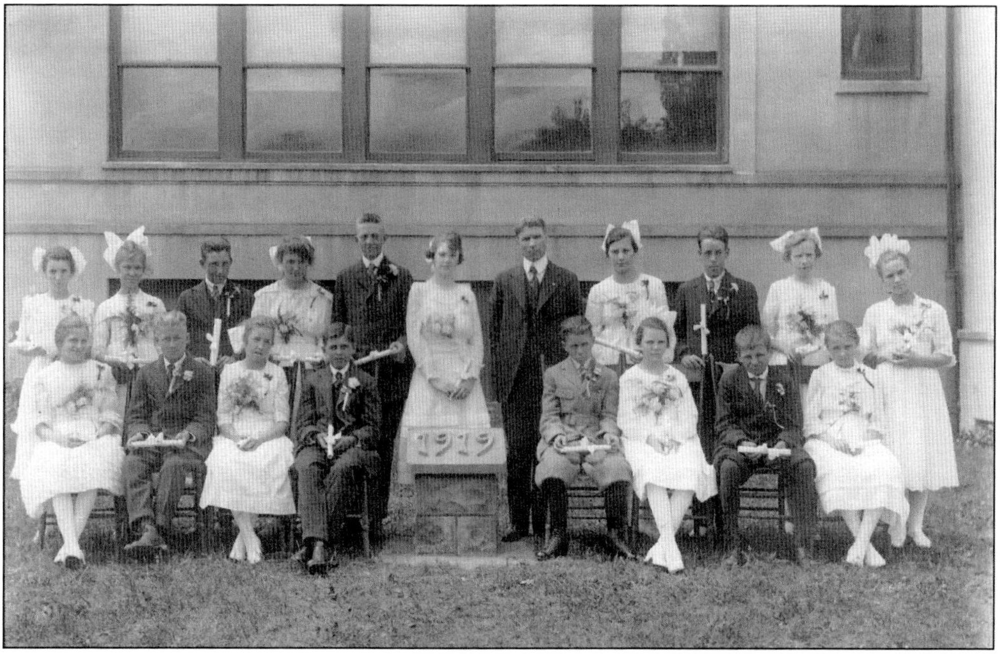

Canby had one grade school when Howard H. Eccles came to teach with just two other teachers. From 1893 to 1913, Eccles taught in three schools: the White School near Hubbard; Riverside School; and Mundorff School, just east of Molalla Forest Road. In Canby, all 12 grades were taught in this school until the Canby Union High School was built in 1926. Here is the eighth-grade graduating class of 1919.

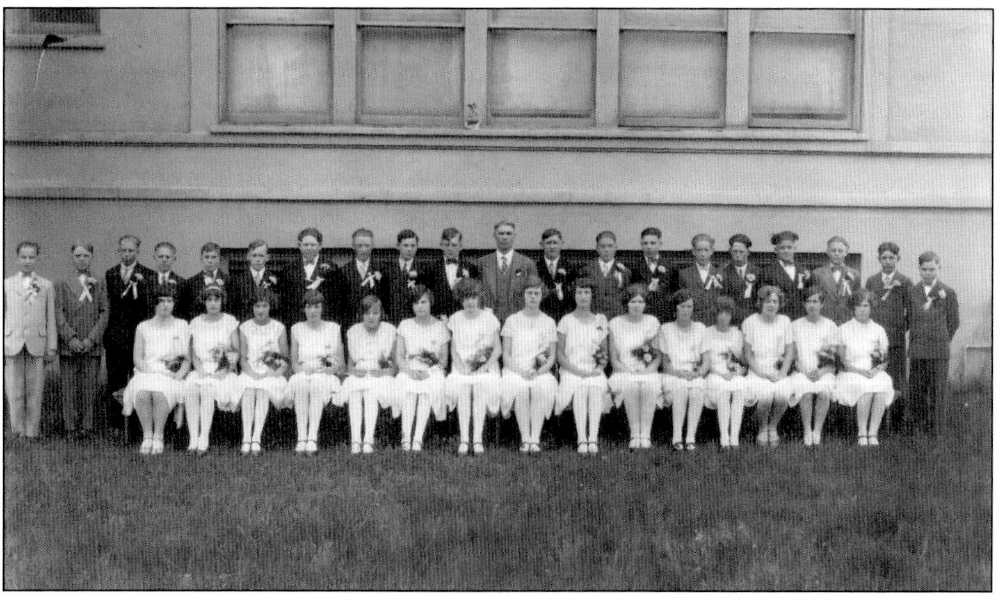

This school building, constructed in 1875, was located on North Grant Street. Shown here is the 1926–1927 eighth-grade graduation class with Howard Eccles, the principal and teacher. Howard H. Eccles was involved with Canby schools from the time he was 17 years old until he turned 73. Because of his dedication to the students and their education, a new elementary school built in 1956 was named after him.

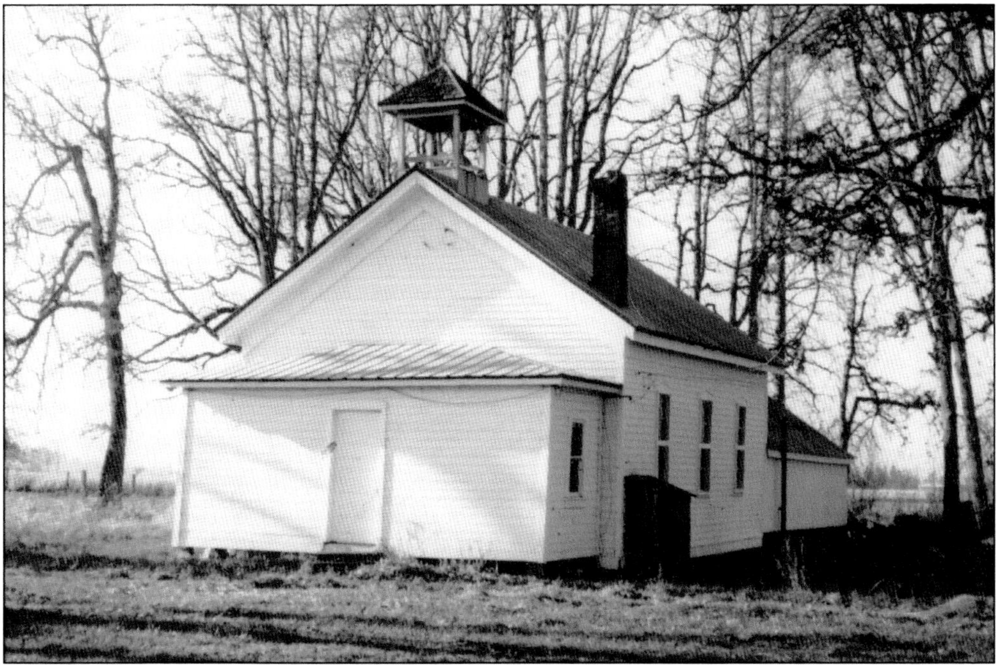

This is the Marks Prairie School in District No. 38, on Mark Road in Canby. It was built in 1900 and restored in 1948. On May 15, 1879, the Mark family set aside two acres of property for a school. It was no longer a schoolhouse in 1946, when the school district joined Canby. The Marks then gave the former school to the Marks Prairie Community Club; it became a meeting hall.

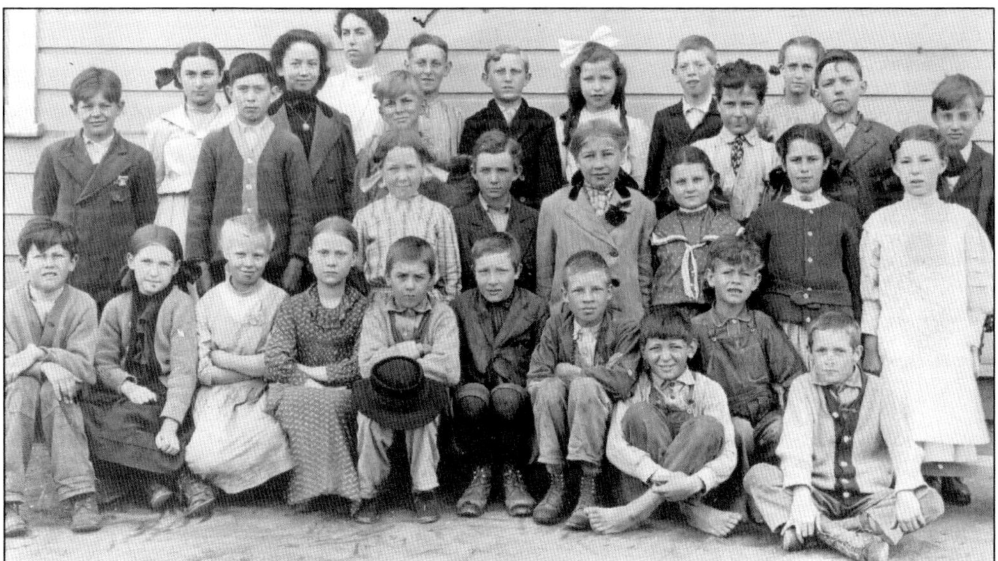

These elementary students were going to school in Canby around 1912. The teacher for this class was Adeline B. Wyeth. The student next to the teacher (with a mark above his head) is Canby-born George Dewey Cox (1898–1988). He was the 14th child of Oregon pioneer parents born in 1852 and 1853. They owned a nursery on the corner of NW Avenue and Ivy Street.

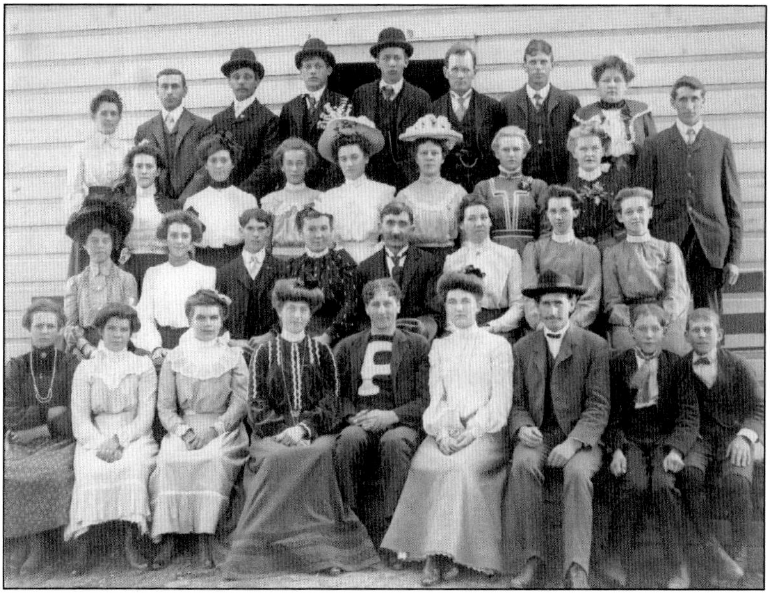

Needy, an area near the town of Canby, was home to a young people's literary society. Many young folks from the area would attend. The member of this group pose in their best clothing for an October 1903 photograph in front of the Needy schoolhouse.

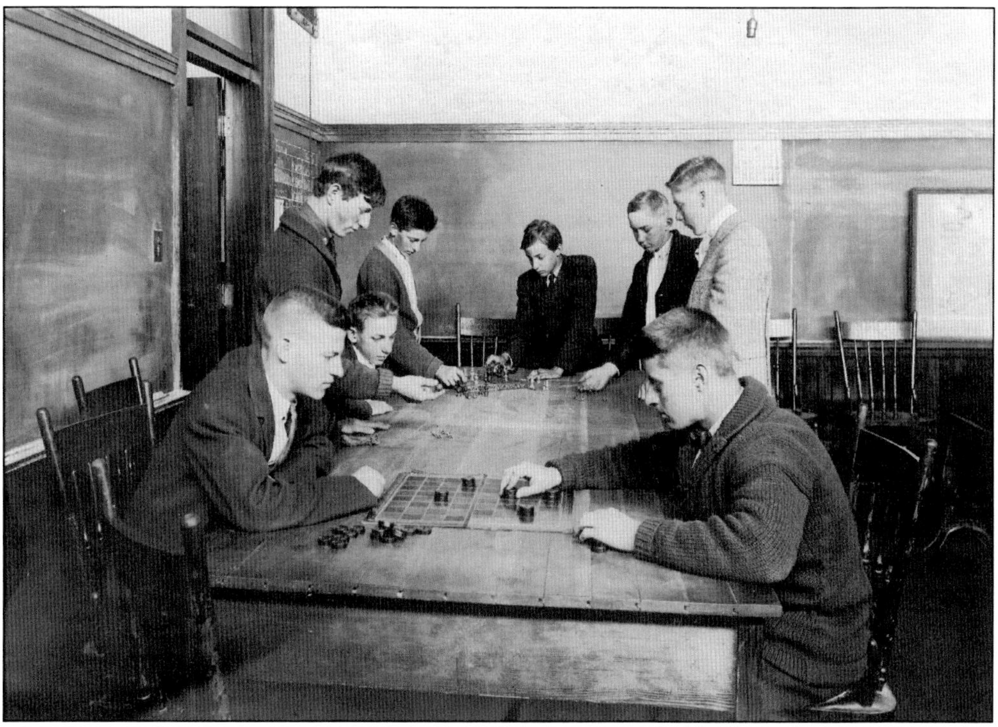

The first high school in Canby was built in 1890 on the corner of NW Fourth Avenue and Grant Street. Shortly after Canby was incorporated, a new, larger building was used; the Canby Union High School was put in its place in 1927–1928. A huge fire destroyed it in 1974. Here are some of the Canby High School students playing checkers and chess around 1915.

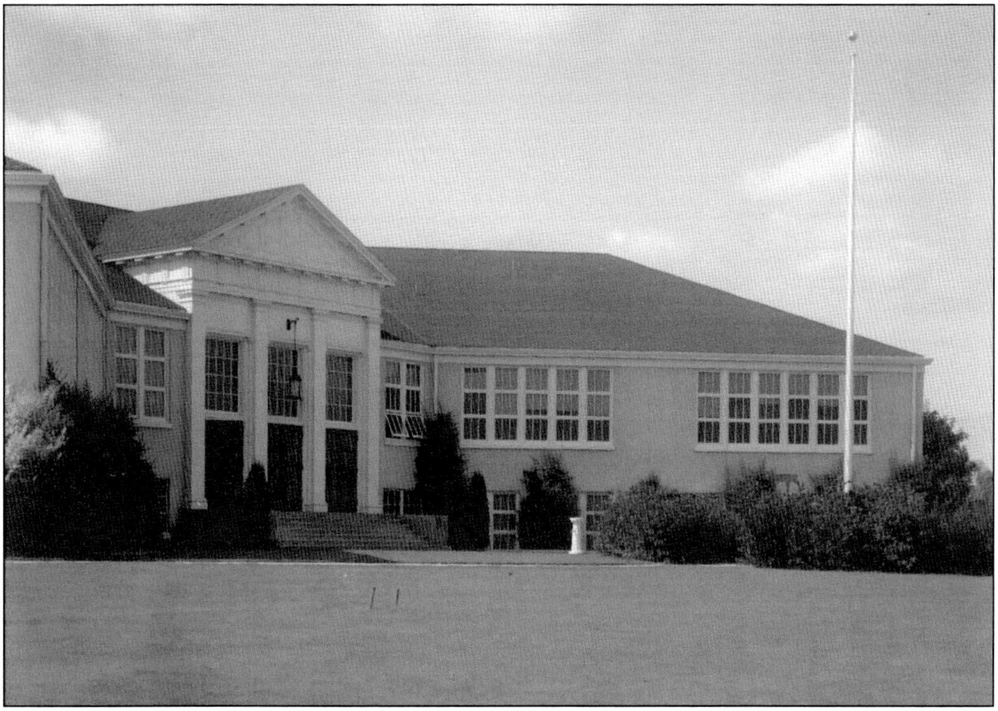

George Henry Brown of New Era and his brother, William W. Brown, the legendary "Horse King" of Eastern Oregon, gave the original Canby High School District 30 acres of land in order to build its first high school. George Brown was a strong advocate for education. He was known as the "Potato King" because he was a pioneer agriculturist of potatoes and one of the first cultivators to ship potatoes in carload lots to other states. Potatoes soon became a major export for Canby. This was the main entrance to the new Canby Union High School a year after it was built on February 3, 1928. One hundred and fifty students attended this school that year.

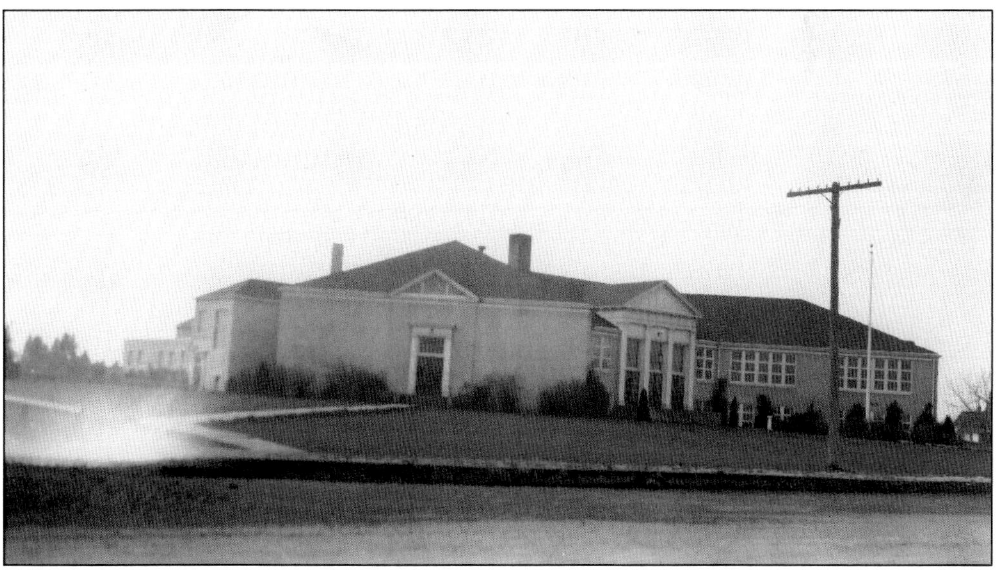

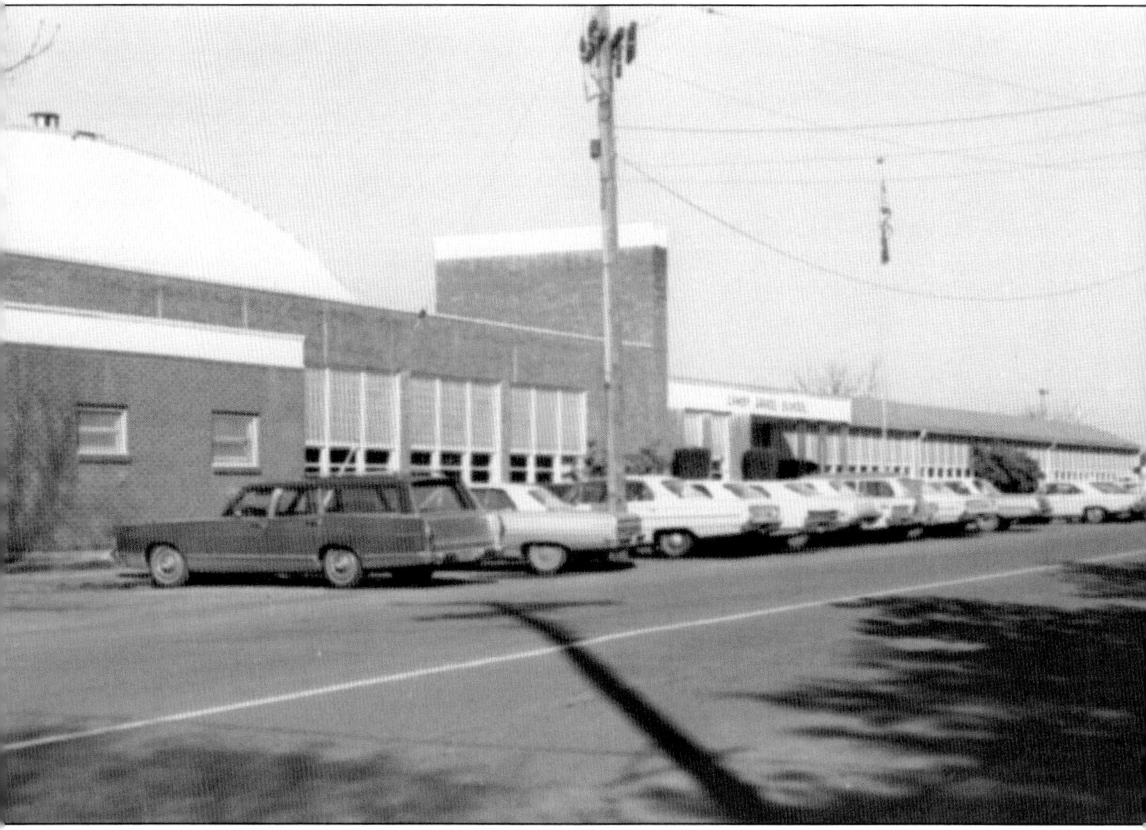

This is the school built in 1947–1948; it is located on North Grant Street in Canby. This was the second school built by School District No. 86. It was the first brick building to be used as a school by the district. In 1976, this elementary school was renamed for William Knight (1839–1922). Knight came to this region with his father, Joseph, and three brothers in 1868. William built the first frame schoolhouse in Baker Prairie in 1875. Five years later, this original 24-block of land became a part of Canby. William's 1874 home still stands on Fourth Avenue, as does the 1890 Knight Building on NW First Avenue, the first meeting place for the city council.

Three

Getting to Canby
Trains, Ferries, and Automobiles

The Oregon & California Railroad was developed in the 1900s. In 1870, it built the first bridge across the Molalla River west of Canby. The first train went over it in September.

The first ferry to Canby is believed to have run from the Champing Pendleton claim in the 1840s. River transportation was more efficient than packing wagons and riding on the muddy roads or pathways.

In 1914, the Canby Businessmen's Club began a ferry service. Clackamas County took it over in 1916. The county managed the ferries from the Riverside District to the end of Mountain Road until 1946. In 1953, the county reopened the Canby Ferry service. It used a steel-hulled boat named after an early leader, Millard Jerome Lee. The ferry service is still in operation.

Clackamas County built the Knight's Bridge in 1877. It was condemned for traffic use in 1944. In 1947, it splintered and fell into the river below. In 1964, the county constructed a steel and concrete bridge just downstream from the original span.

In 1901, E.D. Olds created a wooden covered crossing downstream from the railway bridge to transport automobiles and people between Barlow and Canby. This was used until a newer bridge was built on Highway 99E, and even then, it was working until the mid-1920s.

By 1919, the first two-lane bridge over the Molalla River between Canby and the town of Barlow was built. It was coordinated with the completion of the Pacific Highway from Portland to Salem. When two lanes became four lanes in 1963, a second bridge was constructed to carry the southbound stream of traffic, leaving the earlier bridge for the northbound flow. Since 1919, one can go to Canby by ferry, train, bus, or automobile.

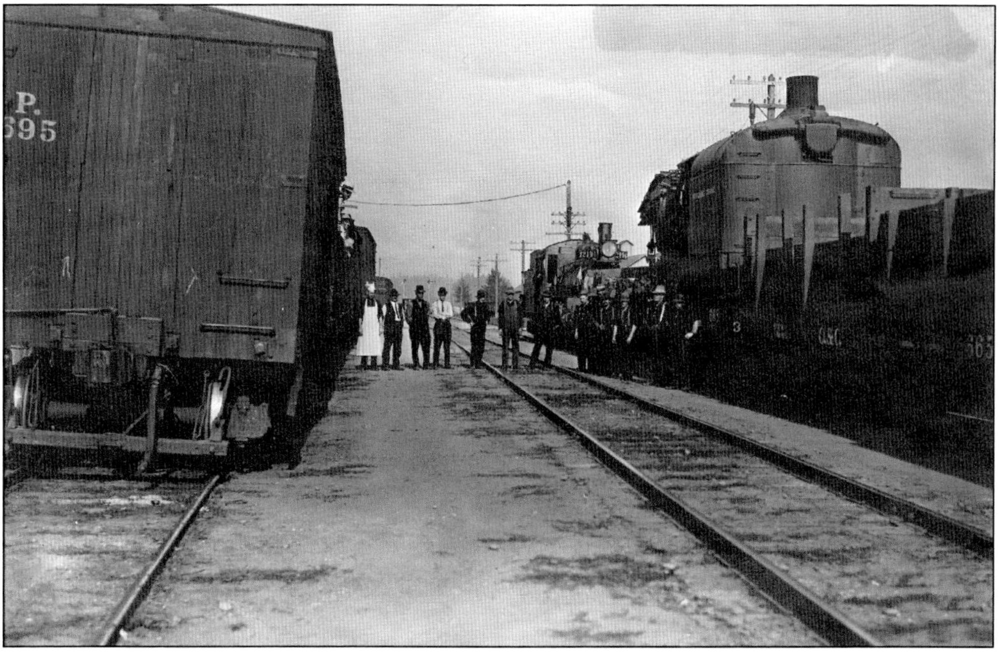

A Southern Pacific wrecker crew was sent out to clear debris from a collision on a trestle over the Molalla River between Canby and Barlow. This area of the river is the main route to the Willamette River, which runs along the northern point of Canby. Traffic was blocked for only one day. This photograph of the work train was taken at the Canby Station in 1908.

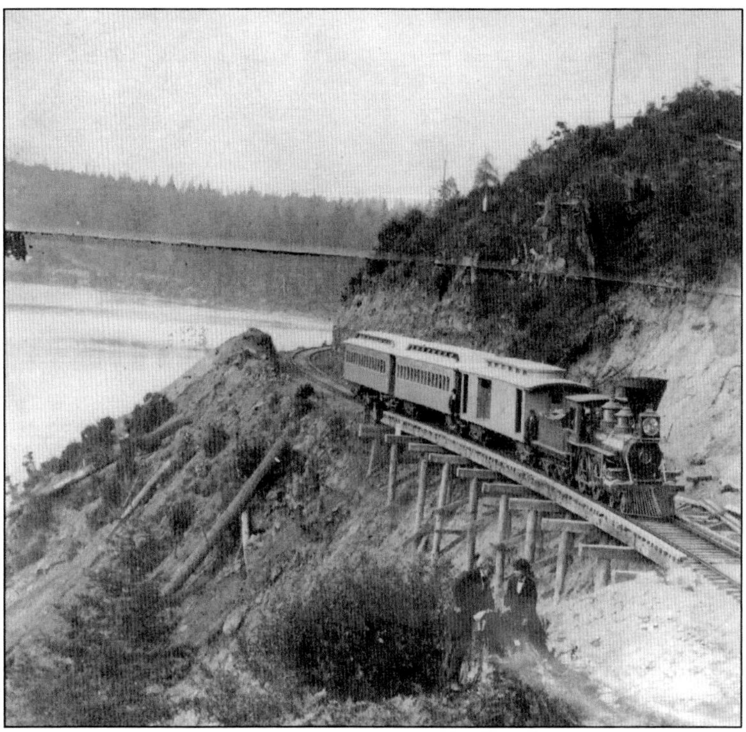

This is a section of the Oregon & California Railroad between New Era and Canby in 1870. R.E. Strahorn, a freelance railroad builder, constructed a rail line called the Strahorn line from Klamath Falls towards the east in the early 1900s. In 1927, the Southern Pacific purchased the line, and in 1928, the Interstate Commerce Commission told the Southern Pacific to sell half of its interest to the Great Northern Rail Line.

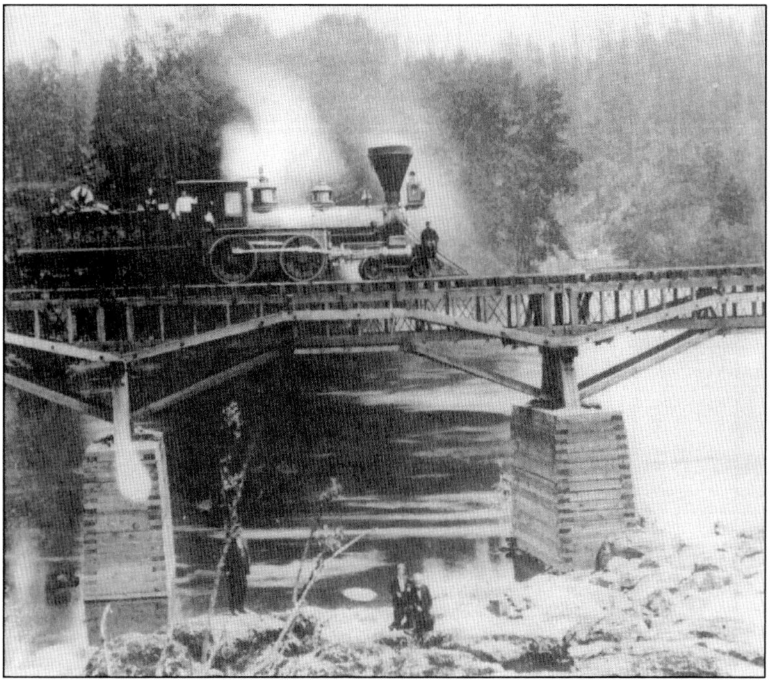

Heading towards Canby at 4:30 p.m. one Christmas Eve, a funnel-stacked steam train plugged across the 370-foot wooden Clackamas River Bridge, a typical early railroad bridge with trestles over the Clackamas River. This bridge, built by Henry Theisen, who was in charge of construction, washed out and was quickly replaced to allow trains to run through Canby.

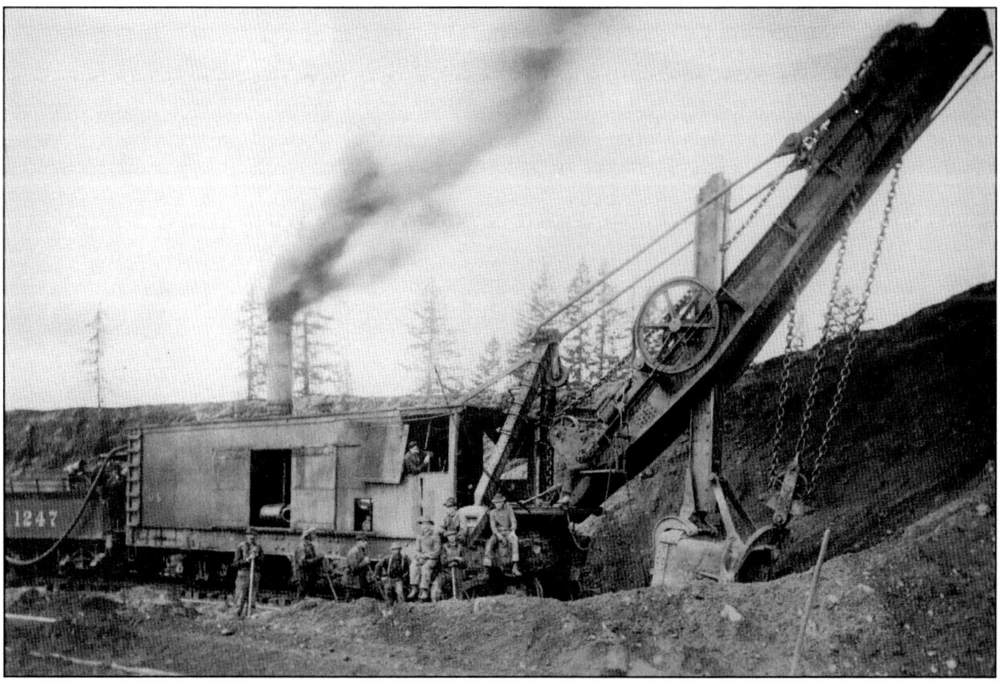

Due to the volume and seasonality of precipitation in its valley, the Willamette River has often flooded. The bridge, not yet complete, was washed out by the wild waters below. The piers and masonry work were severely damaged. In order for government land grants to not be lost, the bridge was quickly reconstructed. Here is a steam shovel in the railroad pit in Canby.

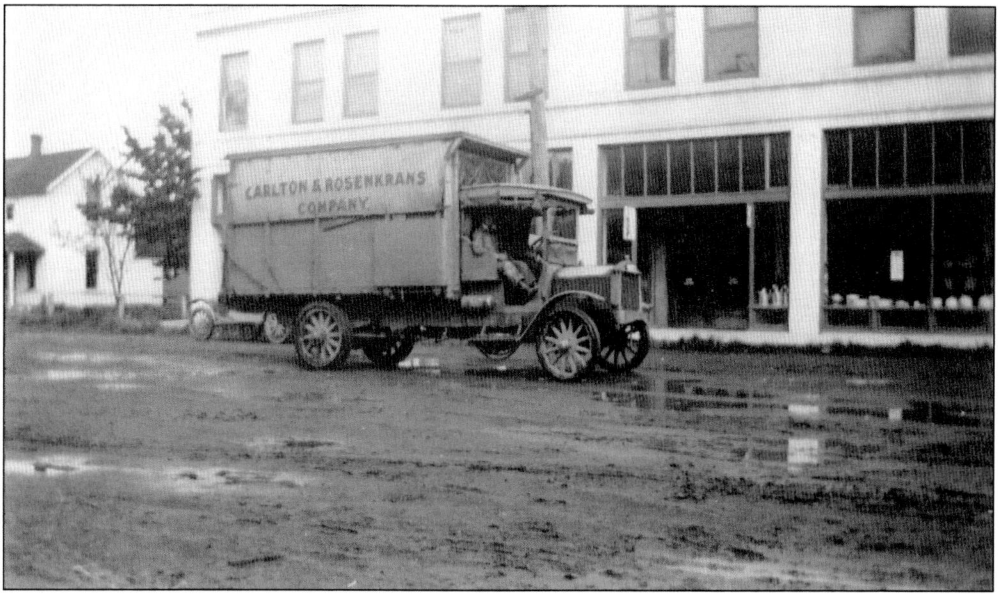

The Carlton & Rosenkrans Company had the first motorized delivery wagon in Canby. It was used for delivery to the company's huge store. Jacob A. Giger, a city councilman from 1935 to 1938, was the driver. The store replaced the horse-drawn wagon it had used up until 1912 with this new vehicle. The truck is shown here parked on NW Second Avenue, across from the store.

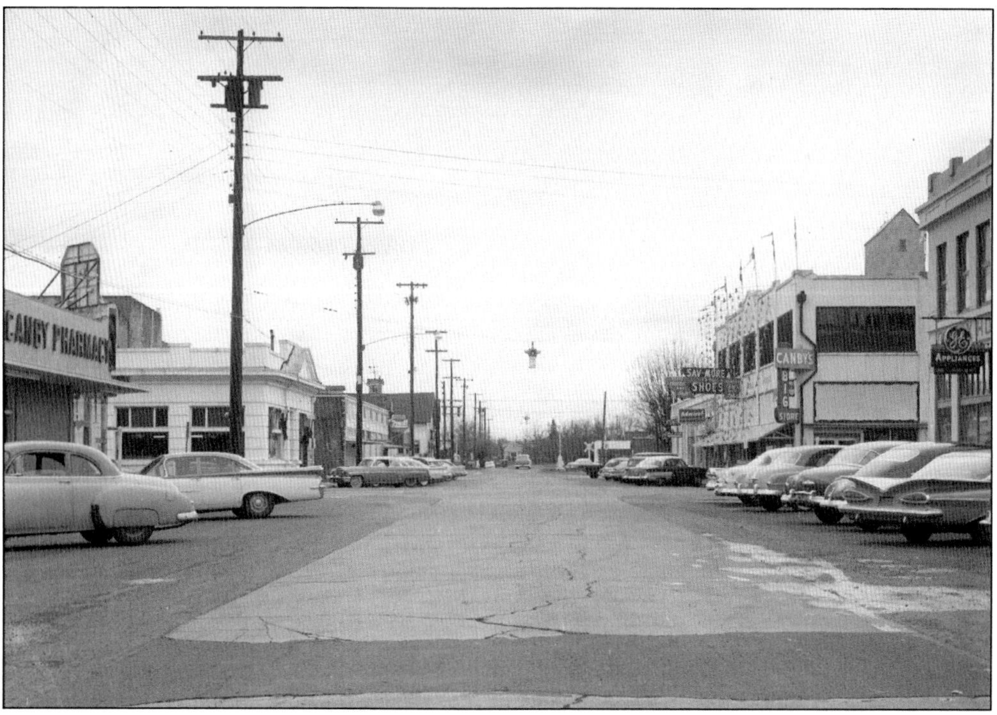

Around 1959, the businesses show the growth and changes in Canby. On the right is Canby's Big Store, where the Carlton & Rosenkrans Company had been located. This 1912 building was remodeled in 1974 after a destructive fire. It is now the Graham Building. On the left at NW Second Avenue is the Canby Union Bank, built in 1914 as the First National Bank of Canby.

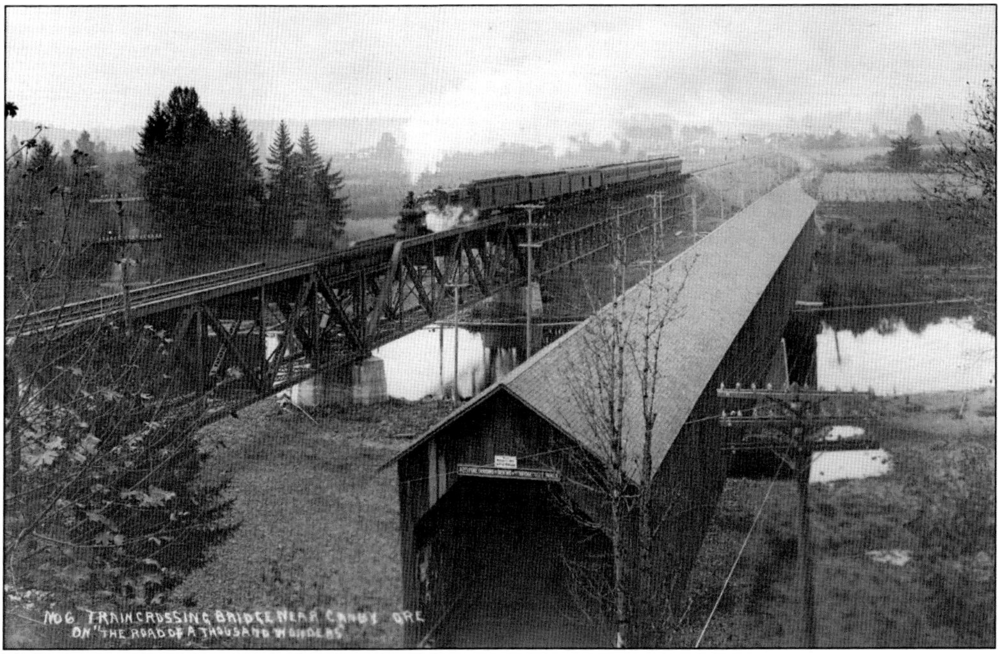

A train is crossing the bridge on the left over the Molalla River near Canby around 1900. The covered bridge, one of three over the Molalla River to Canby at that time, was there from 1901 to 1925. It carried pedestrians, livestock, and automobiles on the early highway up towards the Willamette Valley.

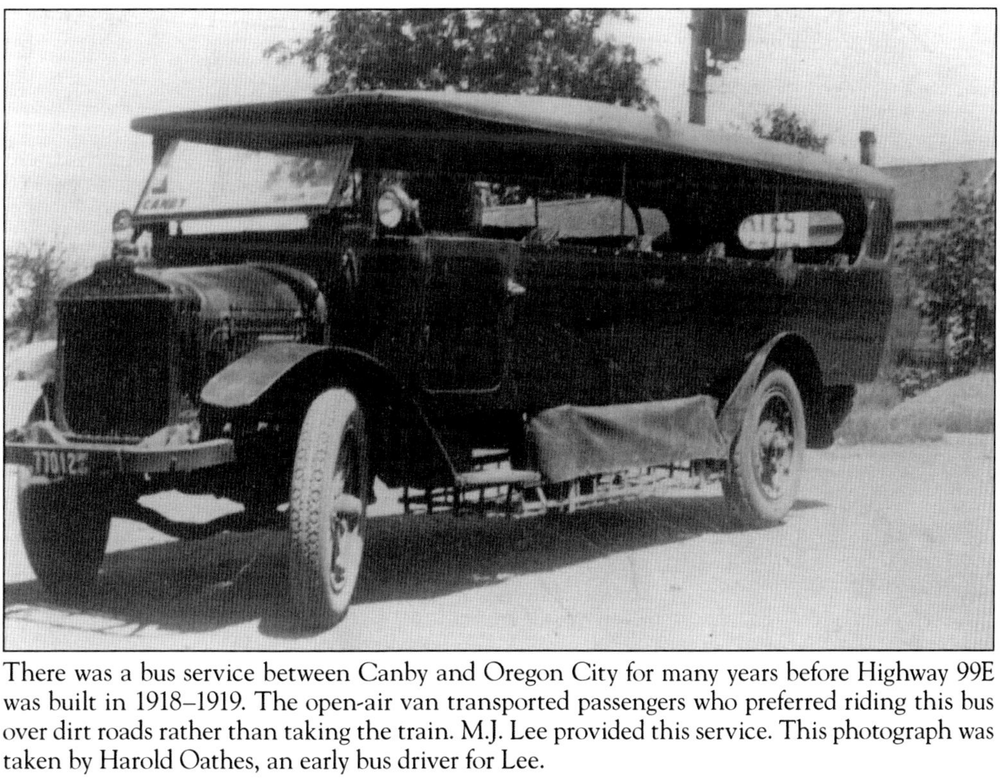

There was a bus service between Canby and Oregon City for many years before Highway 99E was built in 1918–1919. The open-air van transported passengers who preferred riding this bus over dirt roads rather than taking the train. M.J. Lee provided this service. This photograph was taken by Harold Oathes, an early bus driver for Lee.

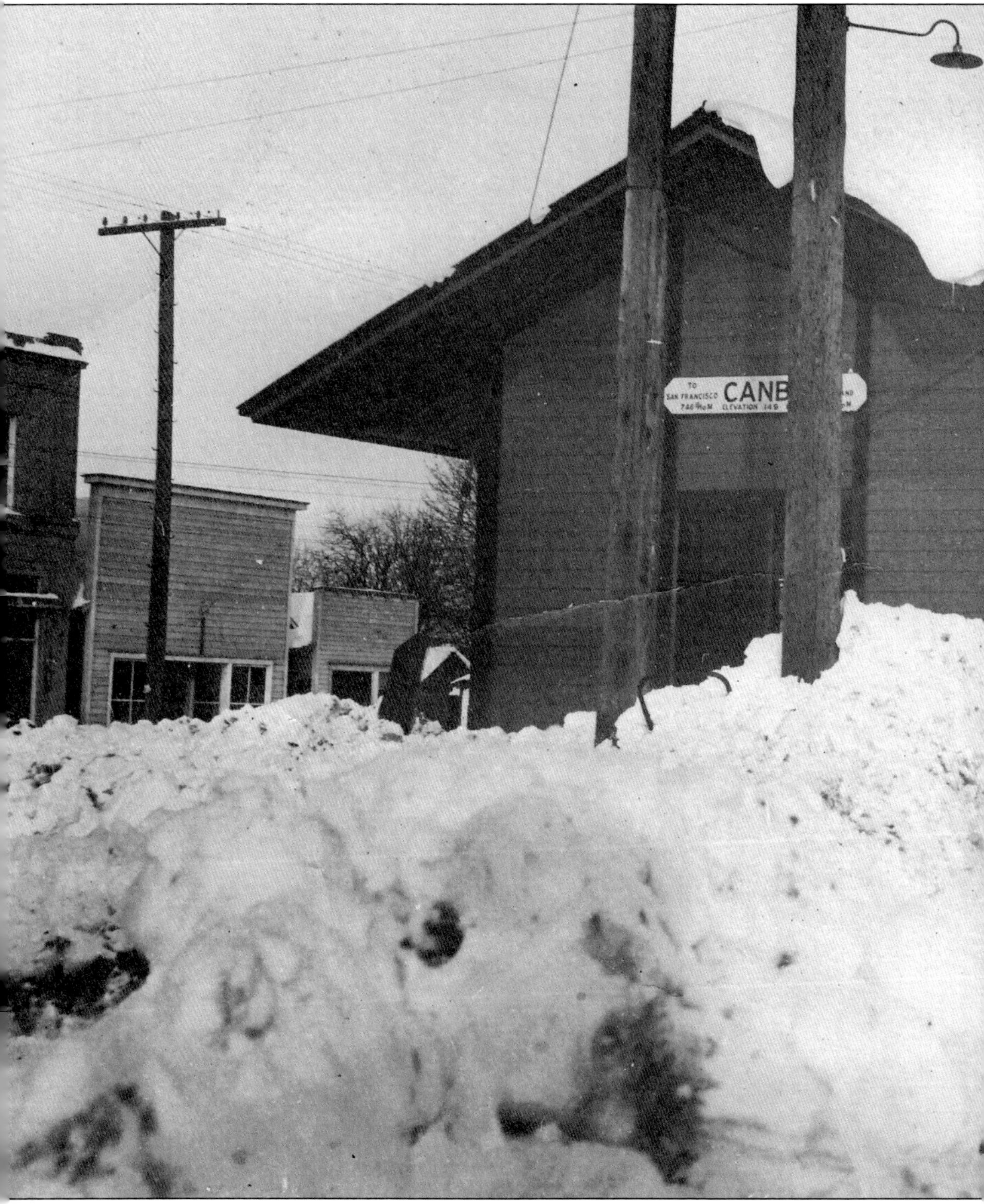

Built in 1893, the Southern Pacific Company Depot, style No. 11, replaced the first depot, which was knocked down in a windstorm in 1891—the same year it had been constructed. It remains one of the oldest railroad stations in Oregon. Trains then carried thousands of carloads of grains, potatoes, and other farm crops. Canby Depot accommodated both passengers and freight and also offered telegraph service. This photograph displays a record snowfall that came in late 1919,

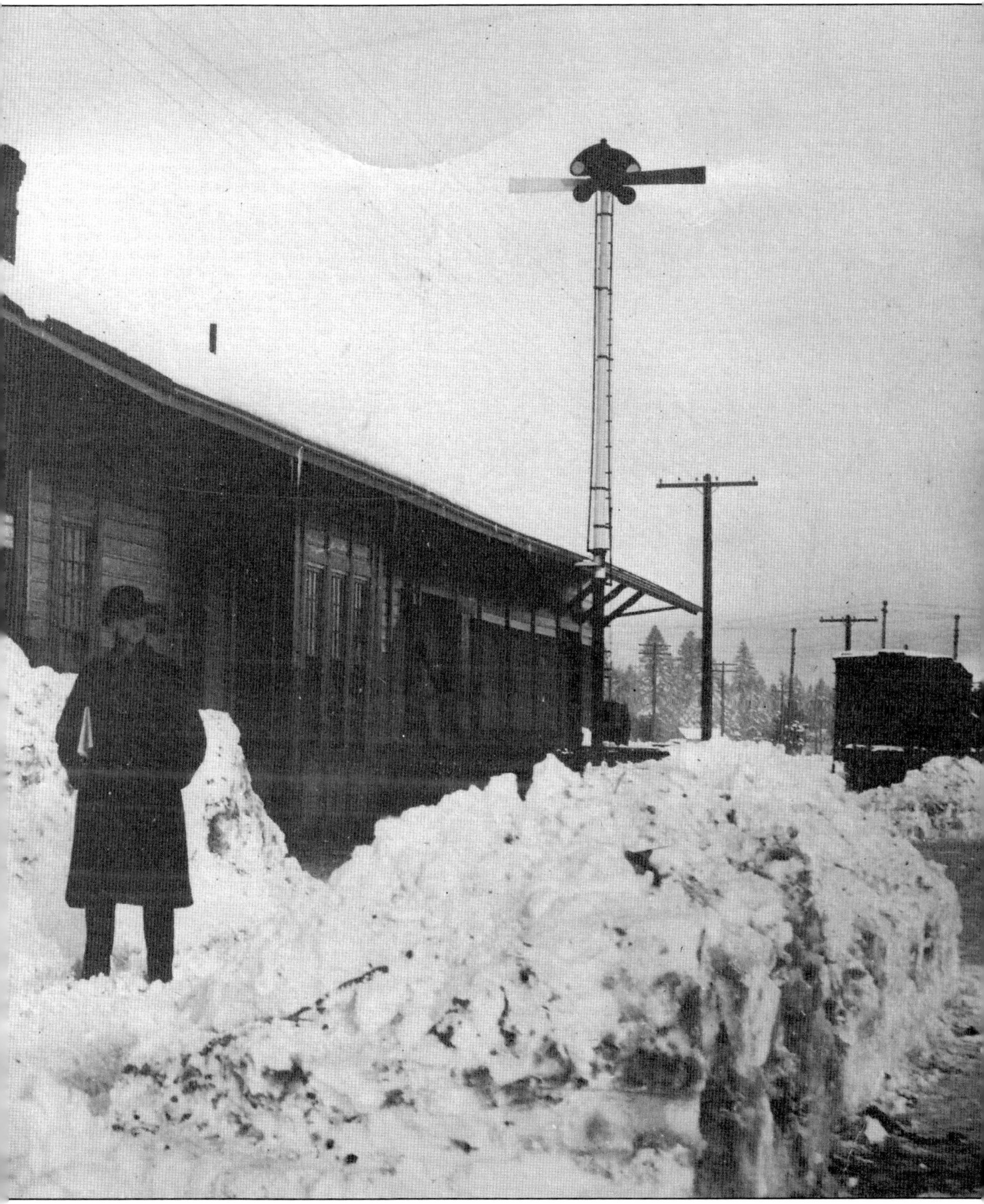

disrupting all train travel for three weeks. Standing by the depot is Hoyt N. Brown, the Southern Pacific agent. The station was closed on August 4, 1976. Southern Pacific donated the building to Canby on condition that it be moved from its original site at NW First Avenue and Grant Street. It was moved in 1983 to NE Fourth Avenue and became the Canby Depot Museum.

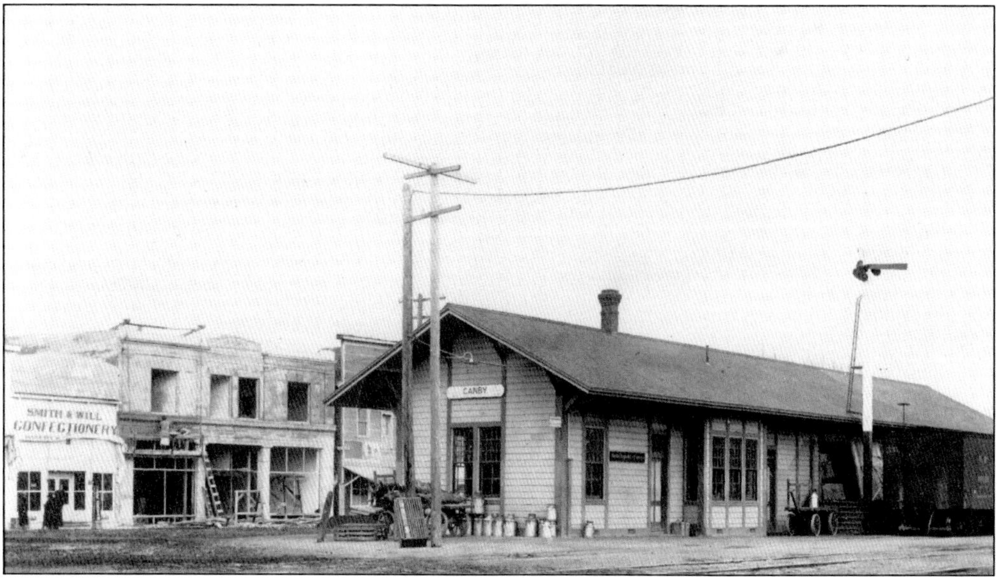

As more people settled in Canby, by 1871, merchants and retailers opened warehouses and shops, such as the Will & Smith Confectionery and Bakery. This was a great location right next to the train depot. Here, the company could sell its home-baked breads, pies, and cakes to the local townsfolk and passengers arriving on the trains.

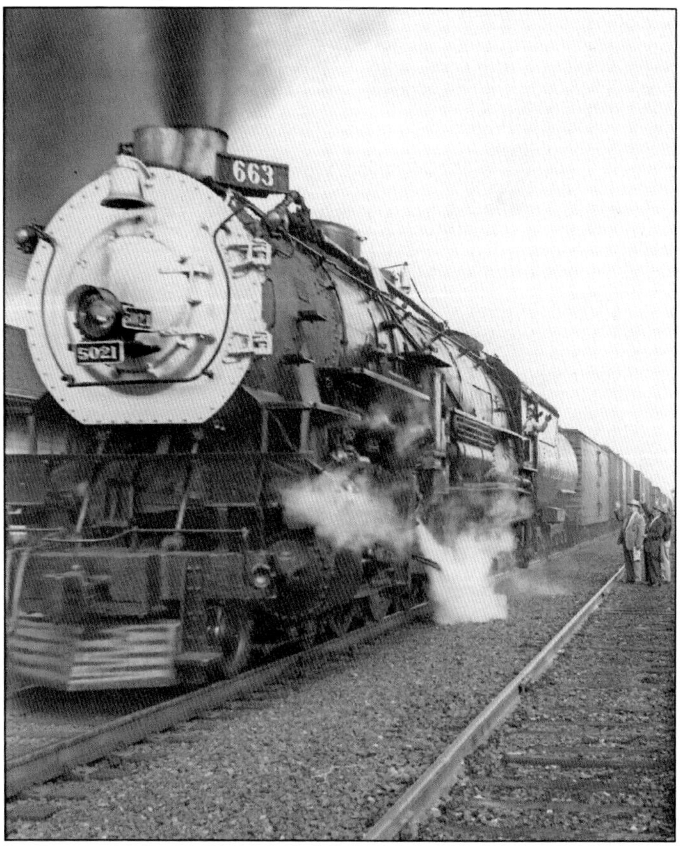

Southern Pacific locomotive No. 5021 has a steam engine. These trains were built between 1925 and 1927 for the Southern Pacific Railroad. They were used in both passenger and freight service and ran the rails from east to west, stopping in the Canby Depot along the way. The final service years of No. 5021 were spent mostly near Portland, Oregon. It remained in operation until 1955.

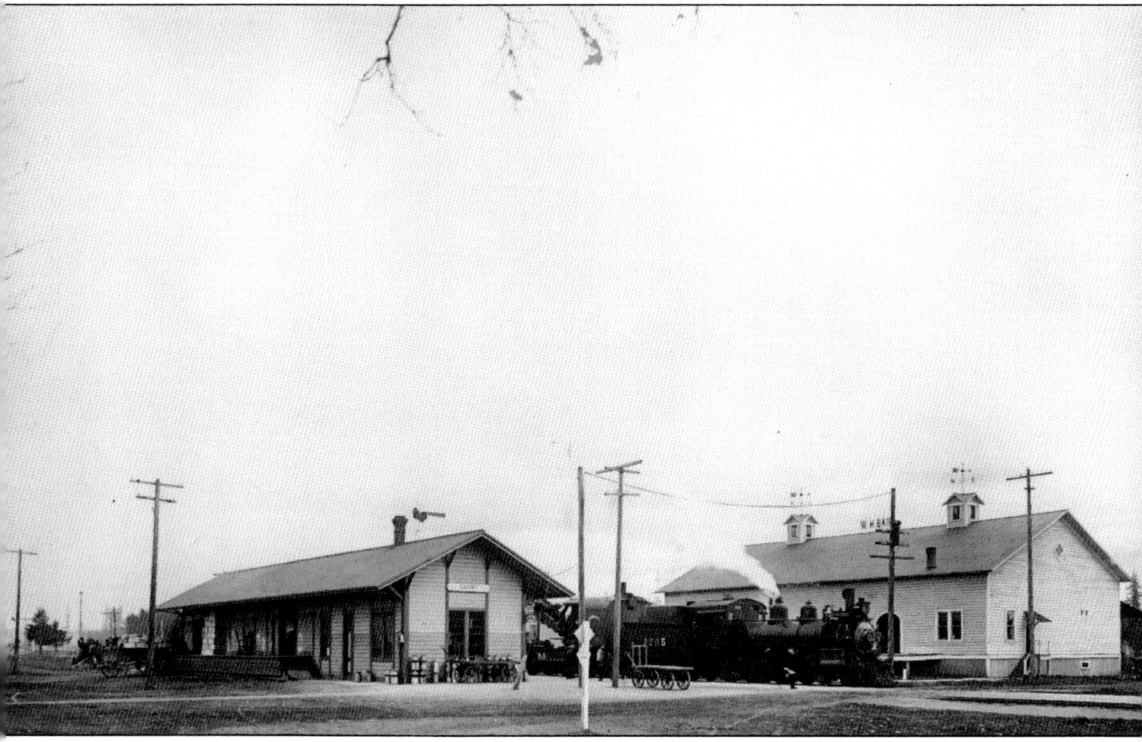

William H. Bair ran much of the business market and the local government in Canby. He was born in 1873 just six miles south of Canby. W.H. Bair ran a wholesale produce business and a meat trade. His shop was so successful that he added a branch in the town of Woodburn. He added smaller shops around the area until 1902. After that, he closed out his companies and went into wholesale produce in Canby. The building next to the train depot was torn down in 1987. The Southern Pacific contractor, Frank Dodge, built a modern warehouse across from the O.P. freight depot. Bair was also a member of the Canby Commercial Club, the Oregon City Commercial Club, the Portland Chamber of Commerce, and the Oregon Chamber of Commerce. He was vice president of the First National Bank of Canby, director of the State Bank at Canby, and the director of the State Bank of Portland. He was a director of the Clackamas County Fair Association and had been treasurer of that body for many years.

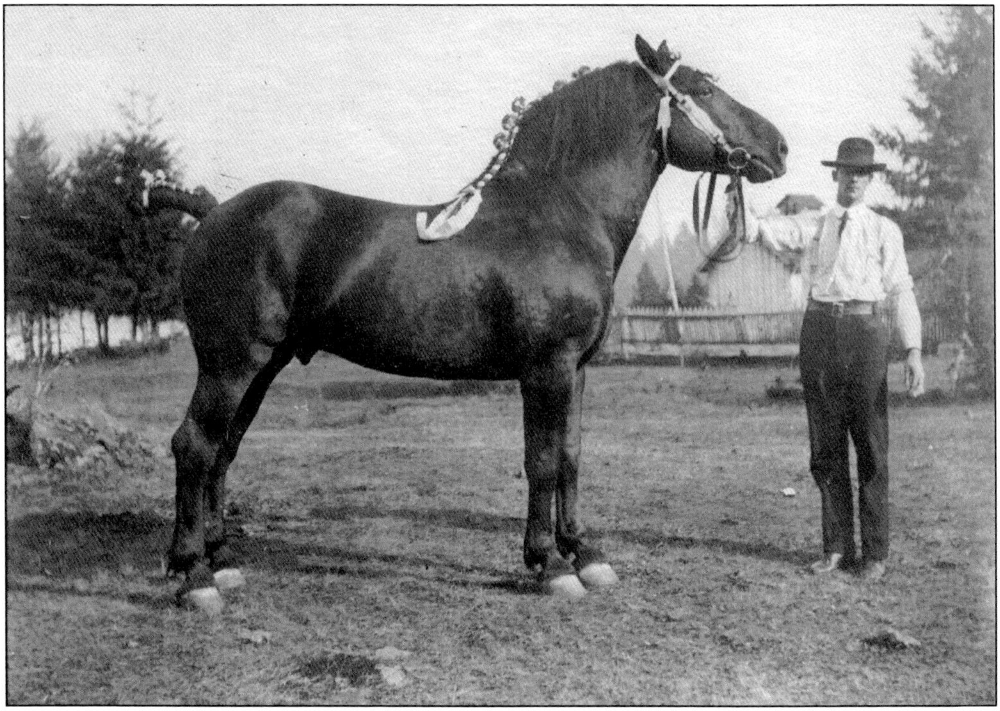

The Clackamas County Fair has been around for over 100 years. It was created through the hard work of the Canby Commercial Club and outstanding businessmen of Canby and the local area. The first official Clackamas County Fair was held in 1907 at Gladstone Park, later known as the Seventh-day Adventist campground. In 1908, the Clackamas County Fair Association planned to expand and began selling membership certificates at $5 per share to provide funds to purchase a larger area in Canby. The Clackamas County Fairgrounds now sits on 40 acres of land across from the train depot. The fair has been and continues to be one of the biggest events in Canby. Above is Charles Hamilton and his grand champion stallion at the first Clackamas County Fair in 1907. Below are high-wheel sulkies at the first Clackamas County Fair in 1907.

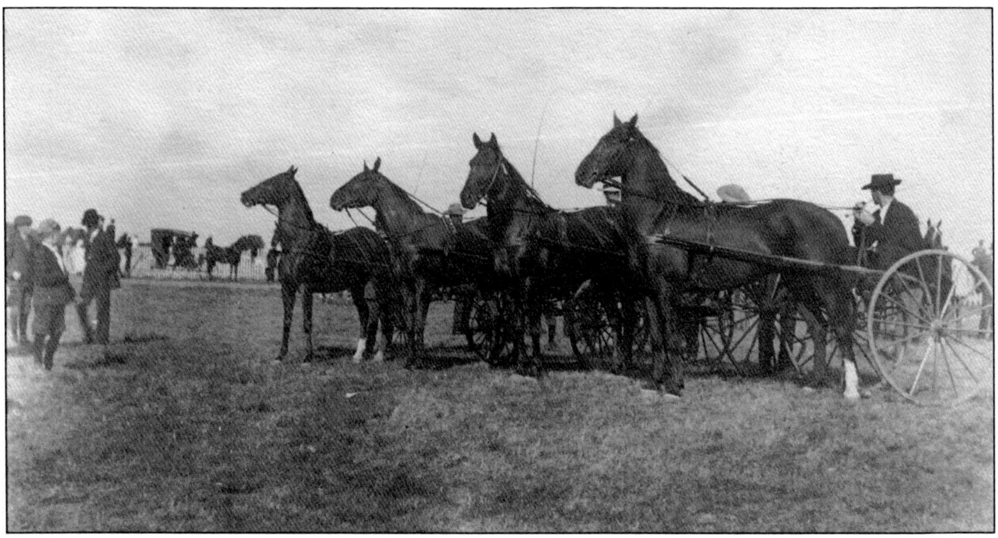

Carl Joehnk had only missed one Clackamas County Fair since it opened in the town of Gladstone in 1907. He made the official opening for the 63rd Clackamas County Fair in Canby at the fairgrounds in 1969. During the years he lived in Canby, he was a 4-H Club leader. Both he and his wife, Helen, were very active in several Canby activities.

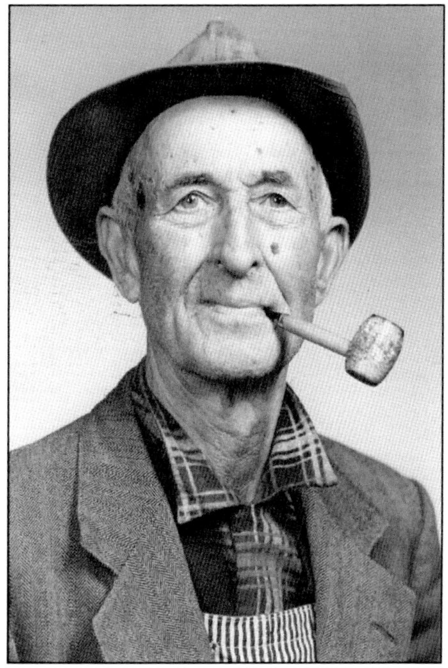

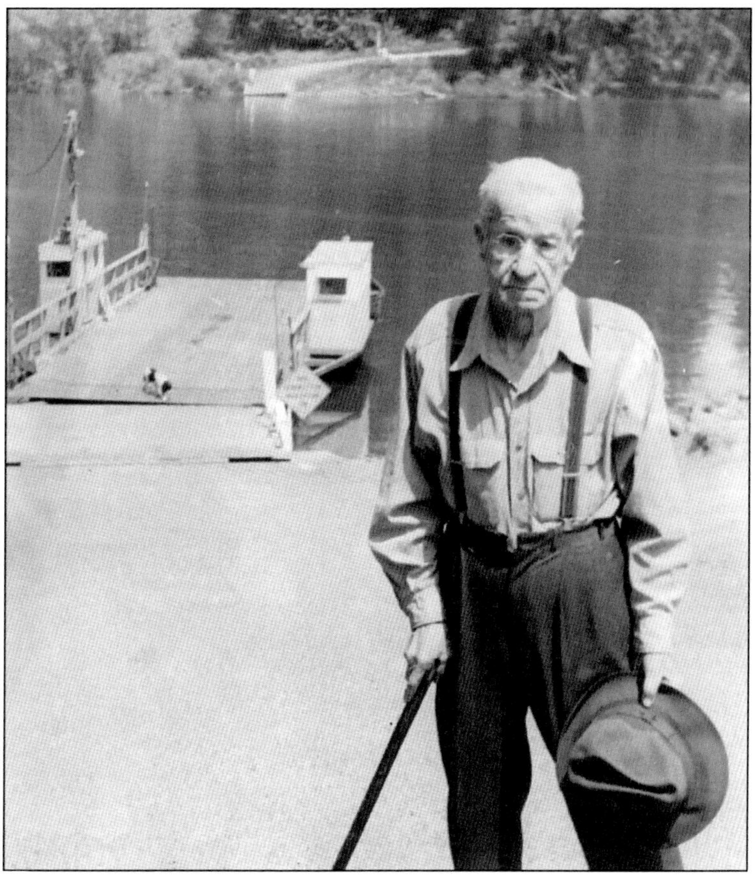

The Canby Ferry has been around since 1914. It is one of only three operating vehicle ferries left in Oregon. The current ferry, the *M.J. Lee II*, is the fifth craft to transport passengers, freight, and vehicles on the Willamette River between the towns of Canby and Wilsonville. Here is Grant Criteser, one of the early chief river pilots on the Canby Ferry.

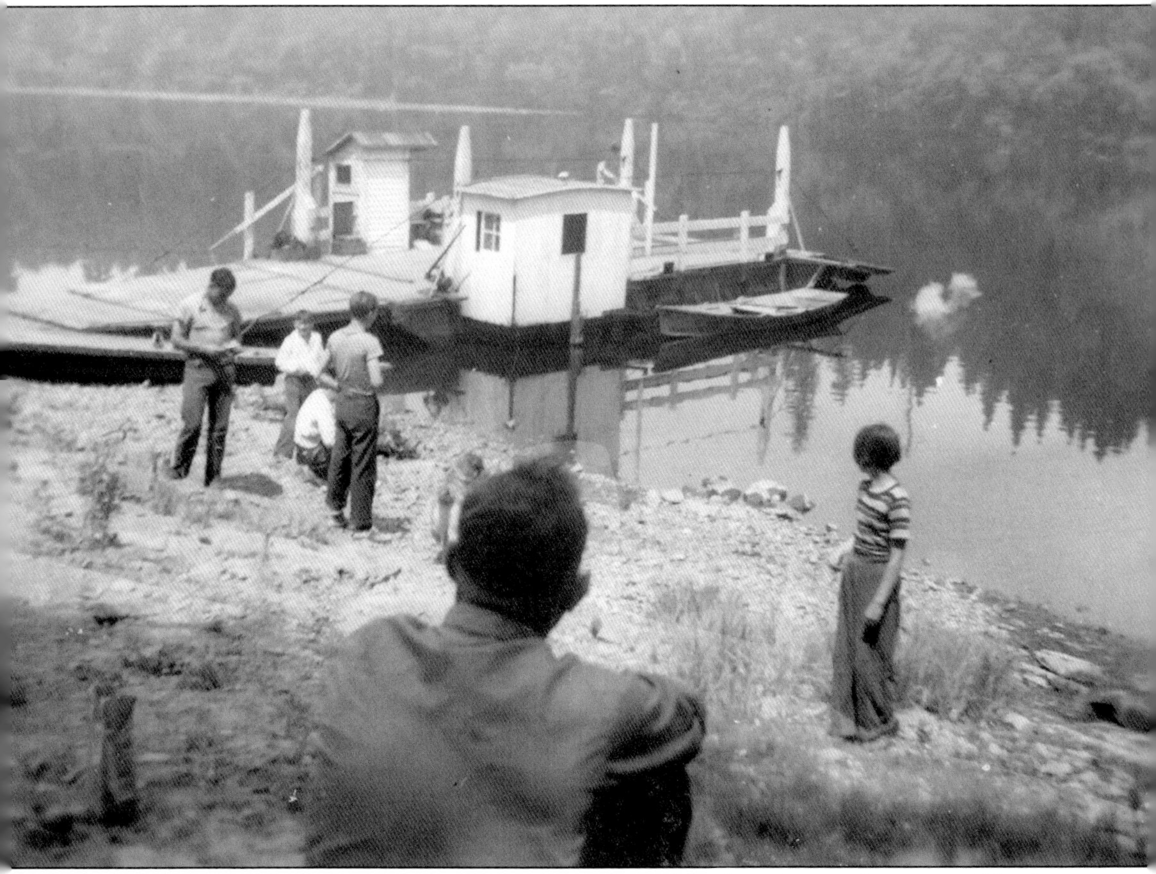

Canby mayor W.H. Bair and Harry B. Evans purchased the first ferry in the town of Newberg, but it was slowing down. It was propelled by a splashboard driven by the Willamette River's current and held on course by a cable. The need for a stronger ferry made the Canby Council authorize money to build a new, gas-driven ferry. The county promised to pay up to $250 for the vessel. Frank E. Dodge's bid of $317 was the lowest, so the county had to barter him down. Dodge built the second ferryboat for the Canby waterway in 1916. Once the 44-foot-long, 12-foot-wide ferry was complete, it actually cost under budget at only $238. This ferryboat was grabbed in a rush of water during a 1946 flood. It was too damaged to replace and was scrapped after 30 years of service.

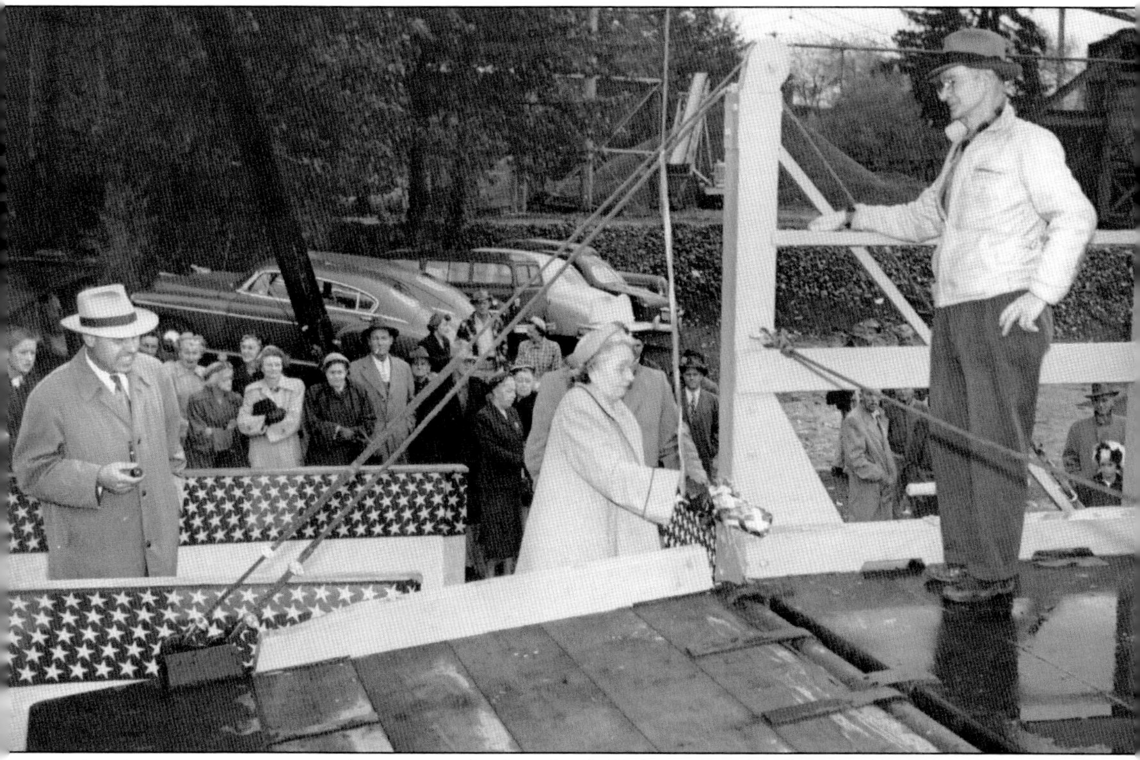

As the ferry service stayed active in Canby, the *M.J. Lee* was added as the latest ferry. It was christened on November 12, 1952, at the boat yard of L.S. Baire & Assoc. in Milwaukie on the Willamette River. Ora Lee Cattley, the granddaughter of Philander Lee, was there for the celebration. The ferry was brought upriver to Canby in July 1953. Clackamas County owns and runs the ferry service as a country road linkage. This ferry was named after the Canby-born Millard Jerome Lee (1872–1959), the first child born in Canby after its incorporation and a first cousin of Ora Lee Cattley. In 1870, their grandparents had sold a 24-block parcel of land for the initial townsite of Canby. William H. Criteser, shown on the right, was the first chief pilot of the *M.J. Lee.* Criteser had spent most of his life on the river. On the left is Wallace M. Telford, the chairman of the Clackamas County Board of Commissioners.

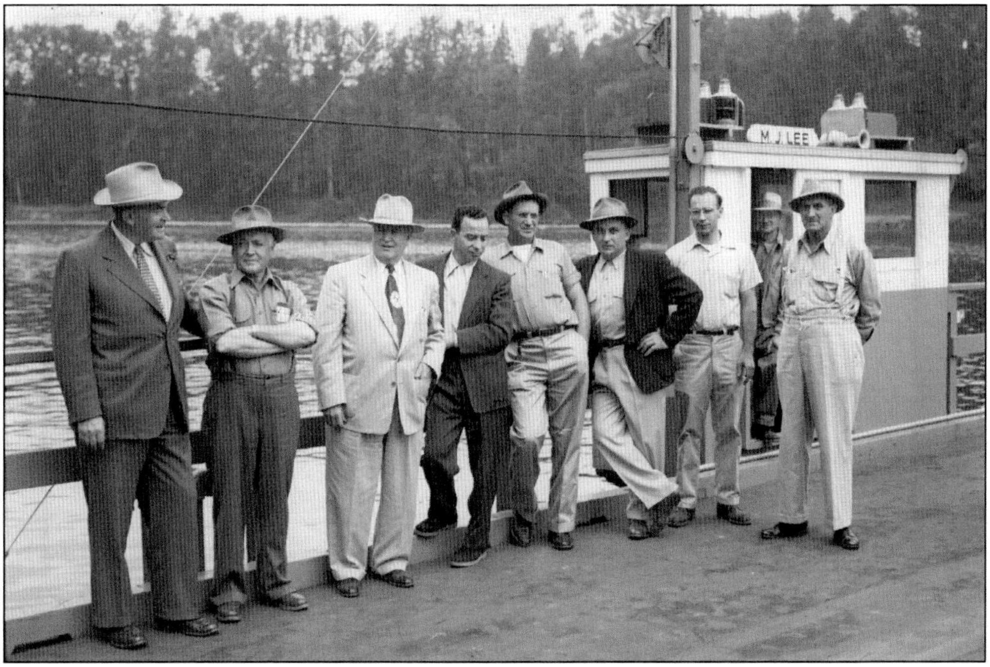

The first official crossing of the *M.J. Lee* ferry was on July 3, 1953. Pictured are, from left to right, Thomas W. Gerber (editor of the *Canby Herald*), Rex B. Eversole (mayor), Wallace R. Telford (county judge), Robert Jones (county commissioner), Vernald Moehnke (county road supervisor), Stan Skoko (county commissioner), Ronald Tatone (city engineer), William H. Criteser (chief pilot, in cabin), and Jerry Baty (county bridge superintendent).

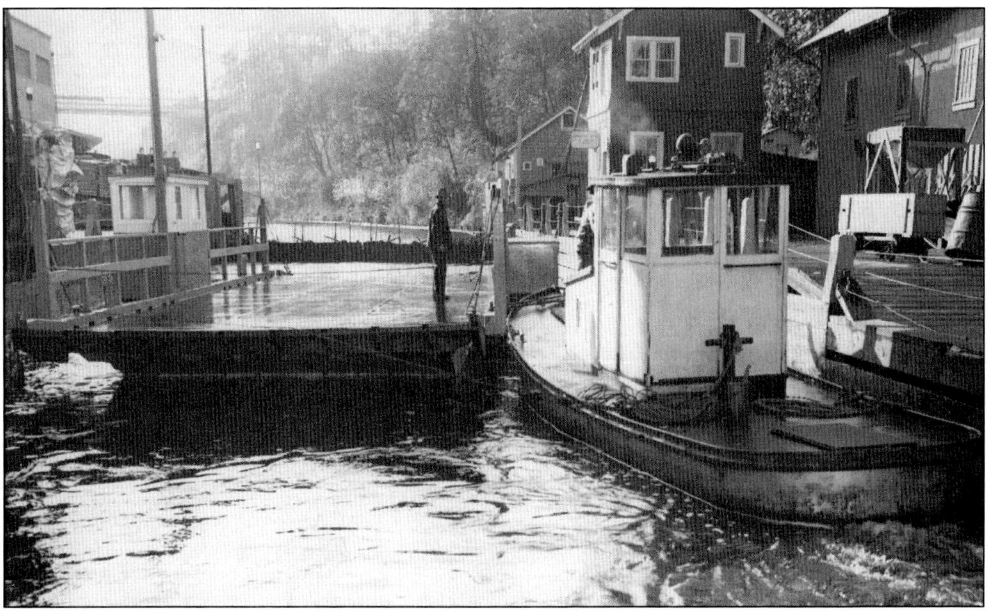

The *M.J. Lee*, Canby's fourth ferryboat, is passing through the locks at the Willamette Falls. It is heading for Canby on November 12, 1952. This steel craft was not put into the water until 1952. It was commissioned by Clackamas County. In December 1995, it failed its Coast Guard inspection; it was replaced on June 20, 1997, by the *M.J. Lee II.*

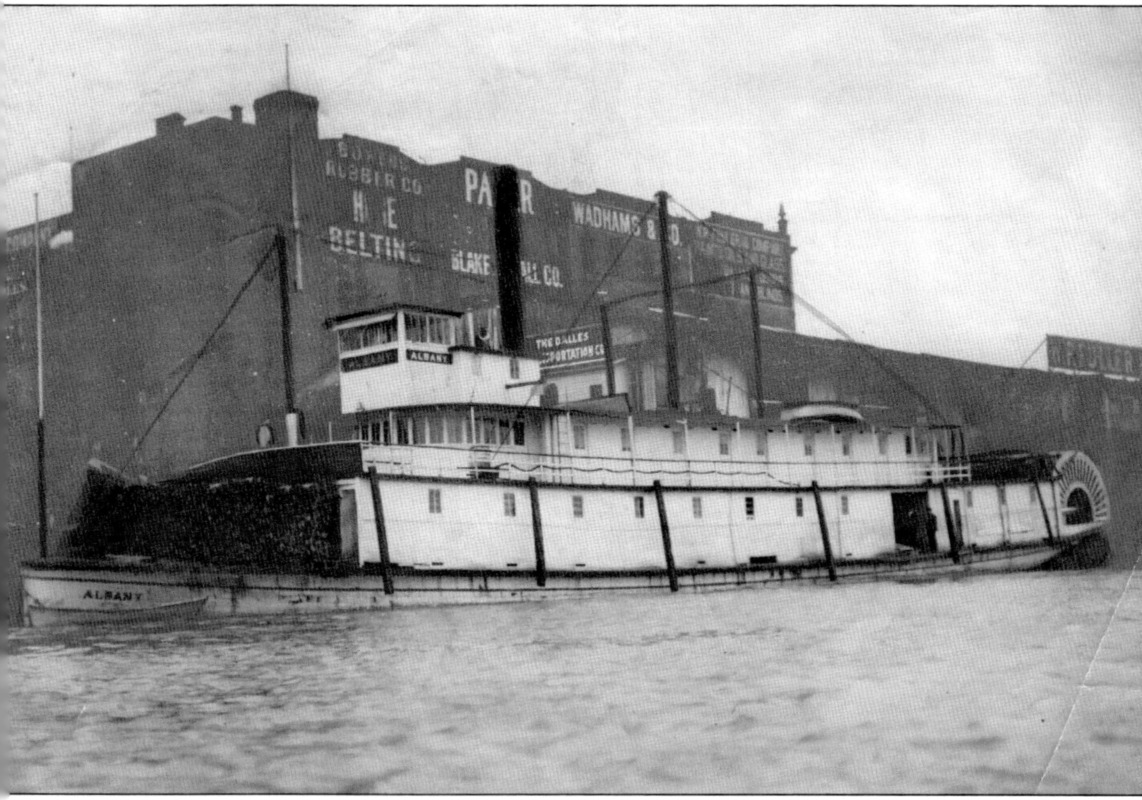

From the 1850s to the early 1900s, the steamboat was the principal transport of the Willamette River. By 1878, around 52 stern-wheel and side-wheel steamers were built along the Willamette, most of them at Canemah, which is located just above Willamette Falls. At first, Oregon City was the farthest upstream point of navigation. As the need increased for water travel, paddle-wheelers began to work above the Willamette Falls. In 1873, the Willamette Falls Canal & Locks Company opened a 1,200-foot-long series of locks that lifted boats around the 41-foot-high falls at Oregon City. The river was then maneuverable by steamboats from the city of Portland all the way to the city of Canby. Here is the stern-wheeler *Albany*, built in 1896, steaming down the Willamette ready to deliver goods. Currently, the locks have been closed by the US Army Corps of Engineers. (Courtesy of Peter Marsh.)

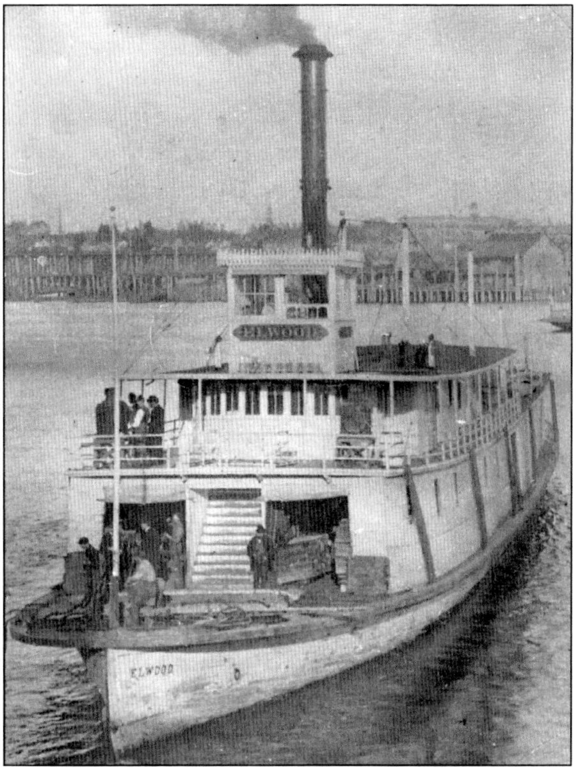

The *Elwood* is an excellent example of a wooden-hulled stern-wheeler. It was built in Portland in 1891 for Abernethy & Company. It carried freight and passengers along the Willamette River as far as Canby. The *Elwood* was 150 feet in length with a 30-foot beam and had a four-foot draft with engines that measured 12 by 72 inches. (Courtesy of Peter Marsh.)

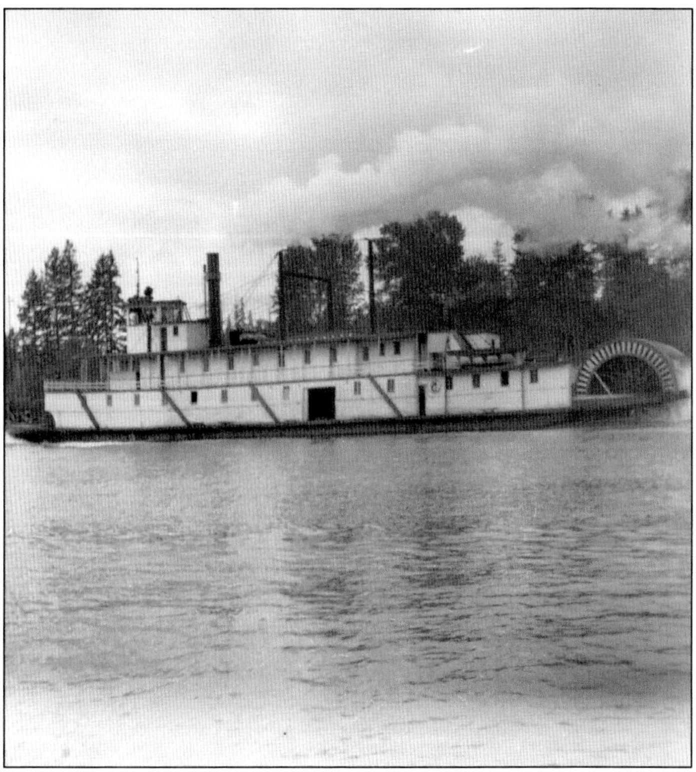

On June 25, 1939, the stern-wheeler *Claire* traveled to Champoeg State Park for the reunion of the Veteran Steamboatmen of America. The *Claire* tossed upriver from Portland, through the West Linn Locks, and past Rock Island. The Canby Ferry followed along to dock at Champoeg. They both returned to port in the evening.

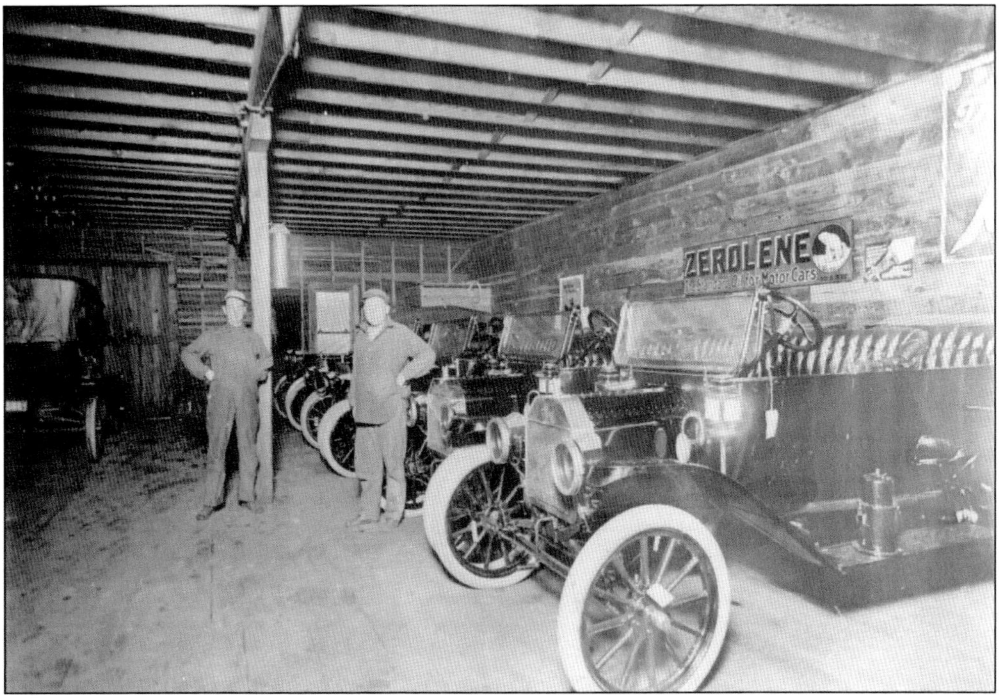

The first automobile manufactured in Oregon was assembled in Canby at a garage shop owned by Frank Zollinger in 1900. It was completed on July 4. The engine of the car was modified from a gasoline-powered wood saw. Shortly after this marvelous invention, Grant White's Fords opened around 1909. This photograph was taken before the 1920 move to its new building on Highway 99E.

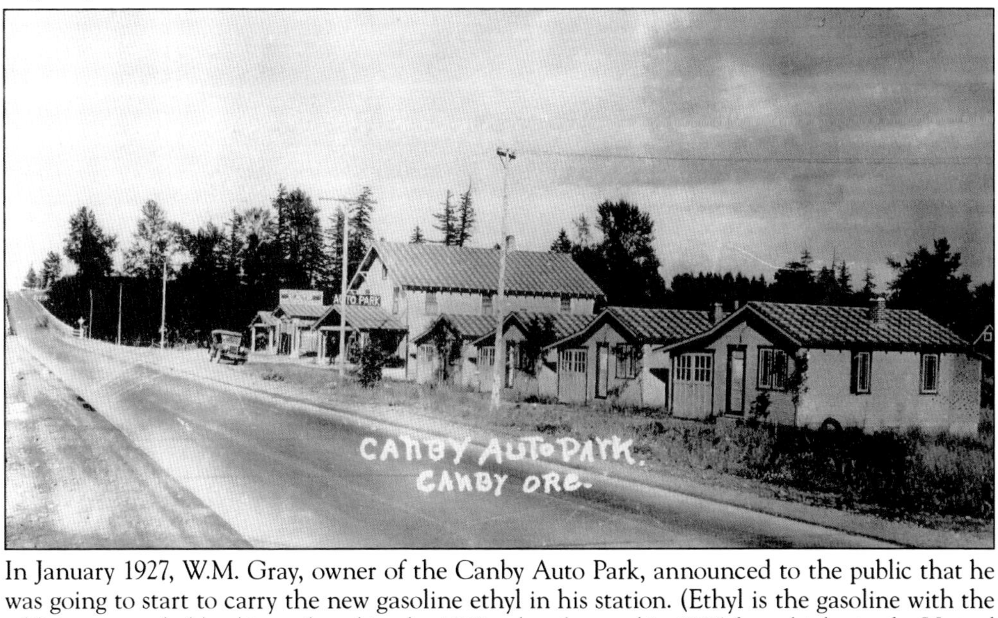

In January 1927, W.M. Gray, owner of the Canby Auto Park, announced to the public that he was going to start to carry the new gasoline ethyl in his station. (Ethyl is the gasoline with the additive tetraethyl lead introduced in the 1920s, then banned in 1995 for vehicles in the United States.) The auto park was just across the two-lane Molalla River Bridge on Highway 99E from Canby. The gas station also offered a hotel and cottages.

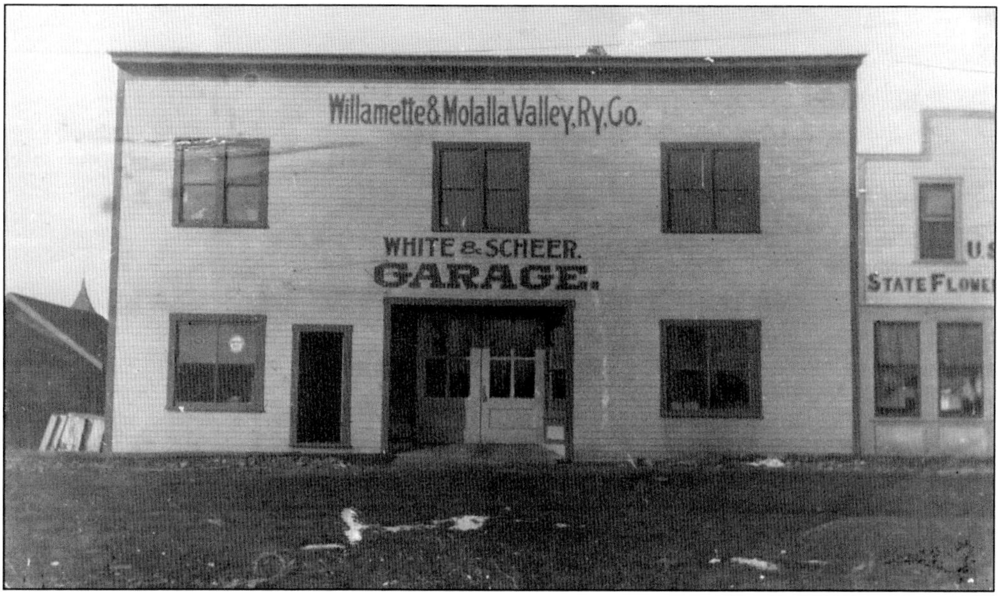

The White & Scheer Garage, owned by Grant W. White and George Scheer, was Canby's first automobile business. It opened in 1910 on NW First Avenue. The shop was on the ground floor, and for some time, Grant lived on the second floor. Edgar "Cap" Smith was White's partner from 1913 to 1917, when the company expanded to carrying Ford, Dodge, and Mitchell cars. In 1918, Maxwells and Happy Farmer tractors were also sold.

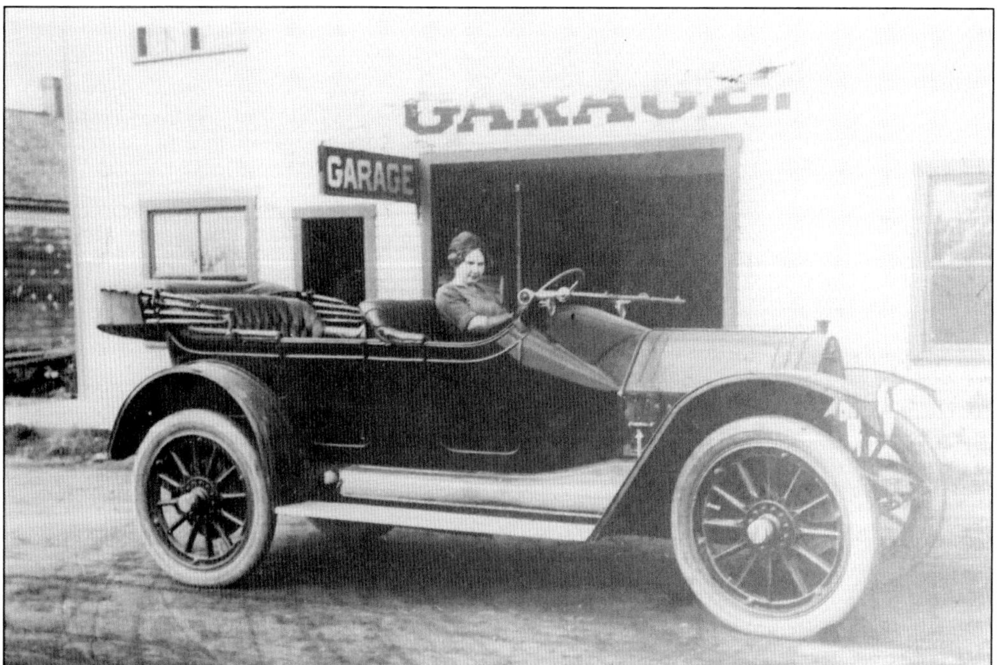

Laura Sandsness Smith shows off her new car in 1914 while parked in front of the White & Scheer Garage. A survey recorded in 1916 counted 39 cars over a 2.5-hour period on the dirt roadway in front of this shop. As the need for more automobiles increased, G.W. White opened the G.W. White Motor Company at 103 SW First Avenue in 1921.

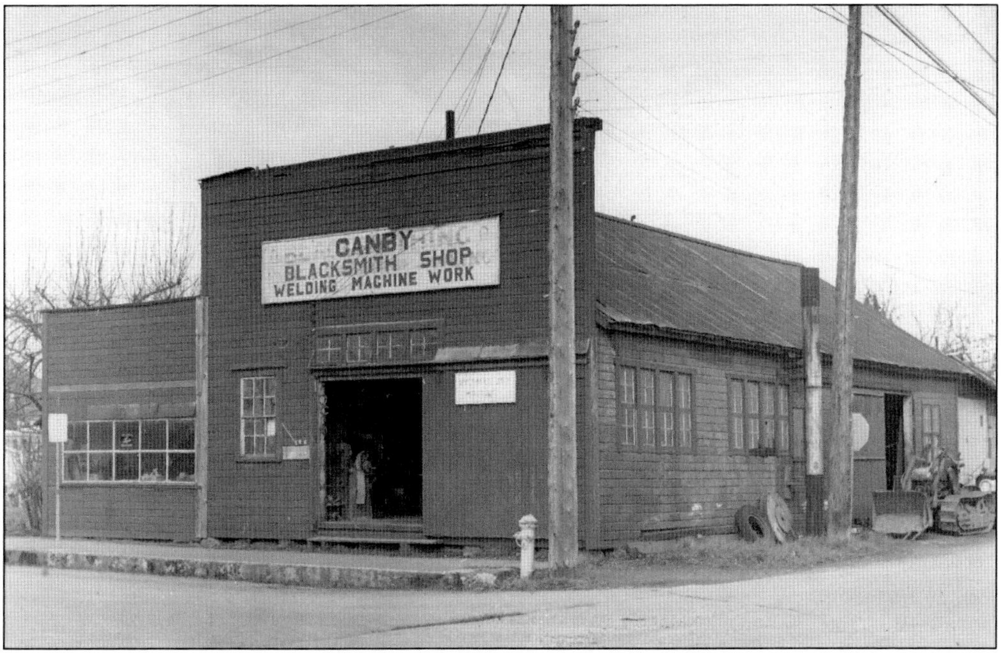

Ralph W. Atwood's blacksmith shop stood for 35 years (1924–1967) on the northwest corner of NW First Avenue and Ivy Street. The shop itself was in business for nearly 70 years. John Zeek built it between 1908 and 1909. The Corvallis Creamery Company added a saloon in 1910, but it did not last very long. Although the business changed owners for years, the building was demolished in the late 1960s.

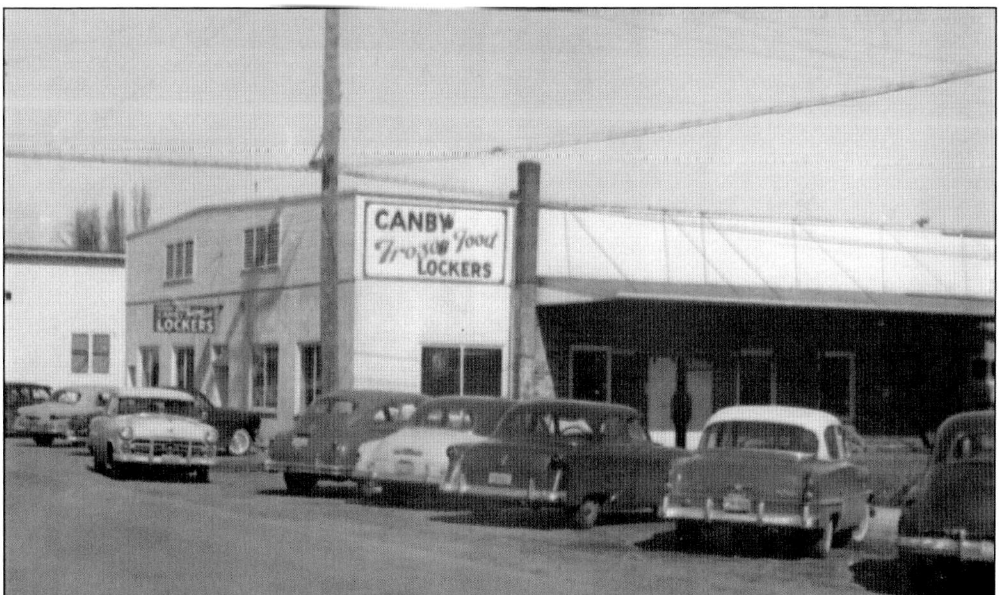

With the railroad running through the center of Canby by 1912, businesses kept opening and growing. Once Highway 99E was built adjacent to the railroad, business became well established. Nothing kept people from shopping on their own downtown streets. Here are several shoppers parked by Canby Frozen Food Lockers in 1946.

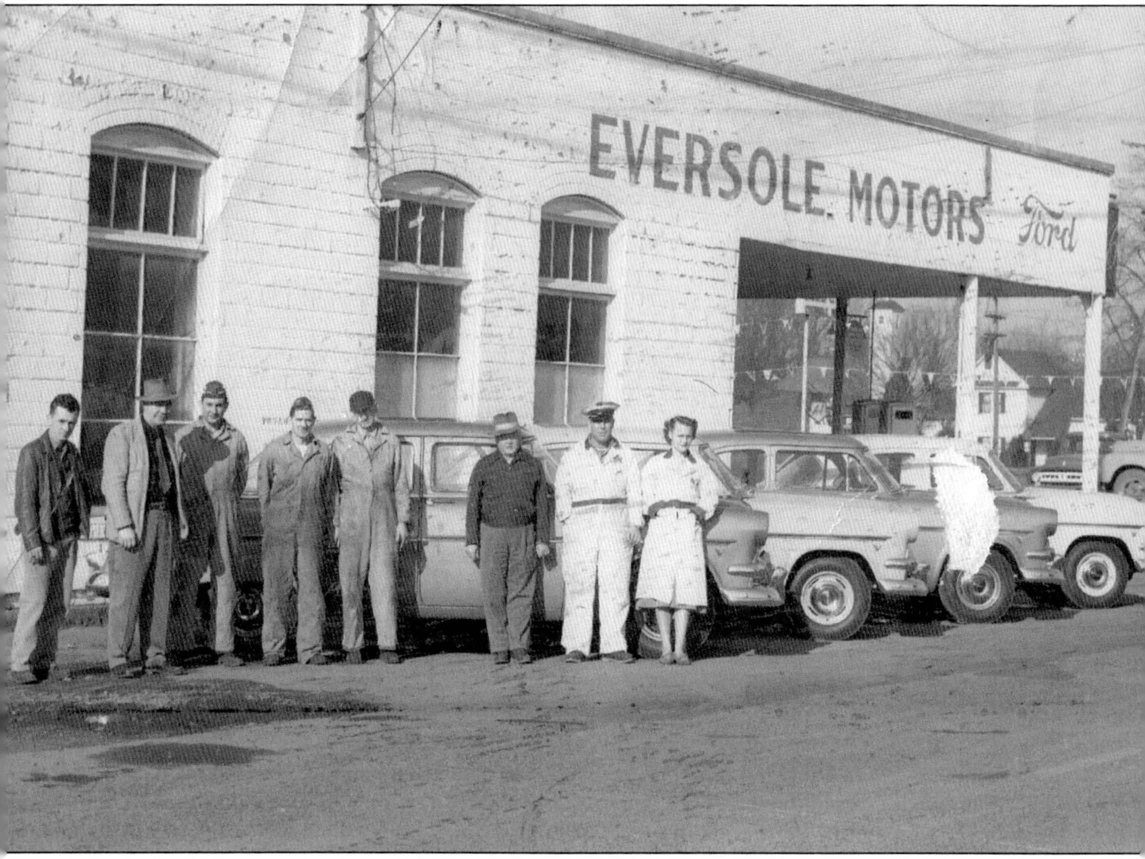

The G.W. White Garage in Canby was the authorized sales agent for Ford cars and Fordson tractors for the southern Clackamas area. It specialized in carrying all of the genuine Ford parts for service. Its motto was, "If you are satisfied tell others—if not tell us." Here is a man next to a Model T at a competing business: Eversole Motors. The arched windows at the left of this photograph were removed a long time ago, initially so that a bay door could be installed for vehicle access. The gasoline pumps are also gone, although the aisles remain, should the current owners be inclined to reinstate filling service. The building continues today as Canby Import Auto Repair at the corner of First Avenue and Ivy Street.

Four

Houses of Worship
Standing Tall over Time

When settlers chose Canby as their home, they also brought their faith and built church communities. J. Wesley and Elizabeth Josyln created a religious meeting place for anyone traveling the valley. They offered to let families camp on their land. Other religious services were held in pioneers' homes and in school buildings. Soon, churches were created for the community. A Methodist reverend, Samuel Mathews, settled in the Canby area in 1880. He helped build one of the first churches, which is now one of the town's most historical buildings. The Pioneer Chapel has housed many different denominations; it continues to be active. Another pre-1900 church in Canby sits on SE Township Road. The German Evangelical church was built in 1893 and has been restored and updated over the years. The Zoar Lutheran Church was built in 1892 on Township Road far from the city limits. In 1911, it merged with Barlow's Zion Evangelical Lutheran and the Bethlehem Lutheran Church of Yoder. This new congregation moved into Canby in 1922. Its current site dates from 1928.

Sadly, some of the original houses of worship no longer exist. The white-steepled Canby Christian Church, built in 1898 at NW Fourth Avenue and Holly Street, was demolished in 1966 and a new building put in its place. In 1903, the Scandinavian Evangelical church was built; it was torn down in 1963. The current Bethany Evangelical Church sits at 450 SE Ivy Street.

Even today, many places of worship stand open and active for parishioners and public celebrations. In every church still standing lies the heart of Canby's past.

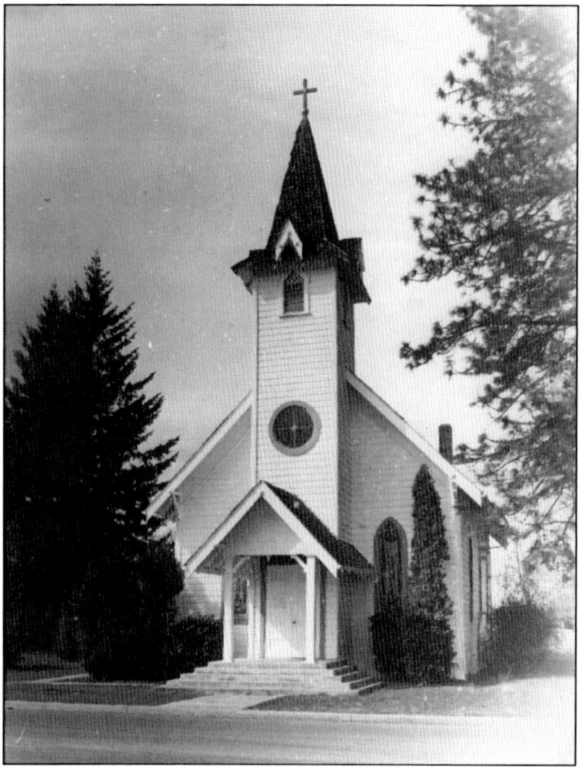

The first church built in town was the Canby United Methodist Church. It was constructed in 1884, but camp meetings began in 1869. When the Methodists were ready to build their own church in 1883, Rev. Samuel Matthews donated lots 1 and 2 of block 8 of his own land. He then became the first minister. The church faced Elm Street between NW Second and Third Avenues. In 1912, a new, larger Methodist church would take its place. St. Patrick's Catholic Church took this lovely building one block north to the corner of NW Third Avenue and Elm Street. When it was relocated, logs were used to support this Victorian building all the way to its present location. It was privatized in 1990, renamed the Canby Pioneer Chapel, and is used for special occasions. Below is a photograph of the structure when it was the Catholic church in 1978.

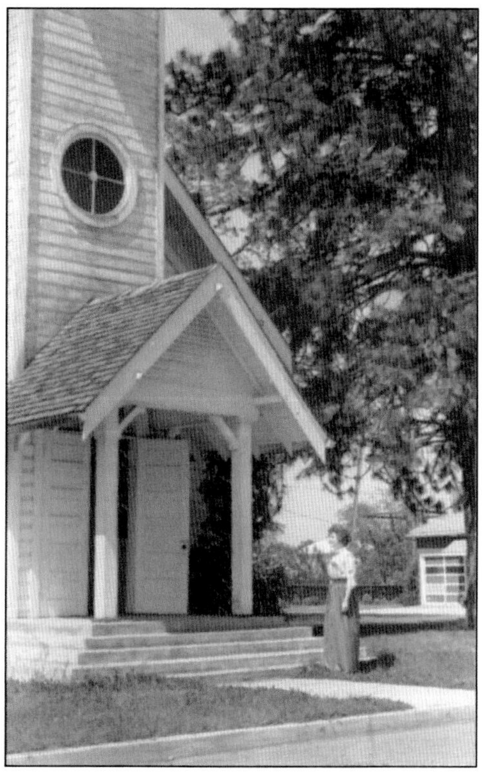

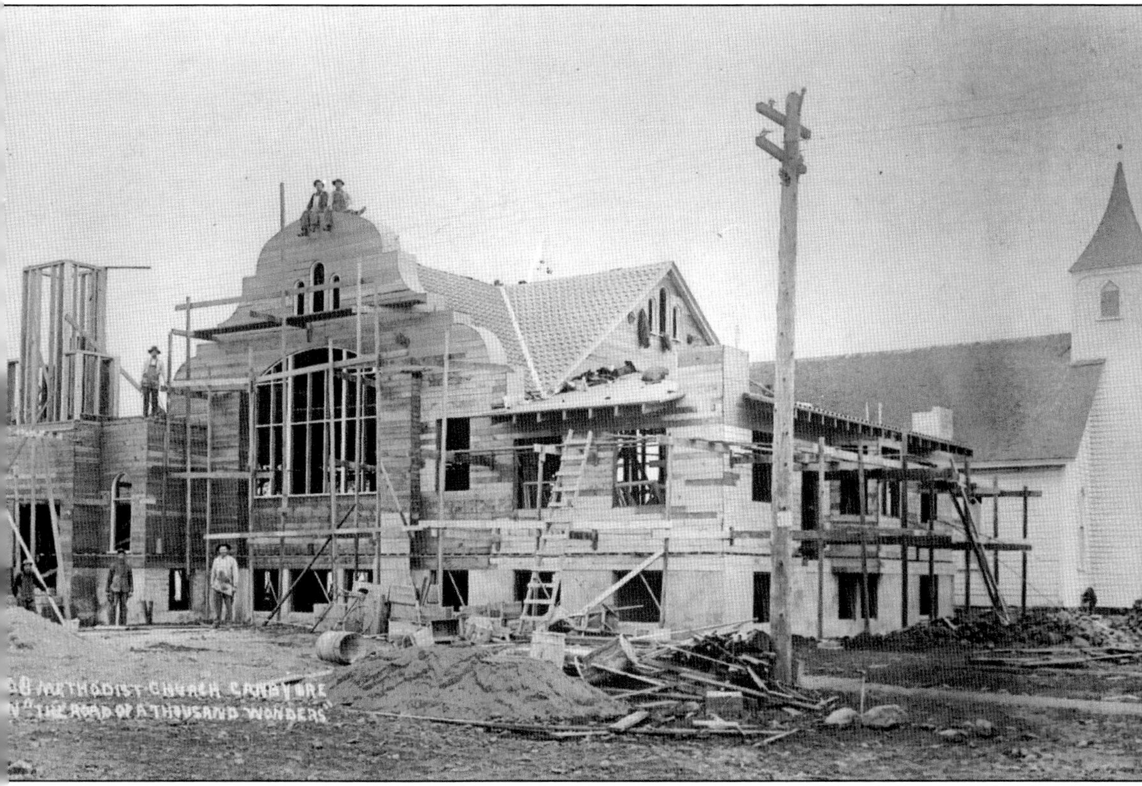

The Canby United Methodist Church has a legacy. Many of the pioneers who came to the Oregon Territory were Methodist missionaries. The first church built in Canby was Methodist (now the Canby Pioneer Chapel). This building was too small for the growing congregation, so a second church was constructed in 1912–1913. This new structure was a Moroccan design. It was dedicated on March 16, 1913. Rev. Andrew Jackson Joslyn, the first preacher, was there for the dedication. Two stained-glass windows were installed as memorials. One was for Reverend Joslyn and his contribution to the congregation; the other one was dedicated to the memory of Cynthia Hosford, who taught Sunday school and was active in the church. Aside from its Sunday services, the church was used for Boy and Girl Scout meetings, senior citizens meals, health care, and many community events. This sanctuary served its parishioners for over 60 years and is still standing at its original site at NW Second Avenue and Elm Street. The stained-glass windows were moved to the new church building in 1981.

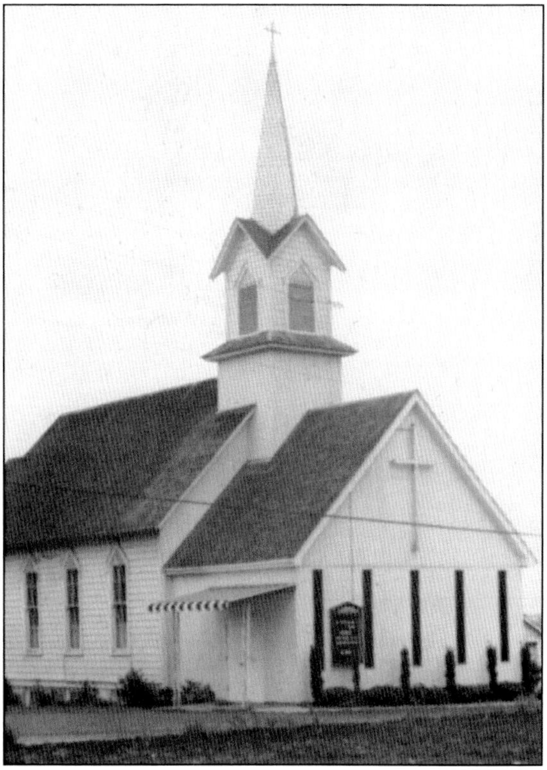

The Macksburg Lutheran Church, shown at left in 1910, was built between 1892 and 1894. It was dedicated on November 11, 1894. It is located in the center of lush farmland on Macksburg Road, near the town of Canby, and situated on a rise of land at the eastern edge of Gribble Prairie. This land lies between Gribble Creek and the Molalla River, a tributary of the Willamette River. The striking feature of this church is its square, shiplap, louvered belfry clad with vertical boards and battens and capped with a belt cornice. The belfry is centered at the north gable end; it has remained unchanged over the years. It is still used on Sundays and for special events. The interior of the church is a compilation of old and new. The altar at the end of the sanctuary is formally displayed with a pointed-arched altar alcove in the center and doors leading to the sacristy and Sunday school rooms. The new parsonage, which still sits next to the church, was built in the early 1930s.

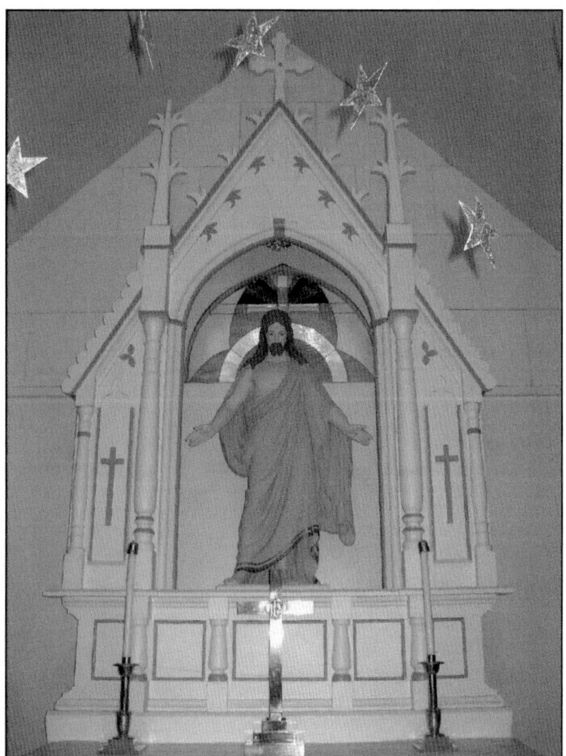

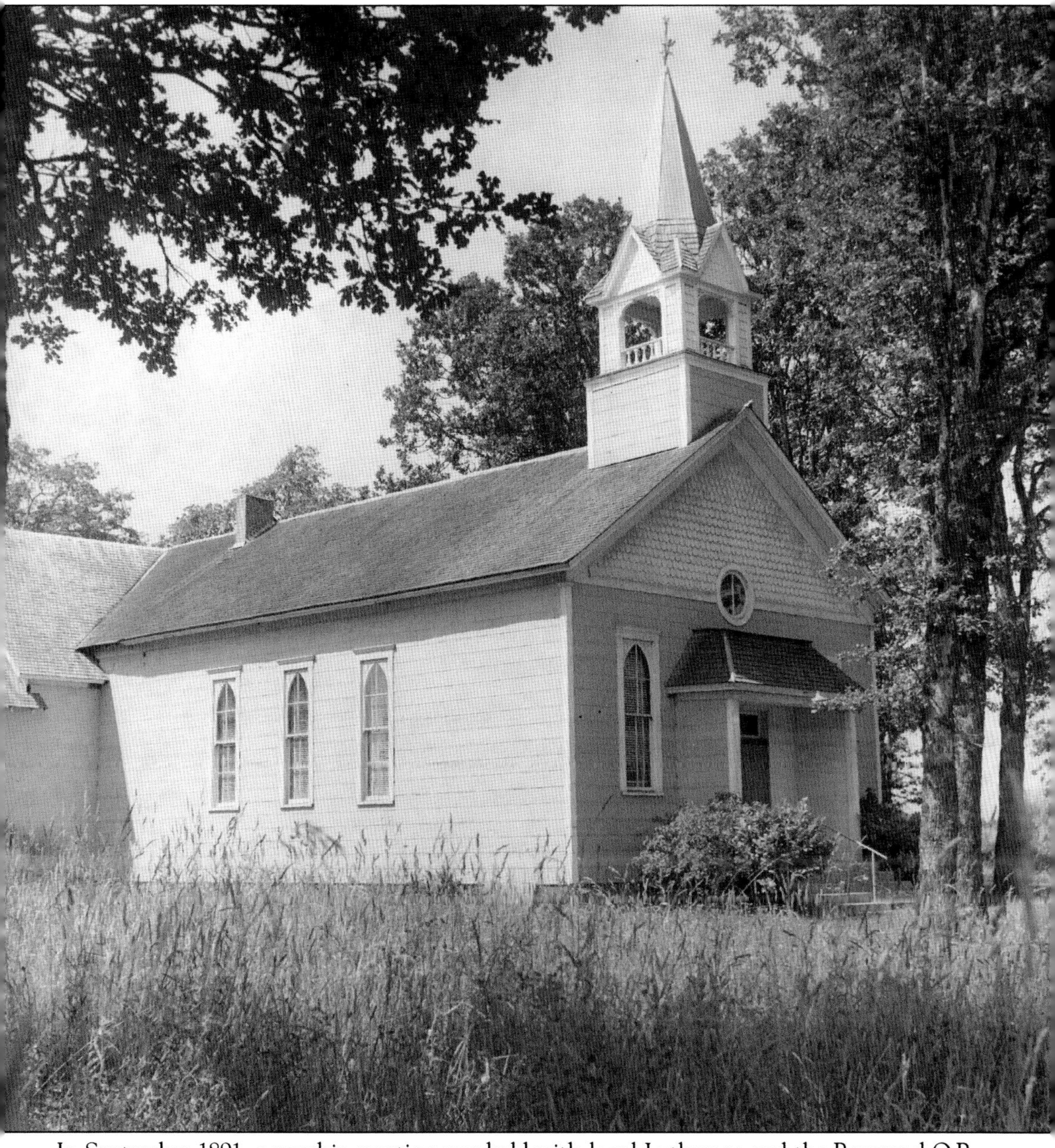

In September 1891, a worship meeting was held with local Lutherans and the Reverend O.R. Sletten in New Era. The name *Zoar* had been proposed on December 2, 1892. On December 29, 1892, the Zoar Evangelical Lutheran Church held its first service in Canby. With a name and a solid group of worshipers, other churches took interest. In 1892, the Zion Evangelical Lutheran Church of Barlow and Bethlehem Lutheran Church of Yoder merged with it. The congregation incorporated under Oregon laws on February 17, 1895. The first chapel was 26 feet square and built on donated land for both the church and the cemetery on Walnut Street. This place is where the Zoar cemetery is currently located. In 1927, the church moved to a new location; this is the church in 1950. By 2012, a new building had replaced it.

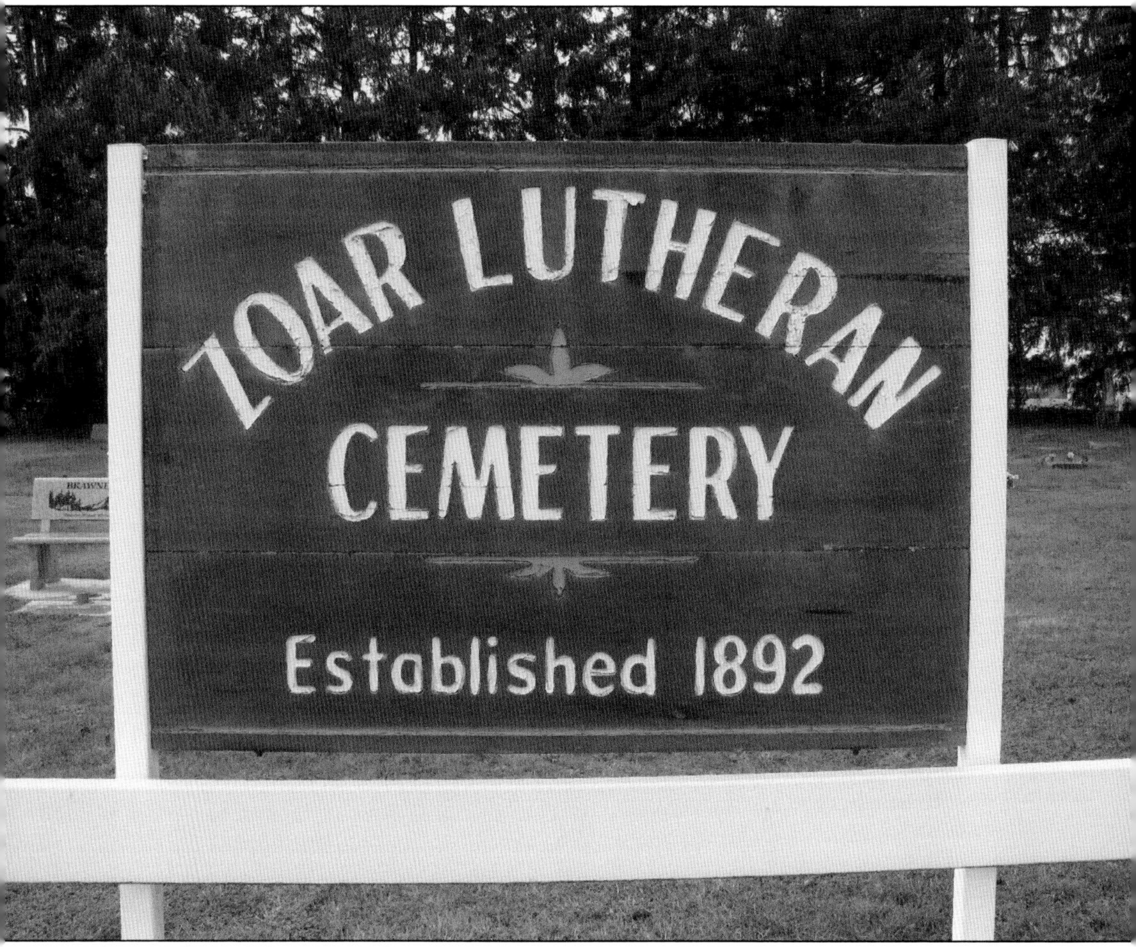

The members of the Zoar Lutheran Church established the Zoar Lutheran Cemetery, also known as the Norwegian Cemetery, on Barlow Road, one and a half miles east of Highway 99E in Canby in 1892. Over 172 loved ones are buried in this graveyard. Although the cemetery is no longer active, the families and volunteers keep it maintained.

The Zion cemetery is more than 100 years old. The Zion Cemetery Association created it in January 1897. The first burial was that of Christian Wintermantel, the person who first proposed the cemetery on January 19, 1897. The Canby Evangelical United Brethren Church owned the cemetery until it became too difficult to keep up, and the city accepted ownership and maintenance of Zion Memorial Cemetery in 1937.

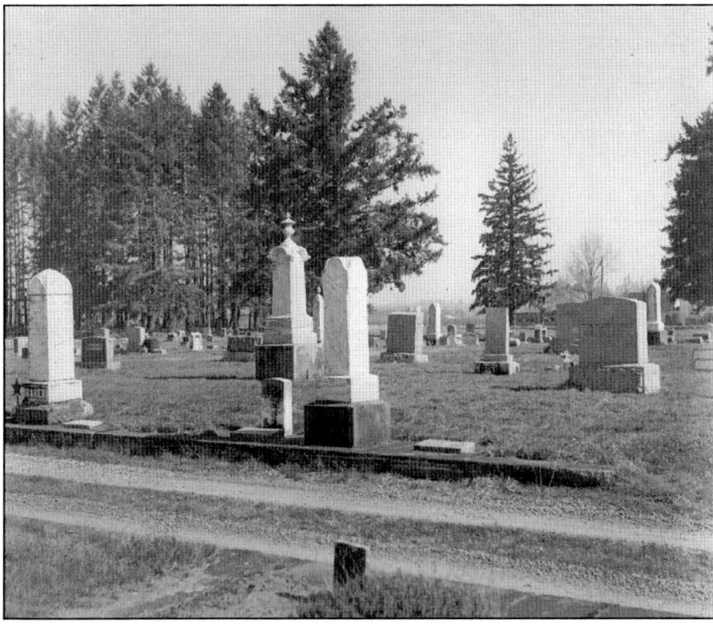

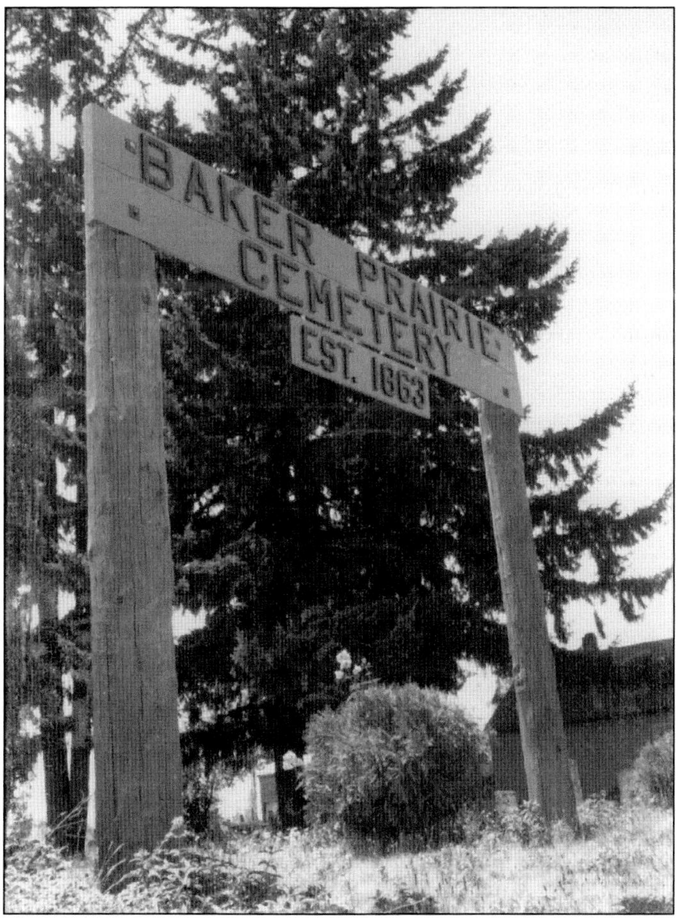

Another early cemetery is the Baker Prairie Cemetery, located on Knight's Bridge Road in Canby. This land was initially a section of a donation land claim owned by Wesley Joslyn. In 1863, for $1, Joslyn deeded one acre of ground on the eastern edge of his land for funeral lots. Most of the graves in this cemetery were laid before 1900. The city takes care of this pioneer cemetery.

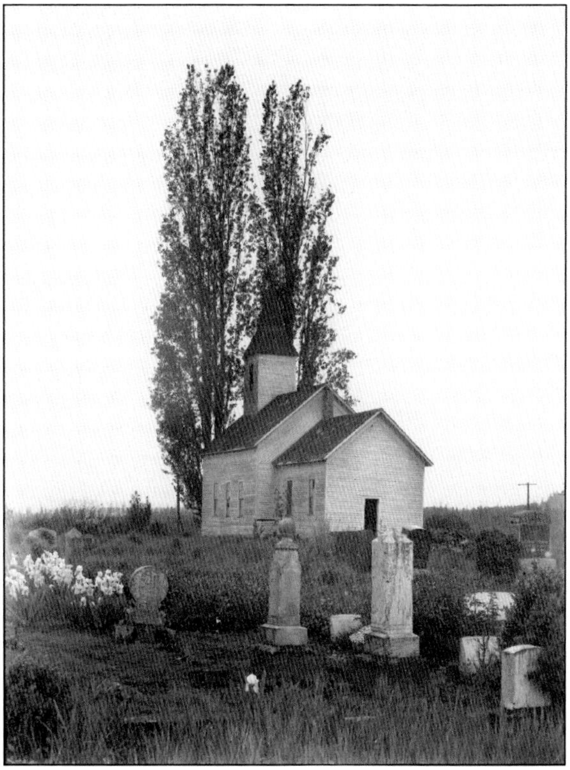

St. James Catholic Church and cemetery was established on January 11, 1883, by Joseph Reif, Andrew Grieshaber, James Leinwander, and Johan E. Bradtl. It sat on a three-acre site near the neighborhood of New Era. Archbishop William Gross dedicated the church on September 6, 1885. The first pastor at St. James Catholic Church was Fr. James Rauw from 1883 to 1888. The two poplar trees were planted in the early 1890s. St. James became a mission in Canby during 1916. The church kept a long history of religious activism in Canby. The church building was razed in 1942. The cemetery became St Patrick's Historic Cemetery, and St Patrick's Catholic Church looks over it. It is a well maintained three-acre plot near the intersection of New Era Road and Highway 99E about three miles north of Canby. It has both historic and current burials.

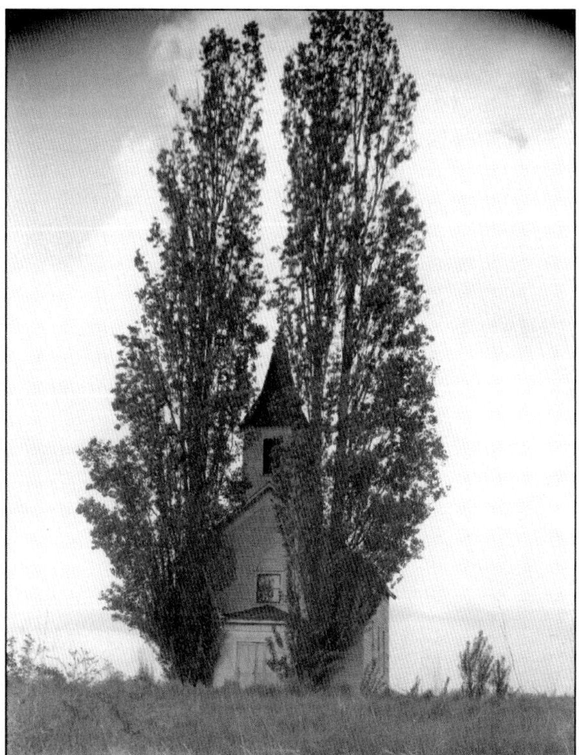

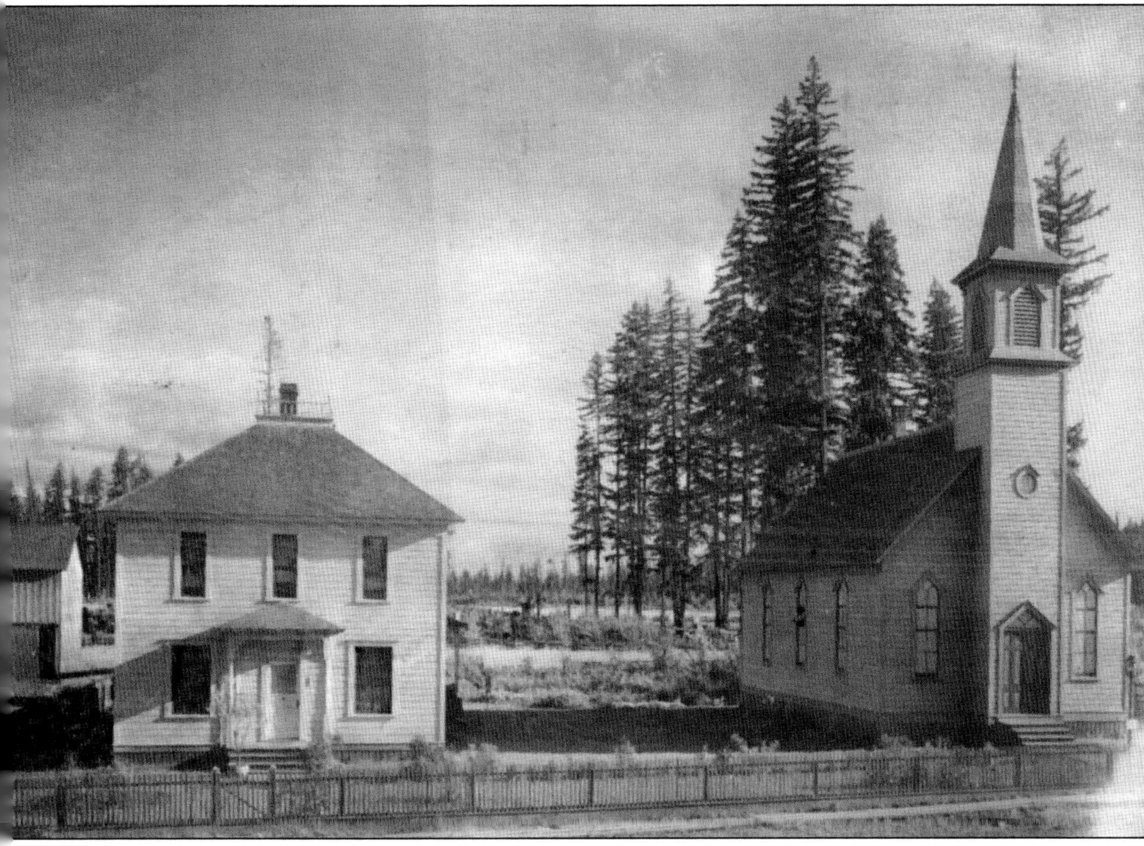

Methodist missionaries arrived in the Canby community in the mid-1800s. Methodism started as a successful camp meeting around 1869 on Wesley Josyln's donation land claim adjacent to the Molalla River. Part of the area was platted into lots and purchased by ministers and other Methodists from around the region. Rev. Samuel Matthews donated his lots 1 and 2 of block 8 to build a permanent church in 1883, and the church was constructed in 1884. While waiting for their church building, the Methodists held their Sunday services and school at the Milton and Cynthia Hosford store. Cynthia Hosford taught Sunday school and was very active in the church community. In her will, she left her property to be sold as a benefit for the building fund. Reverend Matthews was the first minister. The original church was sold in 1912 to the Catholic parish and moved from its original site on NW Second Avenue and Elm Street to NW Third Avenue and Elm. This fine example of an American frontier chapel is still standing at that location.

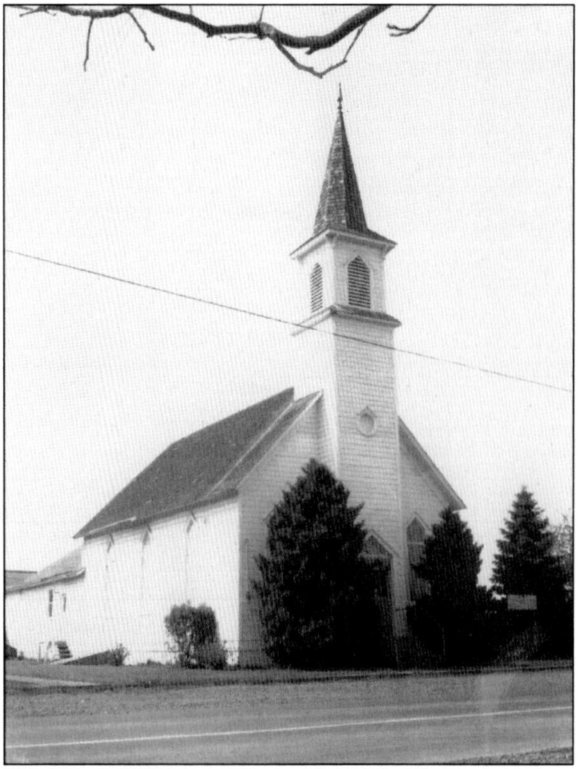

The Canby Evangelical Church of North America had many German-speaking worshippers in 1895. Before a church was erected, followers met in each other's homes. Built in 1894, it was dedicated on Christmas Eve of that year. Rev. Herman Schuknecht was its first pastor. German was the spoken language in this church until 1912. Although its name has changed, it is the oldest continuous church in Canby.

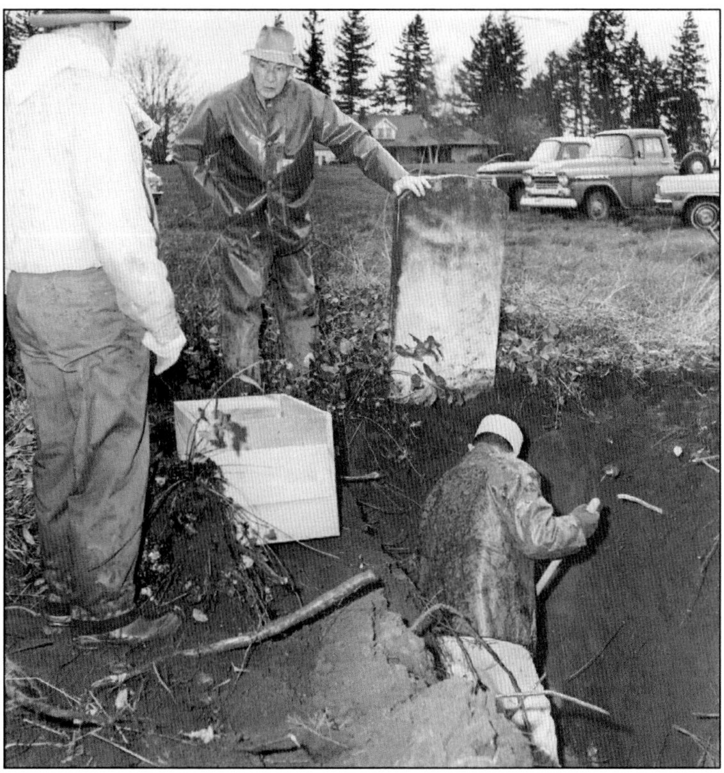

John Tatone (left) and Clayton Yoder watch as the graves of Canby's first pioneer family are transferred in 1966 from the Pendleton Cemetery to Zion Memorial Park Cemetery and Mausoleum. Only three graves were in this family plot: Champion Pendleton died on January 23, 1857; he was 45 years old at his passing. His wife, Phoebe Susan Mann Pendleton, was born on December 31, 1814, and died on May 14, 1882. Samuel R.T. Pendleton, a brother, died on February 28, 1871.

Five

The Families That Settled

Legacies

One of the first Canby settlers was John G. Gribble, who came on the Oregon Trail in 1846. His first home was built in the late 1840s–early 1850s; it was torn down in the 1950s. As the generations of Gribbles grew, the area around them was soon named for this family. Gribble Road runs half a mile north from the original home, and the Gribble Pioneer Cemetery lies three quarters of a mile west on this road.

Another family in Canby is the Kraxbergers. Franz and Carl Kraxberger migrated from Austria to Stover, Missouri, and later settled in Oregon in the 1890s. Soon, the rest of the Kraxberger family joined Franz and Carl. Johans Kraxberger, the father of Franz and Carl, purchased 156 acres in Macksburg, adjacent to the growing town of Canby. There is a road named after the family, and the Walter L. Kraxberger Middle School is located in the nearby town of Gladstone.

The main grocery store still located in downtown Canby, Cutsforth's Market began when Frank T. Cutsforth opened his meat market on NW First Avenue in 1928. His son, Glenn, at only 12 years old, began working in his family's business. In 1937, Glenn married Elsie Egli, and they later expanded the butcher shop. In 1946, groceries were added to the store, and Cutsforth's Market became Canby's third grocery shop. Glenn and Elsie's son, Frank, started working for the market in 1957. After two relocations and three remodels, Cutsforth's Market is still a full-service grocery store in Canby. These families are just a sketch of those who came to Canby and stayed.

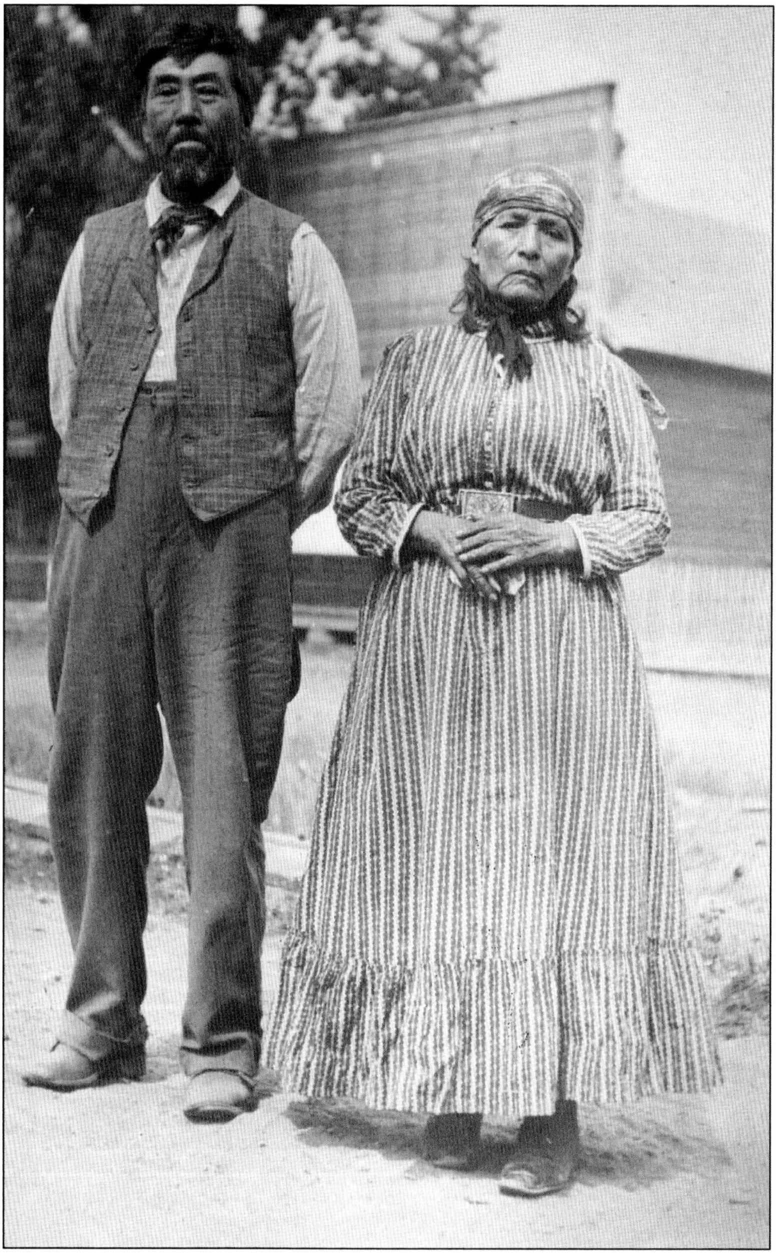

Here are "Indian Henry" and his wife in 1870. Henry was a beaver trapper and a Native American who dealt with the Gribbles for the property that they later filed on for their donation land claim. It is said that John Gribble gave Henry a musket, a pony, and two blankets for the land. Henry then moved to the approximate location of the Nordhausen Farm. As time went on, more donation land claims were bartered with the Native Americans. These claims cornered on the crossroads of the Native American trails and changed the layout of Canby. As the city grew, lumber and farming became the backbone of the community. Without the additional land from the Native Americans, Canby would have been stilted as a city. When the railroad came in, it changed both the pioneers and the Native Americans. The track was 10.2 miles long from Canby to Molalla and was laid by the Portland, Eugene & Eastern Railway Company in 1912–1913.

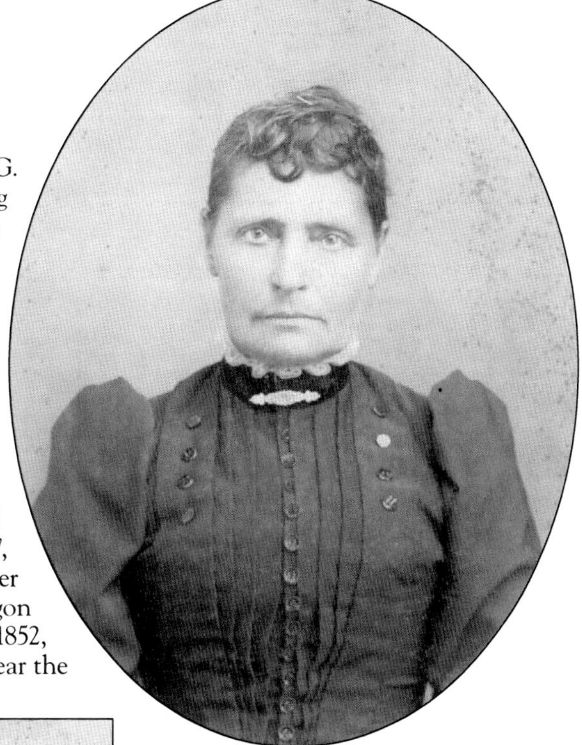

Andrew E. Gribble was the eldest of John G. and Elizabeth Ensley Gribble's eight living children. John came out to the Oregon Territory on October 12, 1846. He had taken a land claim in the spring of 1847 four miles south of Canby. Andrew joined in on the Donation Land Claim Act of 1850 and settled adjacent to his father's land on November 5. This joined land became Gribble Prairie. He married Nancy Ann Riggs on September 19, 1851. The couple had four children. Nancy had spent her early childhood in Missouri. At just 13 years old in 1847, Nancy and her four brothers followed her parents, Daniel and Mahala, in a wagon train going out to Oregon. On March 1, 1852, Daniel filed a land claim of 640 acres near the southwest corner of Andrew's land.

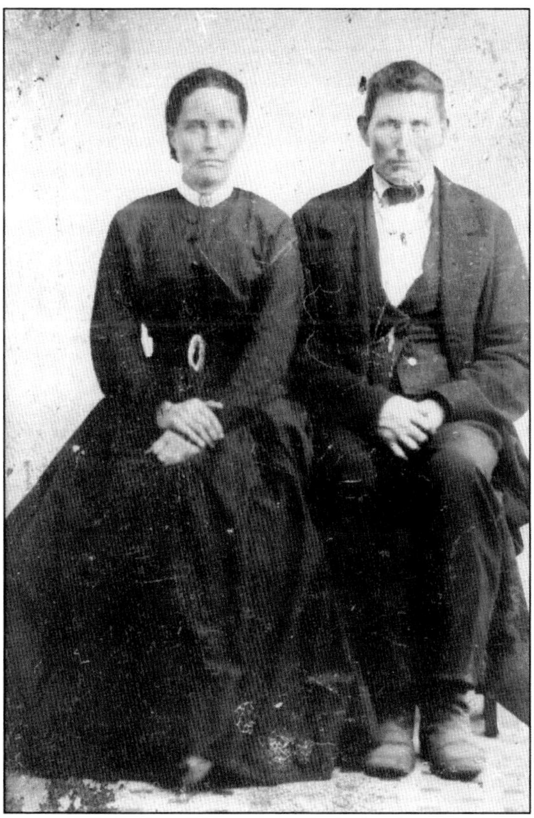

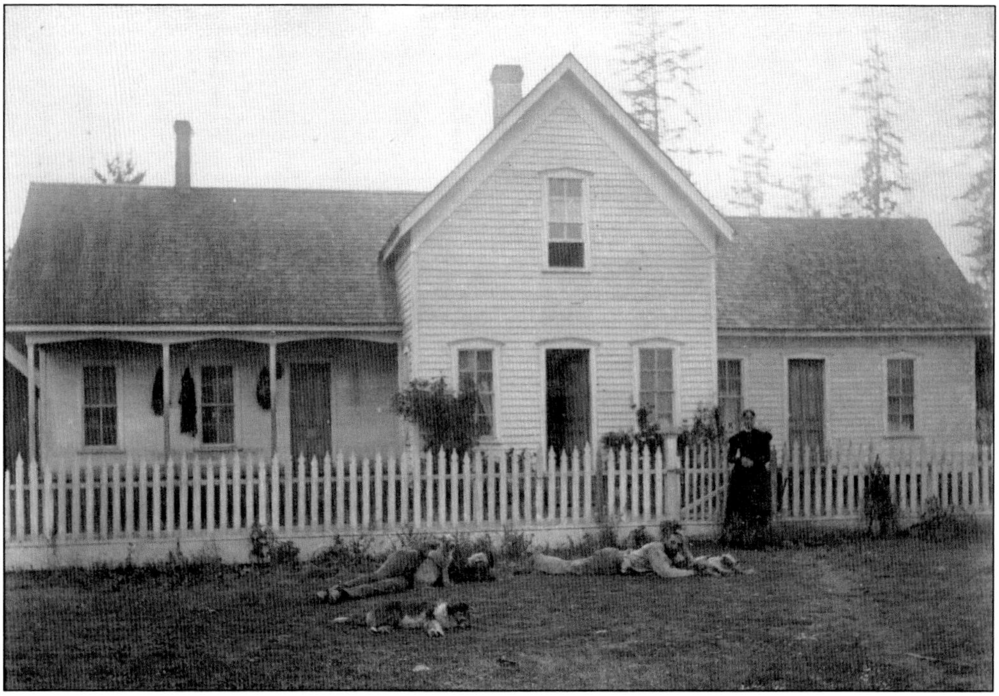

Here is the home of Andrew and Nancy Gribble on their donation land claim. This act, which became law on September 27, 1850, granted 640 acres to married couples arriving in the Oregon Territory before December 1, 1850. Here the Gribbles raised their four children—Ellen Mahala, born on July 30, 1853; Sarah E., born on June 24, 1855; Albert Daniel, born on September 28, 1857; and William, born on September 5, 1862.

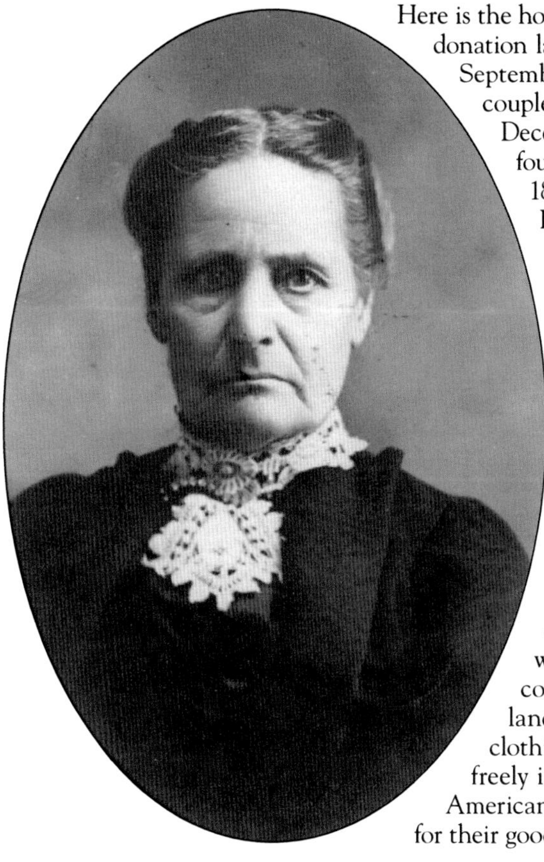

When Andrew Gribble died in 1876, Nancy's children helped her with the land claim. They hired George W. Kesserling, whom Nancy married in the late 1880s. The couple moved closer to Canby and bought six land lots. Nancy was very good with making clothing, spinning, and weaving. She could speak freely in the language of the Chinooks, a Native American tribe. She often traded her handmade rugs for their goods.

Albert Daniel Gribble, the grandson of John and Elizabeth Gribble, who originally brought their family out west, was born in Macksburg on September 28, 1857, to Andrew and Nancy Ann Ensley. His two elder sisters were Ellen Mahala and Sarah Elizabeth, and his younger brother was William. All four children attended school and church and stayed near the family farm as they grew into adults.

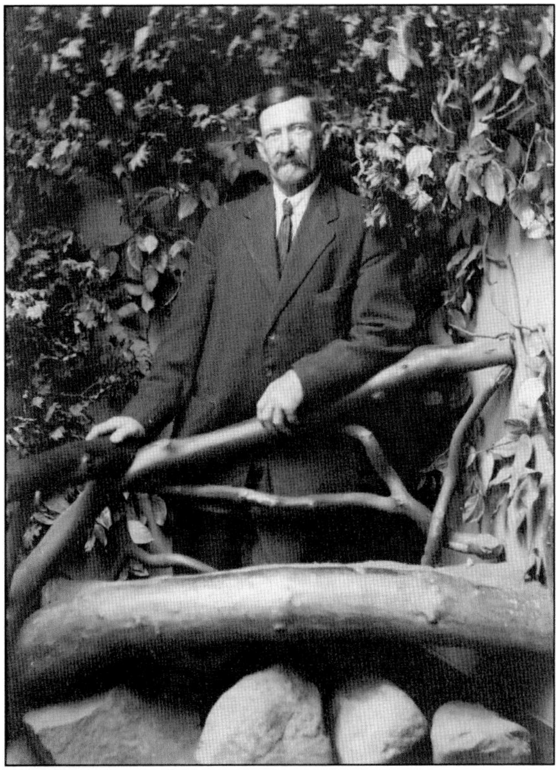

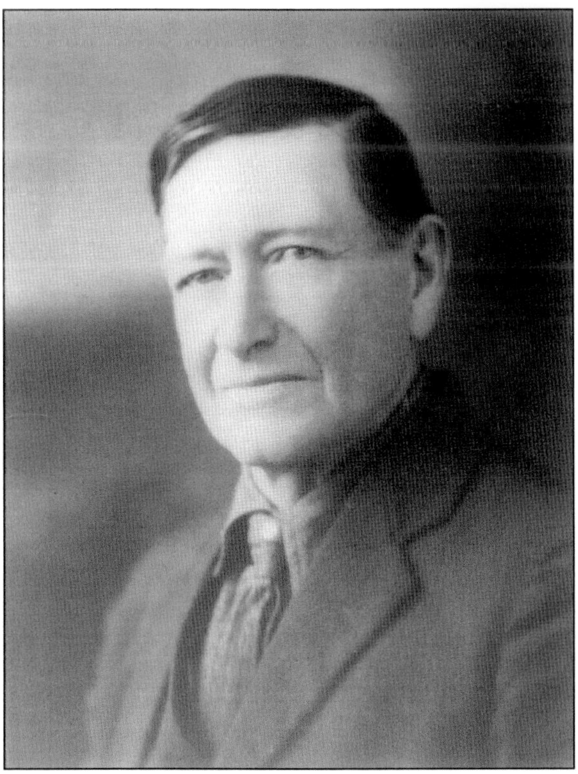

Albert was able to start his agricultural career when he was just 21 years old. When his father, Andrew, died, he inherited his share of the Gribble estate, which was 140 acres. He specialized in growing potatoes, laying out 60 acres for harvest. He grew 10 acres of grass seed for his herd of Jersey cattle. Albert purchased 112 acres of his father's land from his brother, William, in 1894.

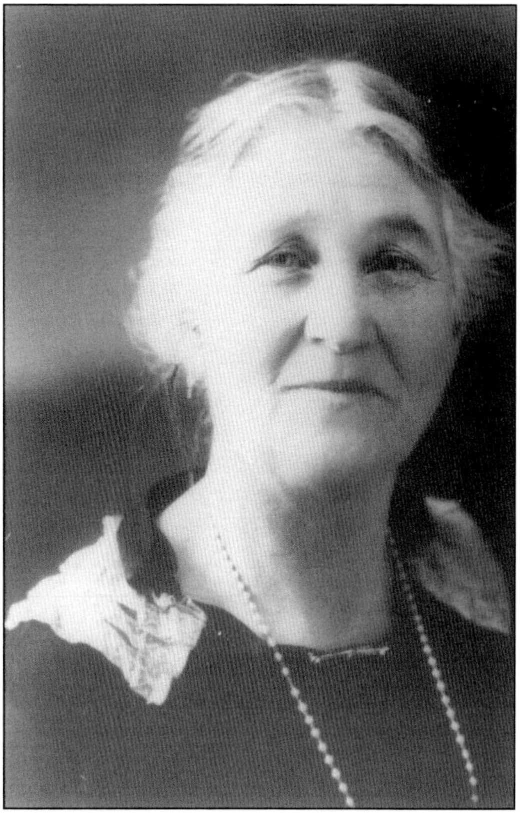

Narcissus Margaret "Maggie" Jesse was born on September 15, 1863, in Smithville, Missouri, to Woodford and Amanda Jesse. Margaret had one younger sibling, Woodford Dennis. Albert Gribble married Margaret in 1885 in the nearby town of New Era. They had 11 children. Albert died on October 2, 1933, and Margaret died on June 8, 1939. They are buried at the Gribble Cemetery, located on Gribble Road in Canby, near their original farmland.

The Gribble family created their own cemetery on Gribble Road when they had to bury their loved ones. There are 126 burials at the cemetery to date, and over 94 graves are within the family. The first gravesite was laid in 1847. The Gribble Cemetery is located on Gribble Road. It is still an active graveyard; family members maintain it. (Courtesy of Daniel Cowan.)

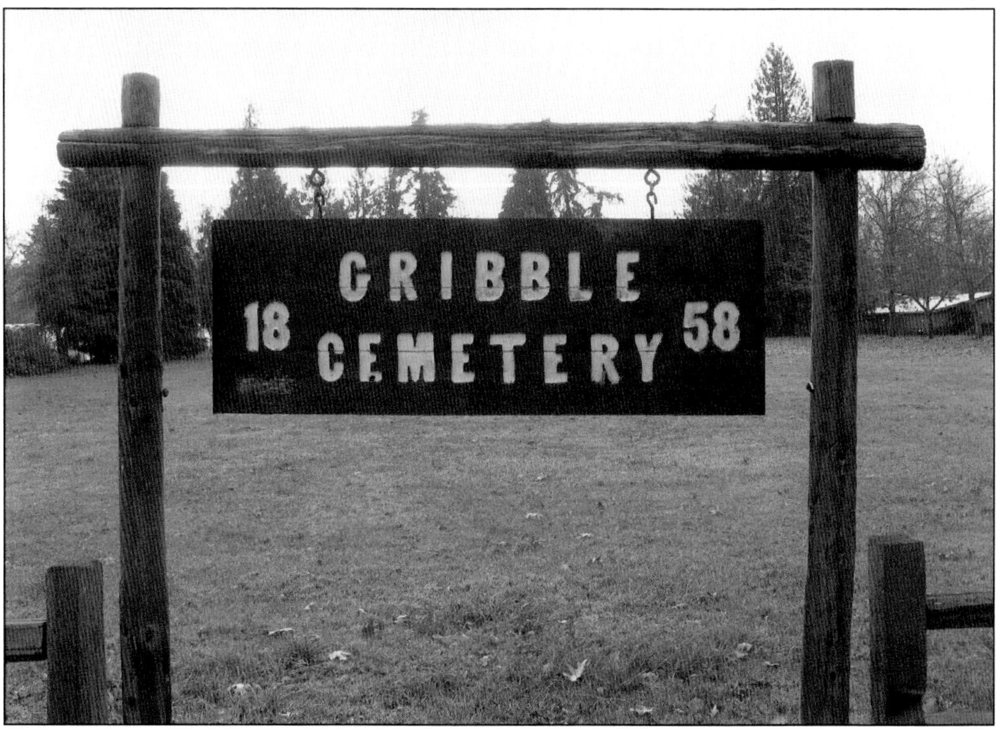

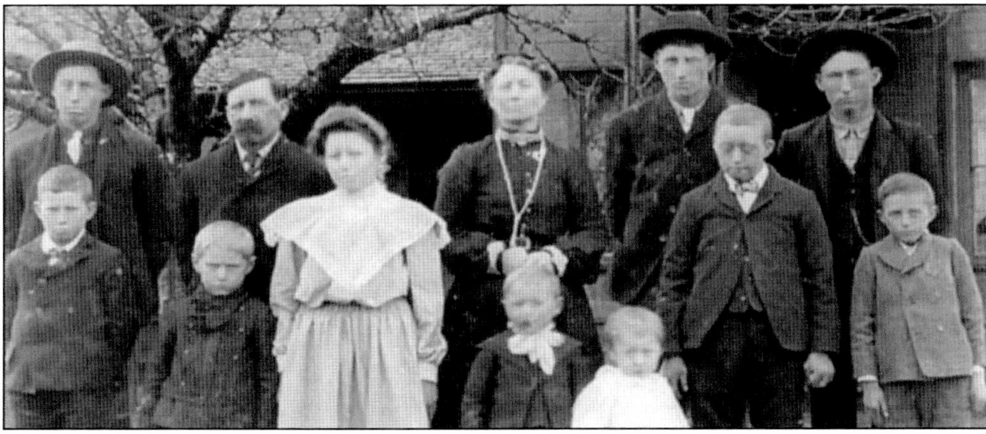

In 1905, Albert and Maggie Gribble gathered with their children for a family portrait on their farm. From left to right are (first row) Andy, Frank, Lena, Estes, Jack, Charlie, and Sam; (second row) Allen, Albert, Maggie, Ensley, and Ralph. As time moved on, some of their children were buried near them in the Gribble Cemetery.

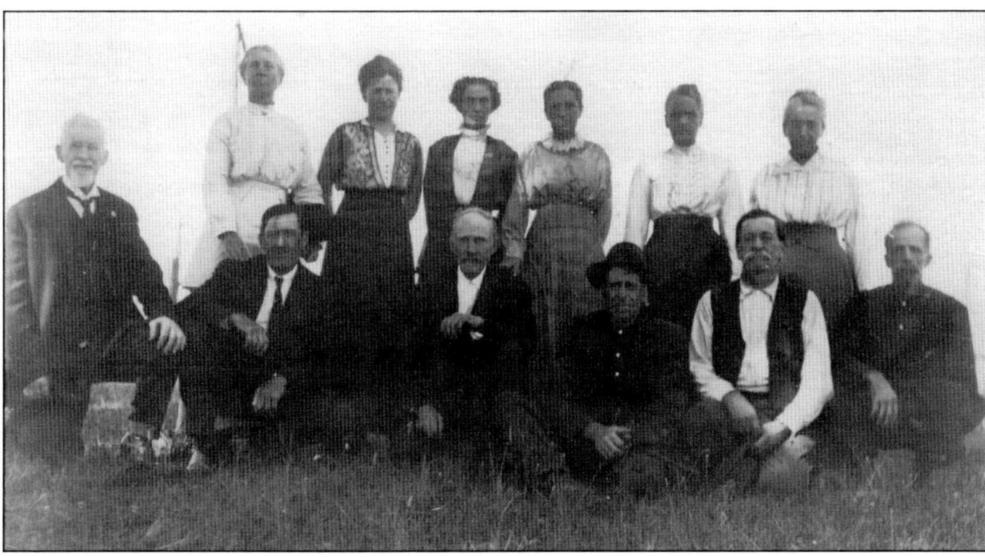

A collective photograph of the Gribble family shows, from left to right, (first row) Bill Irvin, Albert Gribble, John Jesse, Will Gribble, Wesley Riggs, and George Kesselring (Nancy Gribble's second husband); (second row) Maggie Gribble (Albert's wife), Lydia Irvin, Ellen Gribble Irvin (Andrew's daughter), Sarah Gribble, Nancy Riggs Gribble (Andrew's wife), and Mary Wing.

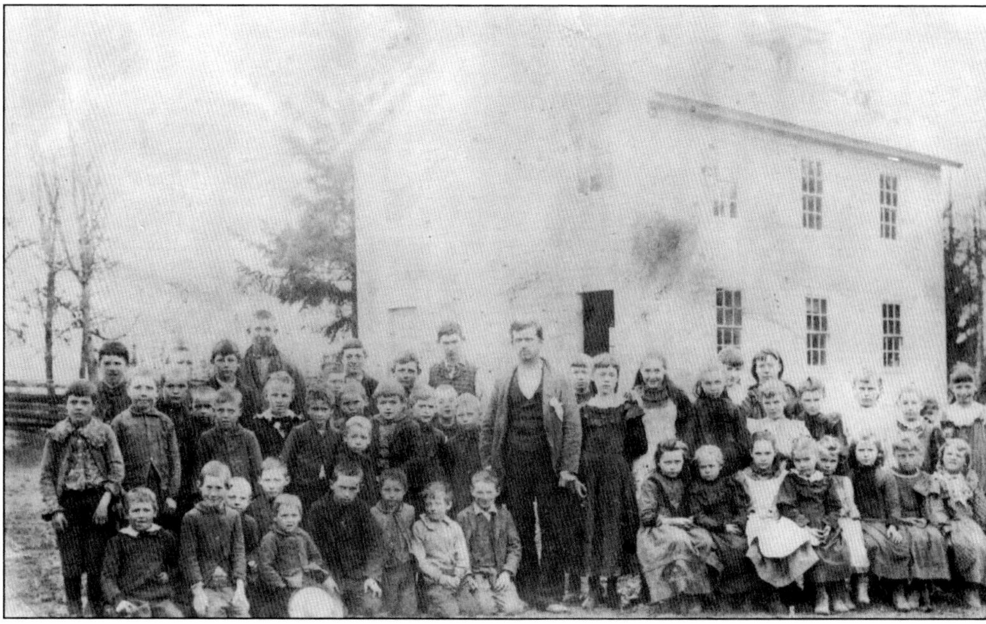

Here is the Macksburg School District No. 20, where many of the Gribble children attended. This is a photograph from 1896. The teacher, standing in the center, is P.L. Coleman. Ralph Gribble is the fourth boy from the left in the front row, sitting to his right is Ed Kraxberger. Just to the left of Coleman is Allen Gribble. The young man in the last row at top left is Otto Kraxberger.

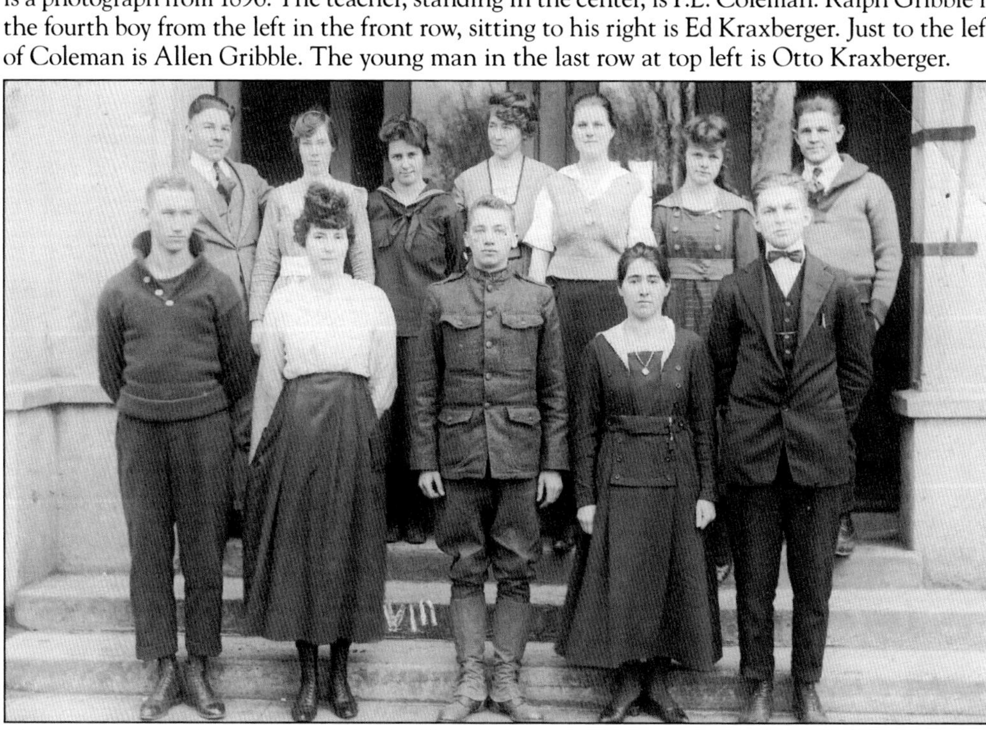

Here is a school photograph of Canby High School graduates in 1919. From left to right are (first row) Roy Zimmerman, Anna Gillmore, John Robins, Laura Pennell, and Kenneth Hornig; (second row) John Gastrock, Mable Gribble, Eva Whipple, Pearl Cartlidge, Agnes Hendrickson, Mildred Dedman, and Wayne Hampton. Also graduating were Edith May, Craig Dedman, and Herman Anthony.

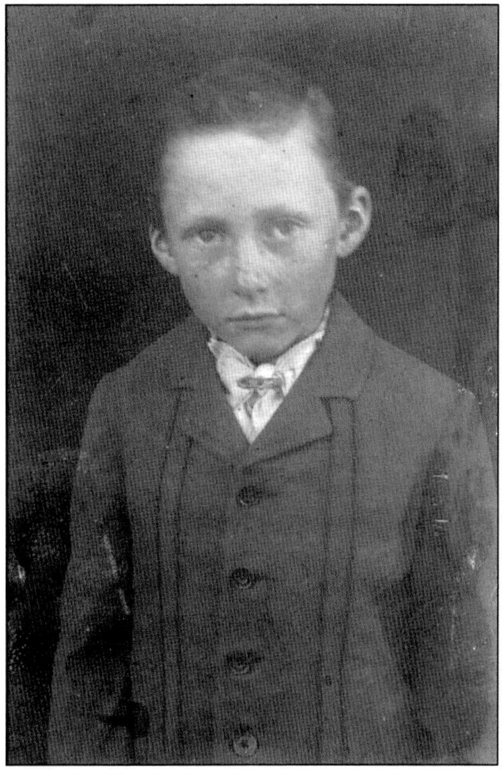

Ralph Gribble was born on October 5, 1886. He was the eldest son of Albert and Maggie Gribble. The couple had nine sons and two daughters. In 1909, the Gribbles had a photograph taken of some of their young sons and a friend of the family. Shown below are, from left to right, Ensley, Samuel, Ralph, Andrew, and William Miller. Albert was a very progressive and resourceful father. In addition to teaching them to work the farm, he also taught his sons about breeding Jersey cattle and Berkshire swine. Aside from teaching their children to work hard on the land, both Albert and Maggie wanted to offer the best school education to all of their children. Schoolwork was as important as cultivating the grain.

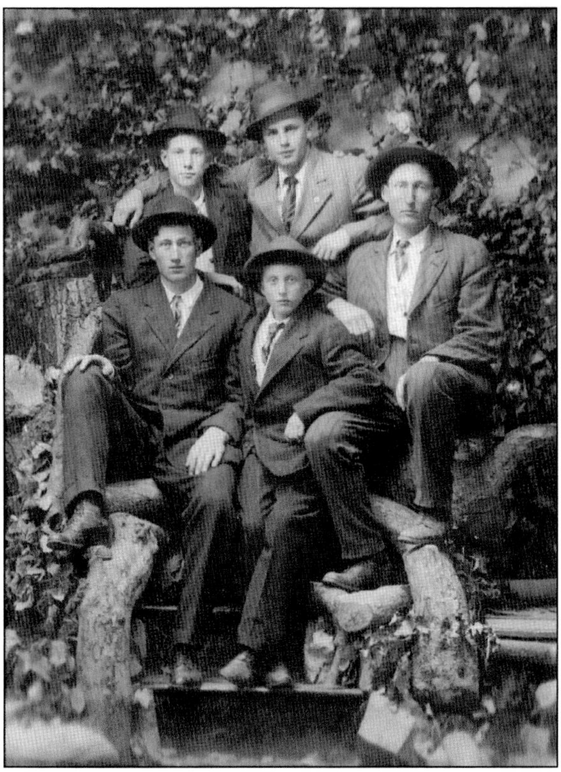

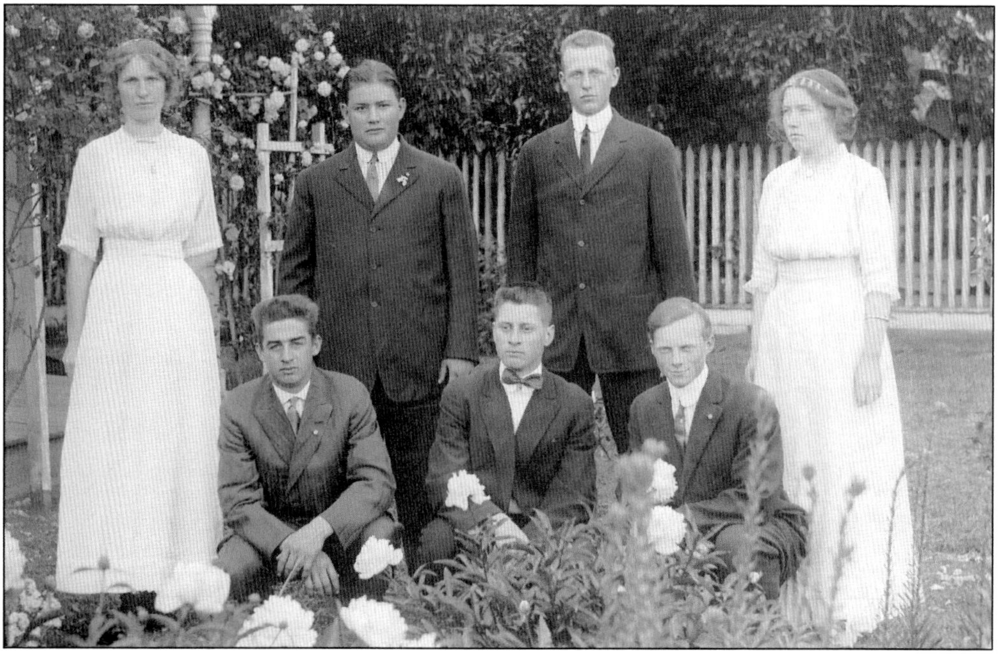

At the beginning of the 20th century, a new generation of Gribbles grew up on Gribble Prairie and went to the same schools their parents most likely attended. The young woman on the right is Lena Gribble (later Mrs. Harry Reynolds), posing with her graduating class of 1914 from Canby High School.

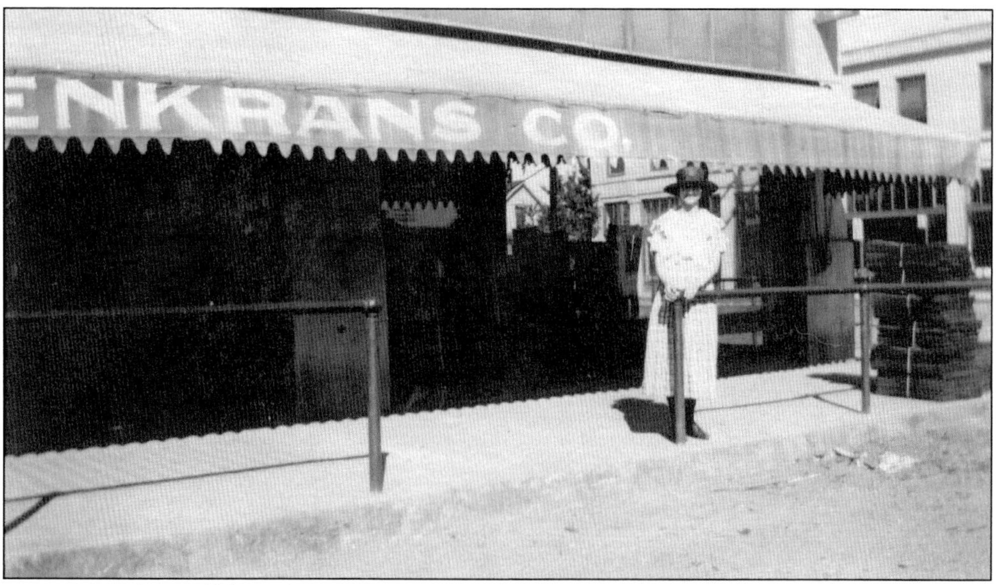

Here is Myrtle Gribble in front of the Carlton & Rosenkrans building in downtown Canby. Carlton & Rosenkrans was founded in 1891; it was the largest retail store in Clackamas County at the time. Myrtle was born on July 31, 1900. She died on June 24, 1992. Myrtle lived a long 92 years in Canby.

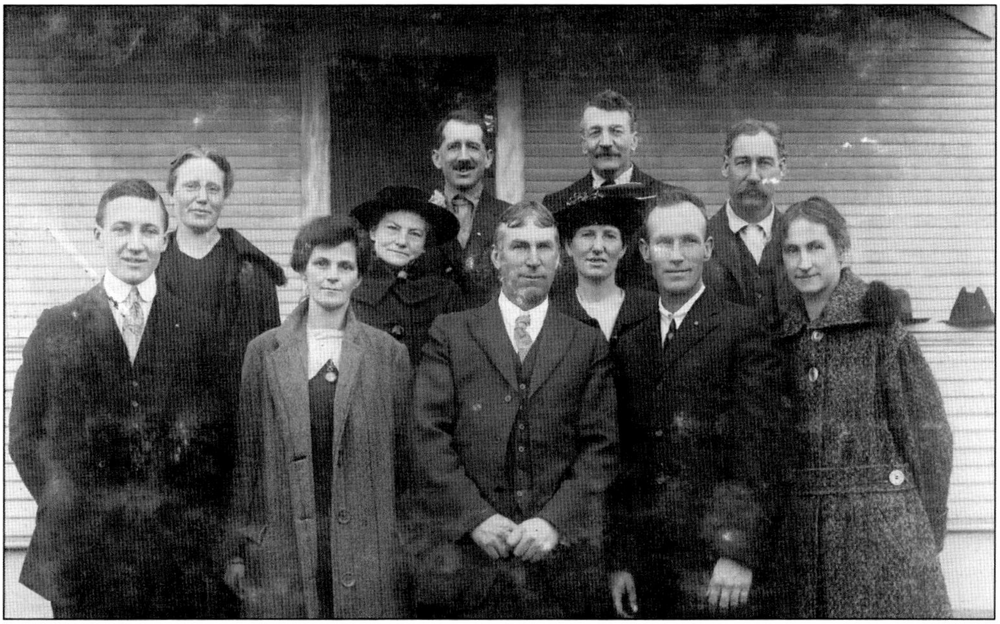

The Gribbles were involved in both the city groups and the community. The officers of the United Artisans Lodge in 1916 are, from left to right, (first row) Clyde W. Kendall, unidentified, Elmer Gribble, Ross Rider, and Florence Stoddard; (second row) unidentified, Mrs. O.R. Mack, unidentified, and Sam Hess; (third row) Irvin Wheeler and Warren C. Kendall.

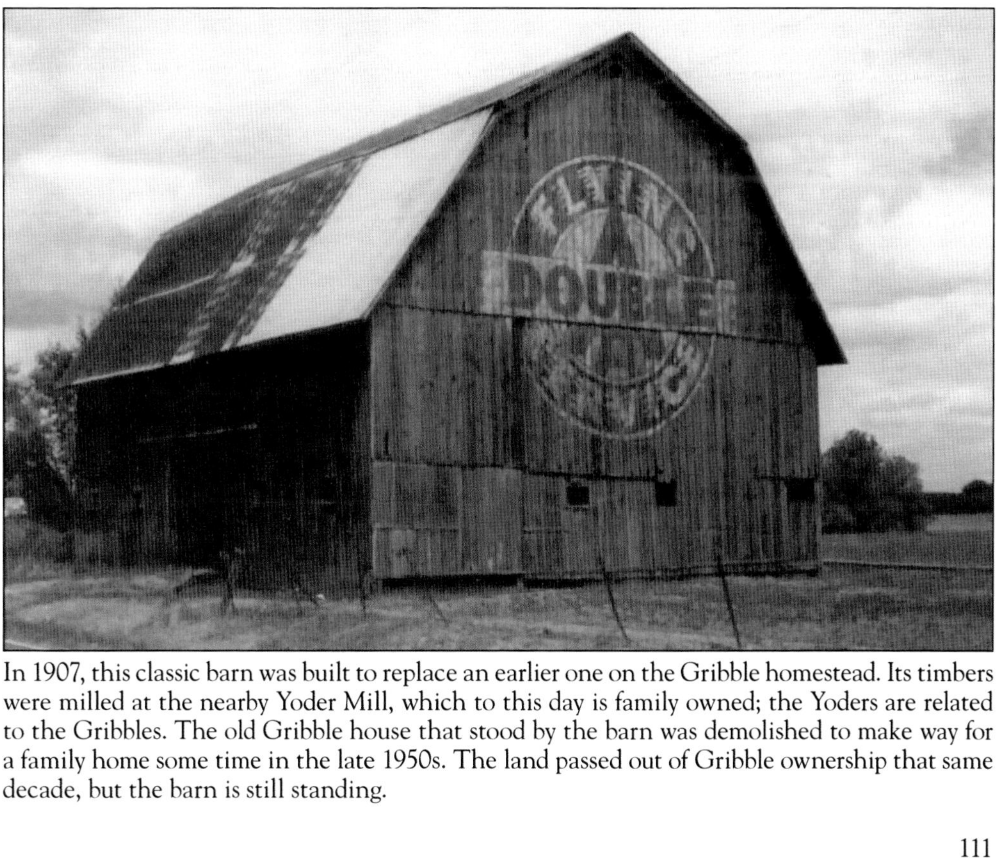

In 1907, this classic barn was built to replace an earlier one on the Gribble homestead. Its timbers were milled at the nearby Yoder Mill, which to this day is family owned; the Yoders are related to the Gribbles. The old Gribble house that stood by the barn was demolished to make way for a family home some time in the late 1950s. The land passed out of Gribble ownership that same decade, but the barn is still standing.

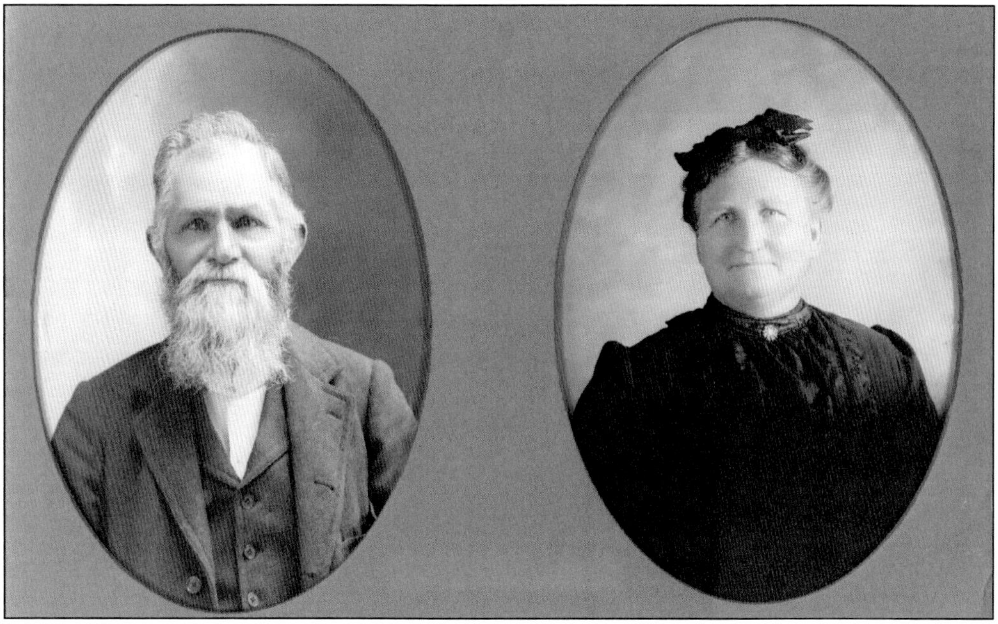

Another family that passed its land on to the next generation was the Lees. Heman A. Lee (born on March 29, 1833, in Jefferson, New York, the son of Philander and Anna Lee) and Eda Elizabeth Tice Lee (born in Iowa on July 10, 1851) both came out in wagons with their parents. Heman was 15 years old when he arrived in Oregon. His father deeded him 52 3/4 acres of his donation land claim in Canby. Heman was Canby's first mayor in 1893 and later served from 1896 to 1899. His son, Milo Heman Lee, was born in Canby on April 5, 1872. Milo married Mary Elizabeth Bonny; they had two children. Milo was a well driller by trade. He and his wife lived their whole lives on the land until Milo had to move to Jennings Lodge, Oregon, to receive medical treatment. He died there four years later.

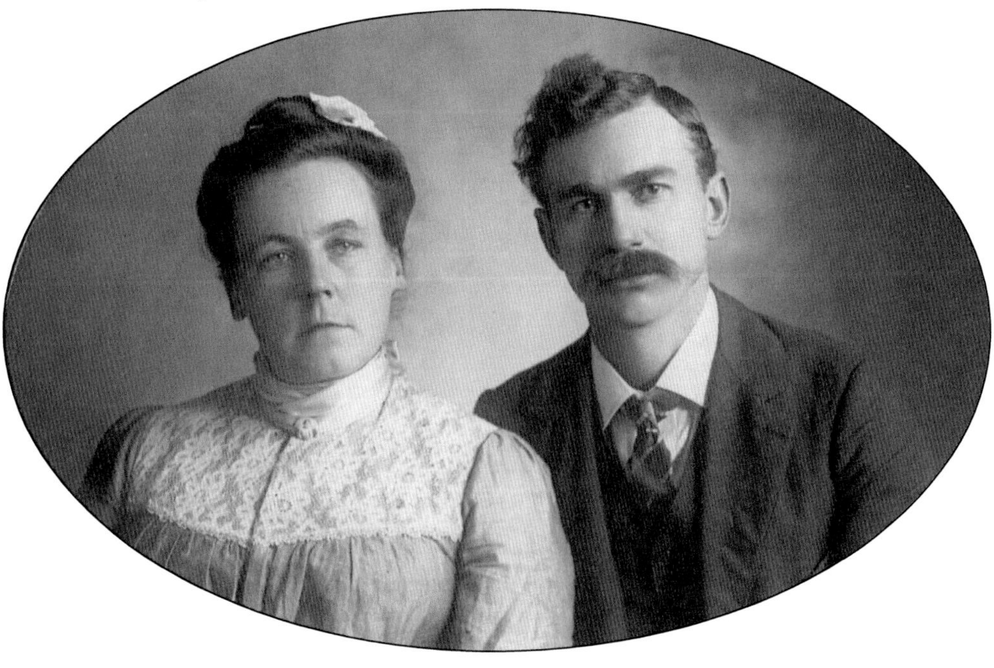

Clara Lee (left), age 19, and Lorinda Lee, age 17, were two of Philander Lee's granddaughters. This photograph was taken in Portland, Oregon, in 1887. These women were the daughters of Heman and Eda Lee. Clara soon after married E.D. Hutchinson and had several children. She later married Ranson Soper. Lorinda married Harry Gilmore, the mayor of Canby from 1904 to 1905.

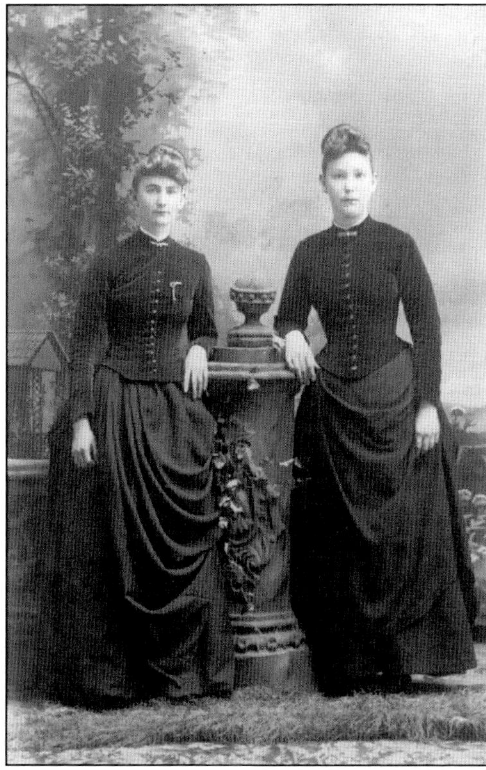

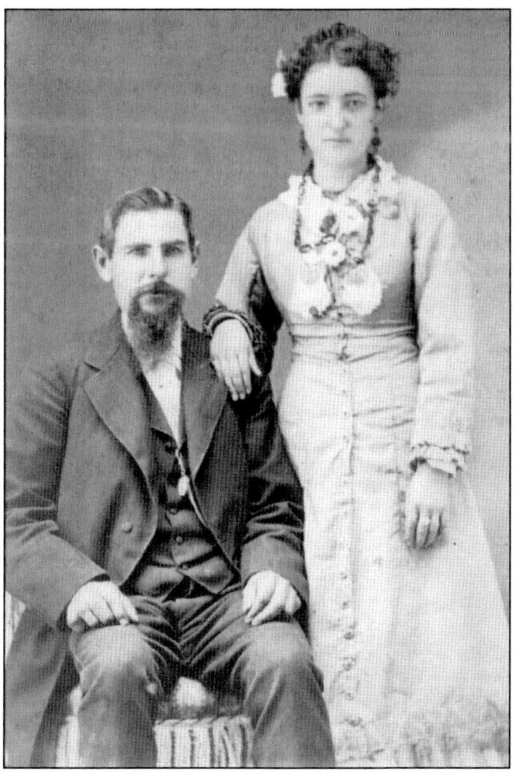

Joseph Knight and Lucetta Birtchet were married on June 27, 1878. They were another young couple with dreams of settling in this new town. Joseph was a shoemaker and also raised hops on his land. He even ran a sawmill. The Knights had 300 acres courtesy of the Donation Land Claim Act to expand their homestead.

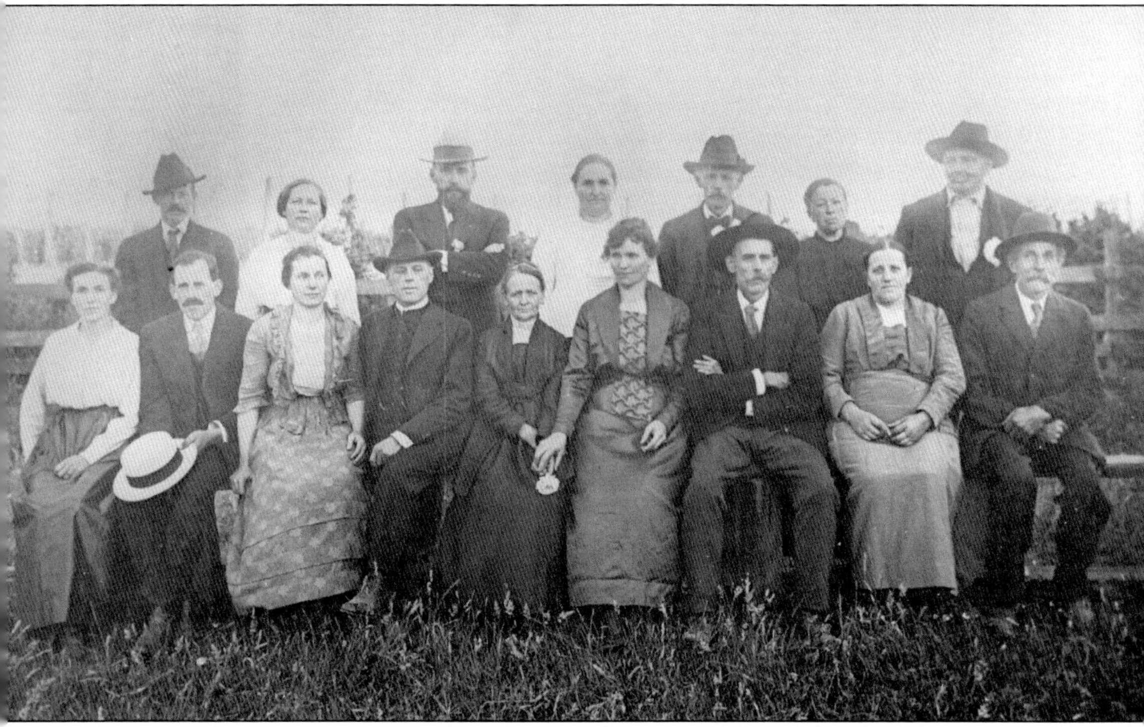

The Kraxberger family line that still lives near Canby began in the villages of Ehlend, Hunsheinz, and Buchkirchen in Austria. Their primary occupations were mostly likely in farming and weaving. The first in this family to come to America was Michael, who had been born in Wels, Austria. He had married Katherine Roiter; they immigrated to Morgan County, Missouri, in 1853. They had four children—Elizabeth J., John G., Michael F., and Theresa. By 1890, as the Kraxberger family grew, the enticement of fertile grounds out west was beckoning. In 1892, John Kraxberger and his wife boarded the newly constructed Canadian Railroad and arrived six days later, June 13, in the city of Portland. By July 15, preparations were made to move the family to their new home in Macksburg. Pictured is the first generation of Kraxbergers' husbands and wives: from left to right, (first row) Augusta, Otto, Nora, Rev. William, Julia, Bertha, Ferdinand, Marie, and John Etzel; (second row) Adolph, Christina, Franz, Emma, Charles, Rose, and Henry Kummer. (Courtesy of Verlyn and Darlene Kraxberger.)

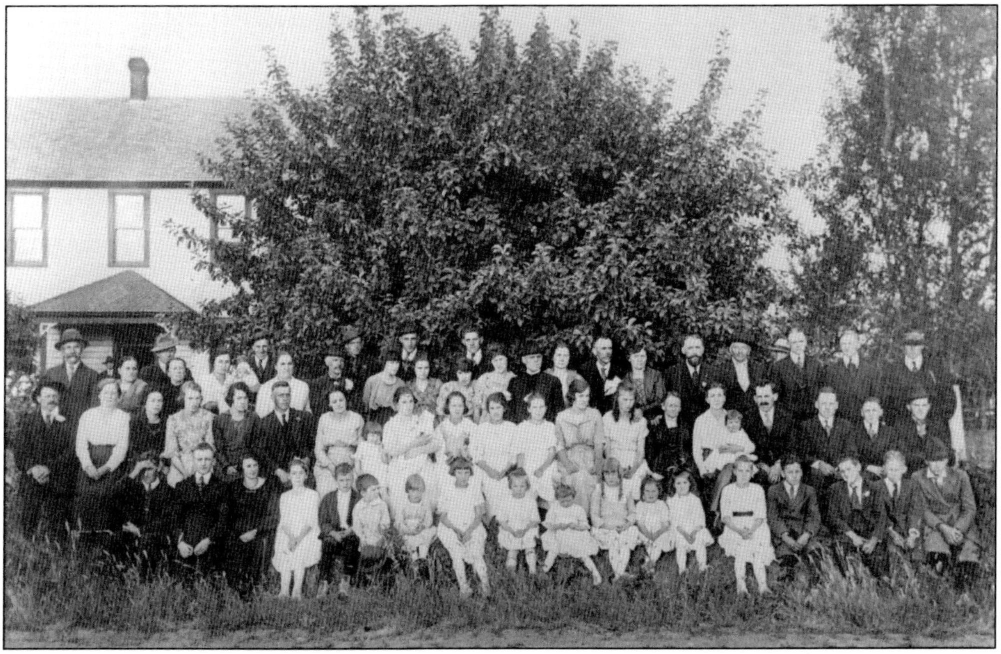

By 1889, more of the Kraxbergers were coming to America. Franz, Carl, and Ferdinand boarded a ship to this new land. They traveled to Missouri and stayed there through 1890. Oregon was offering land deals for newcomers, so Franz and Carl came out west. They met up with others from their family and bought land nearby Canby. Here is a photograph of family and friends on Franz's farm in 1918. (Courtesy of Verlyn and Darlene Kraxberger.)

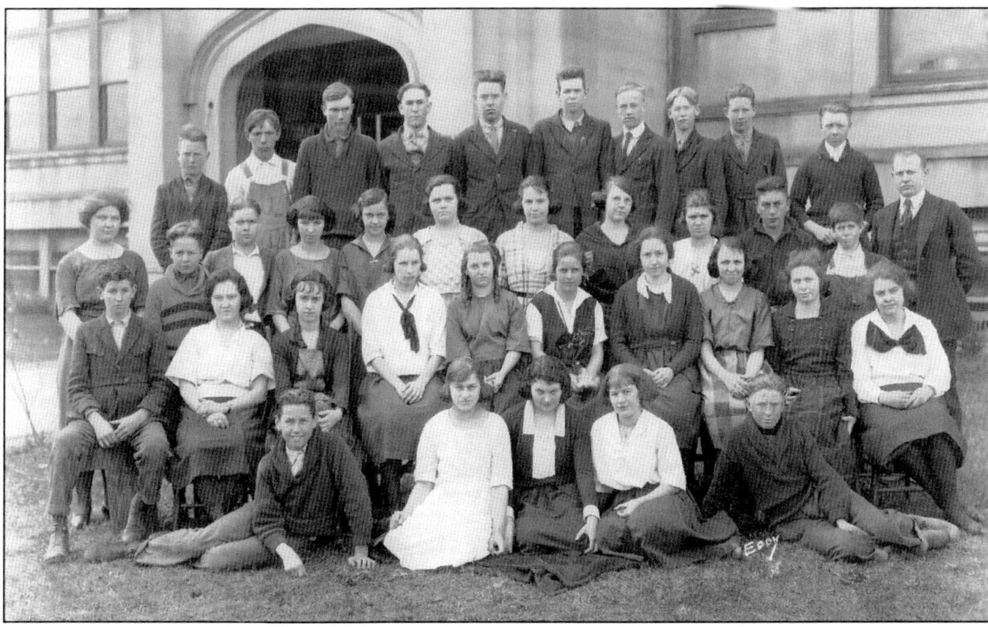

The freshman class of 1922 at the Canby High School appeared to be ready and eager to take on their first year of high school. Sophie Kraxberger is the fourth student from left in the second row. Her teacher was Wayne Gurley. Like her siblings, Sophie would finish high school and settle near her family's farm.

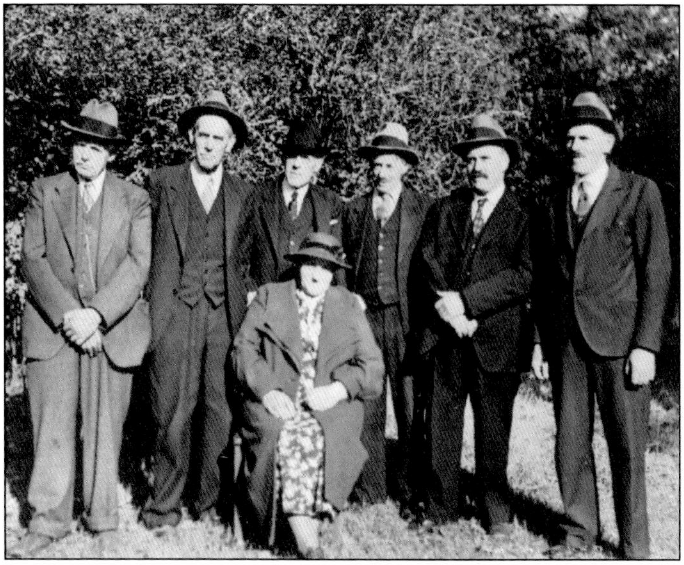

As more of the Kraxberger family came to America and settled near Canby, they stayed together as one large family, much as they were in Austria. Even as the years went by, they kept holidays and reunions as a part of their heritage. Here is a reunion photograph from 1933. Standing, from left to right, are Charles, Ferdinand, Rev. William, Adolph, John, and Otto Kraxberger. Sitting down is Marie Kraxberger Kummer. (Courtesy of Verlyn and Darlene Kraxberger.)

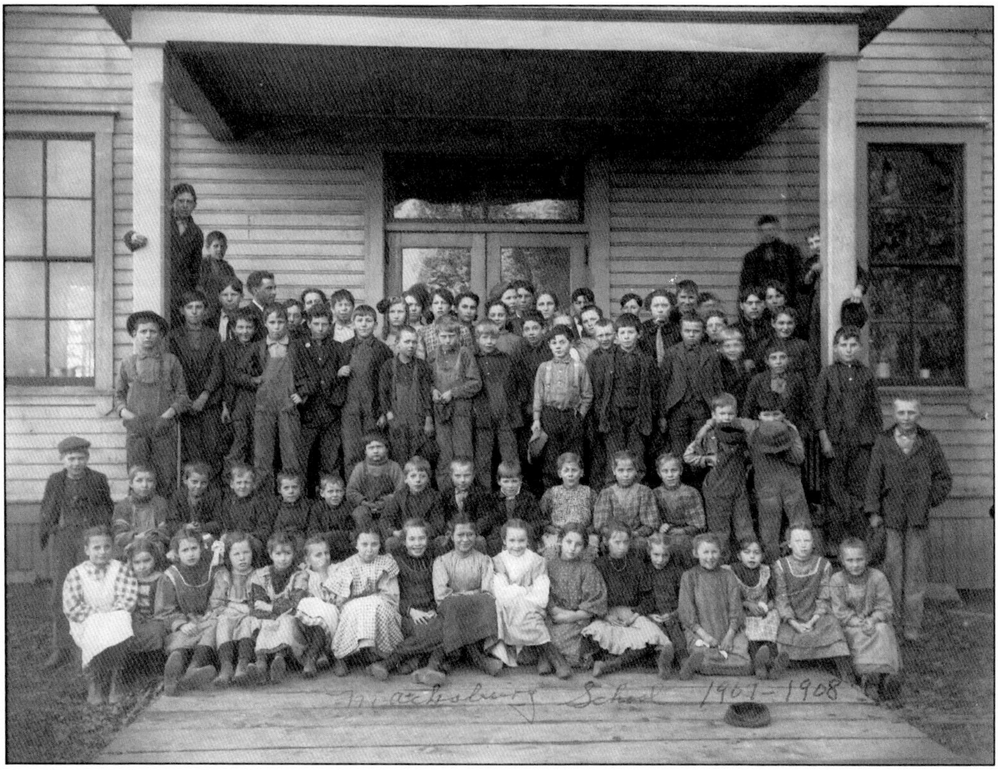

As the Kraxberger family grew, the children continued to work on the farm and attend the local school. In this 1907–1908 photograph from the Macksburg School, Margaret Kraxberger is the fifth child in the first row; Elsie, Nora, and Walberga, are third, fourth, and fifth from the right. Bruno Kraxberger is the second child from left on the second row. In the third row are, from far left to right, Rufus Kraxberger, Sam Gribble, and Lena Gribble. (Courtesy of Verlyn and Darlene Kraxberger.)

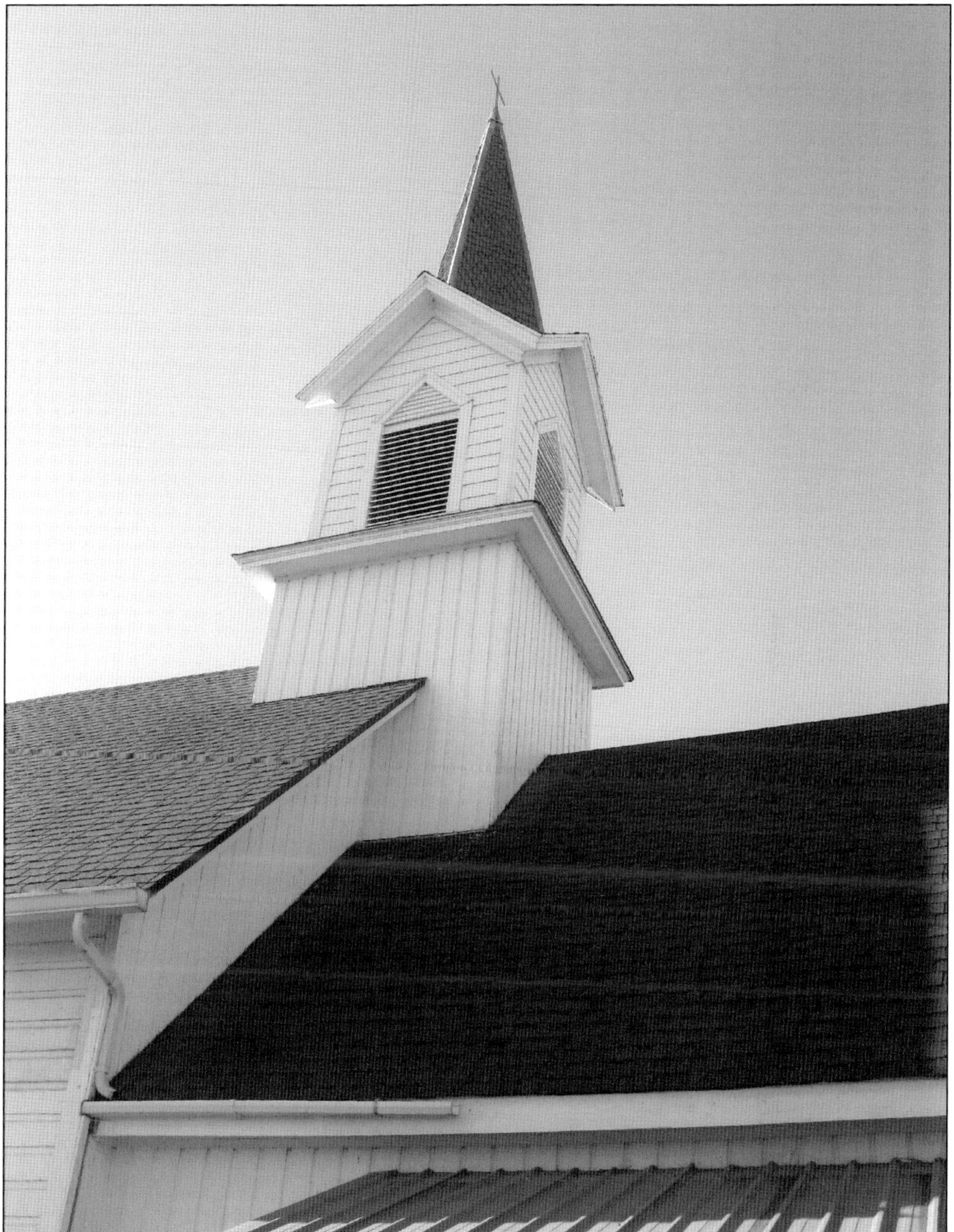

Following their purchase of land and settlement at Macksburg, the Kraxberger family found that the need for a religious community was vital. Before they had a church, every third Sunday, John Kraxberger would bring in Rev. C. Buechler from St. John's congregation in Portland. He was driven by wagon to meet in different families' homes. After the service, he was taken to the Canby train station, where he would grab a locomotive and return home. The first home service was in September 1892 at the home of Albert Klebe. Once the Macksburg Lutheran Church was built, the home services ceased. The German language was used in this Lutheran church until 1929. After that, up until 1943, the services alternated between English and German.

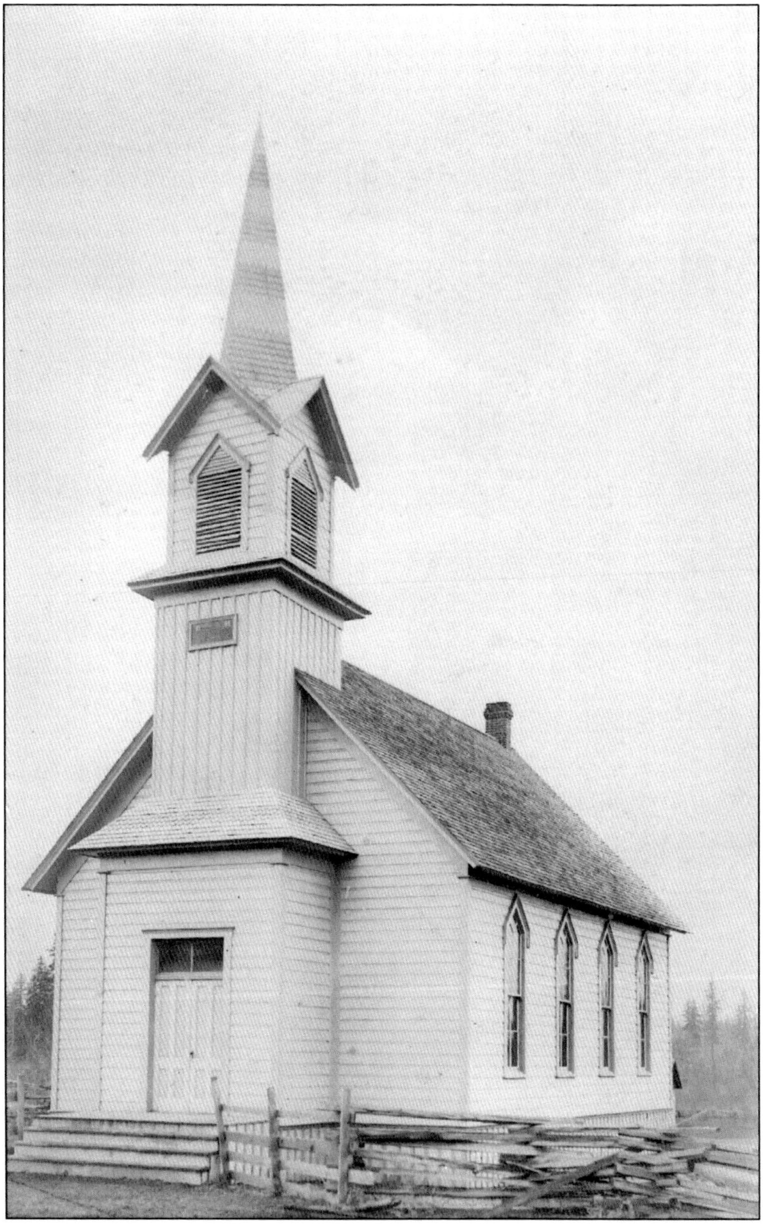

The primary executors of the Macksburg Lutheran Church's affairs were Chris Lorenz, Franz Kraxberger, and Albert Klebe. An acre of land for their new church was purchased from Klebe in 1894 at the price of $50. Johann and Rosina Kraxberger were active in the labor to build a church that was similar to the family church they remembered in their native Austria. The wood-frame Rural Gothic/vernacular structure was a simple rectangle with a tall steeple reaching toward the sky. Four windows on each side were also designed with arches pointing upward. A group of Mennonite carpenters from the Needy area began construction in 1894. The cost was $237, with a lot of the labor donated. When the money came in from the parishioners, it was handed to the carpenters immediately. It is rumored that the family members were assessed proportionately according to the acreage of their farms for their work and donated money. The church was completed and dedicated on November 11, 1893.

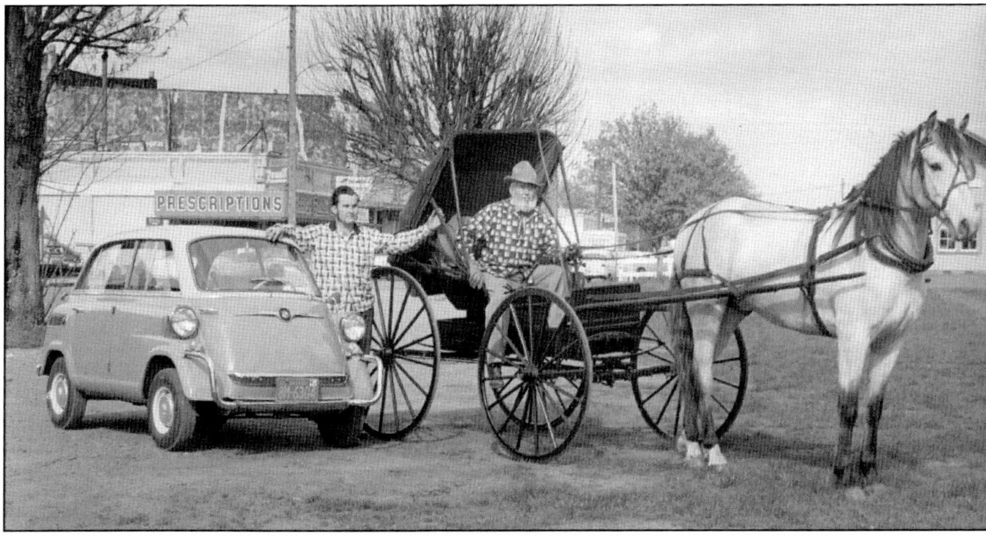

Dale W. Cutsforth was a Milk Creek farmer. On April 23, 1959, he brought his horse and buggy to Canby for his family to see. The buckskin pony's name was Rawhide, and it rode nicely for Dale to come and see his son, Gentry. Gentry met his father with his two-cylinder Isetta automobile. While Gentry bragged about how efficient his German car was on gasoline, Dale reminded his son that Rawhide makes many miles without any gasoline. Dale planned to take his horse and buggy to Salem, Oregon, on Saturday for a riding club parade.

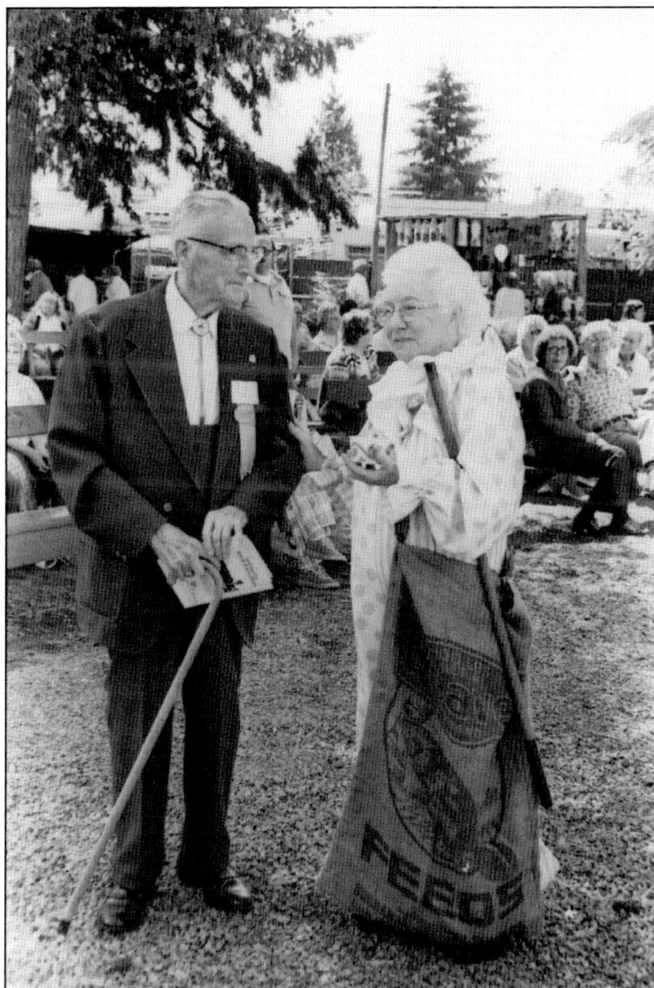

Lillian I. Cutsforth, Dale's wife, was born in 1899. She was always busy at home with her children or helping out in community events. Here she is with George Cattley helping at the Sweet Ade. Her son, Gentry, wrote and published the stories she had cut out and pasted into a scrapbook. Gentry found these stories after Lillian's death at the age of 97.

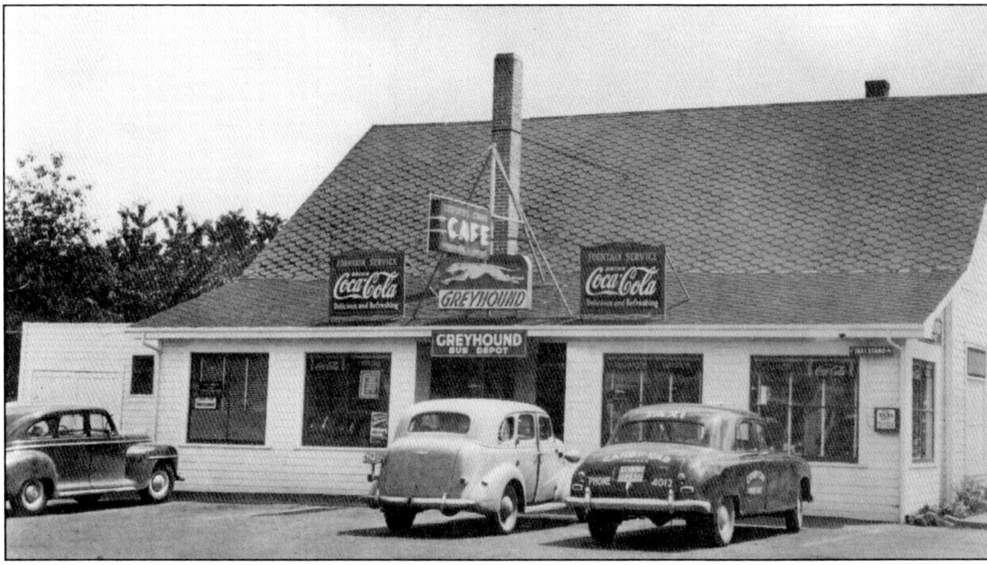

Larry Bradford ran the Bus Depot Café at Cutsforth's Corner. It was a central place to eat, meet friends, and travel. It offered a fountain service, hamburgers, and a lunch stop with a simple deli menu. It was a taxi stand for the Canby Cab Company and one of the Greyhound bus depots for the area.

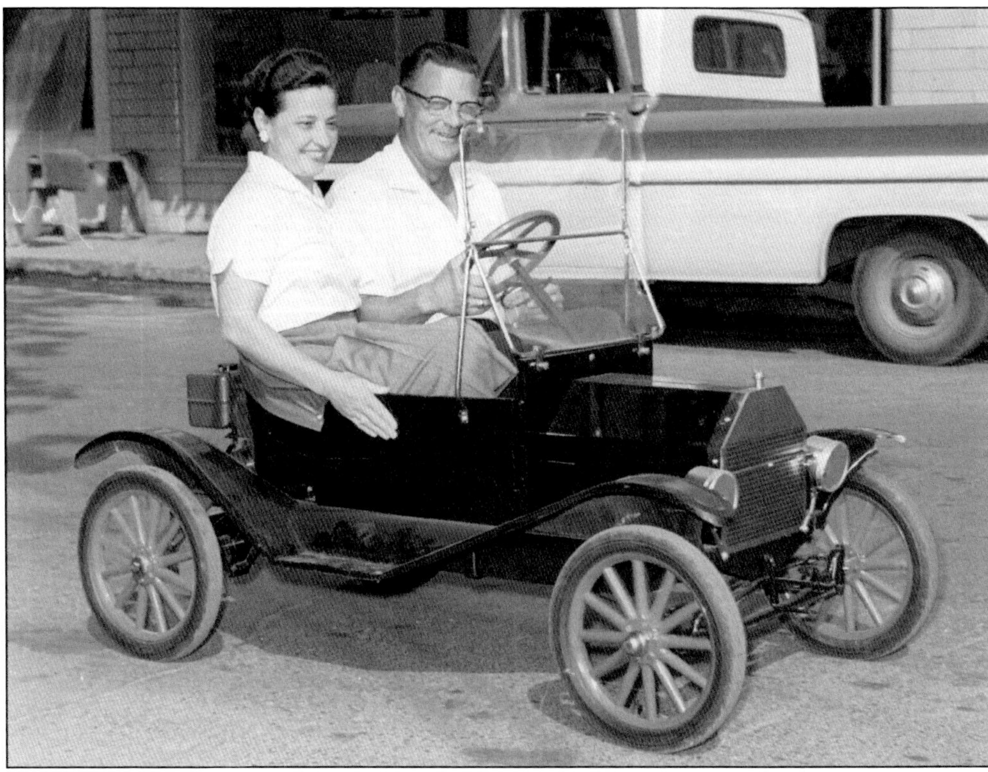

Elsie Cutsforth was always involved in the local festivities and events in Canby. Here she is with Mayor Earl Oliver posing in a midget car during the Kiddie Capers Parade in August 1961. This car was owned by the Cutsforth family and used in the town parades for many years.

In 1928, Frank T. Cutsforth opened a meat market on NW First Avenue in Canby. When Glenn Cutsforth was 12, he began working in the business alongside his father. Groceries were added to the market in 1946, and Cutsforth's Market became Canby's third grocery store. Glenn's son and the current owner, Frank Cutsforth, started working for the market in 1957. Here are the Cutsforths in 1952: Frank, Glenn, and Frank's grandson, Frank D.

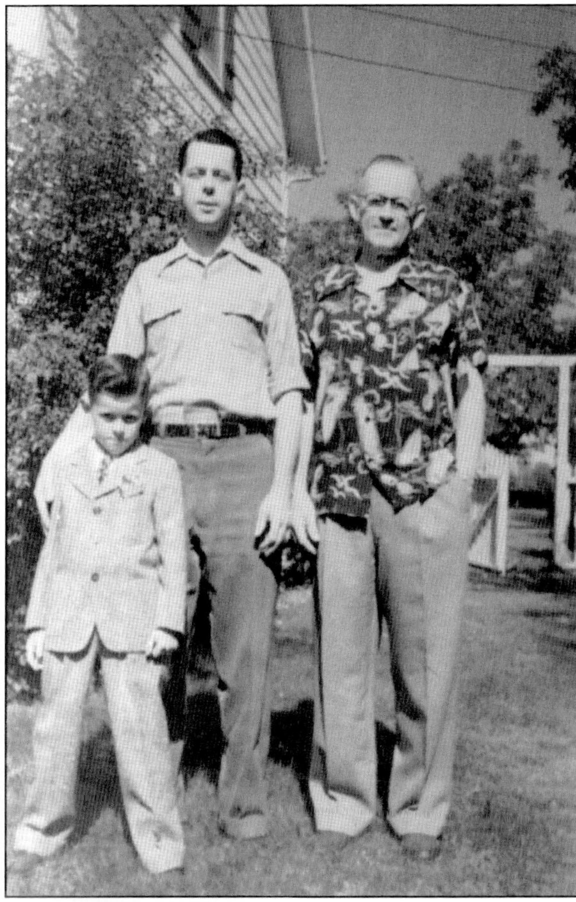

The Cutsforths have kept their deli and butchering up with the most modern tools of that time. The earliest store only offered meat, but Cutsforth's Market quickly became a full-service grocery retailer. Founded by Frank T. Cutsforth in 1928 after he ran a similar business in Gervais, Oregon, it is still active today in Canby. Cutsforth's Thriftway Marketplace will someday be managed by the fourth generation of Cutsforths.

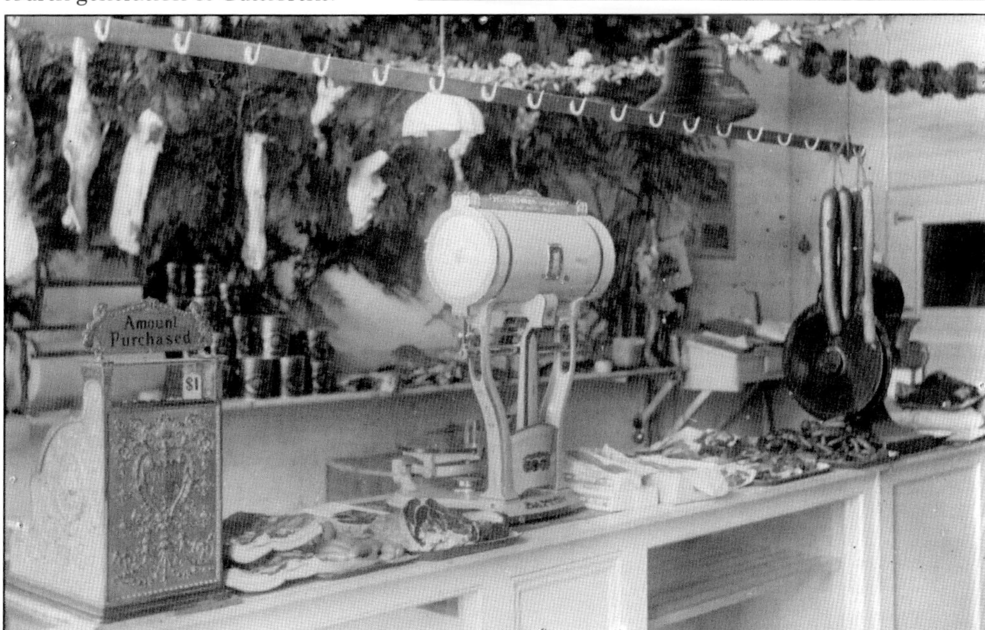

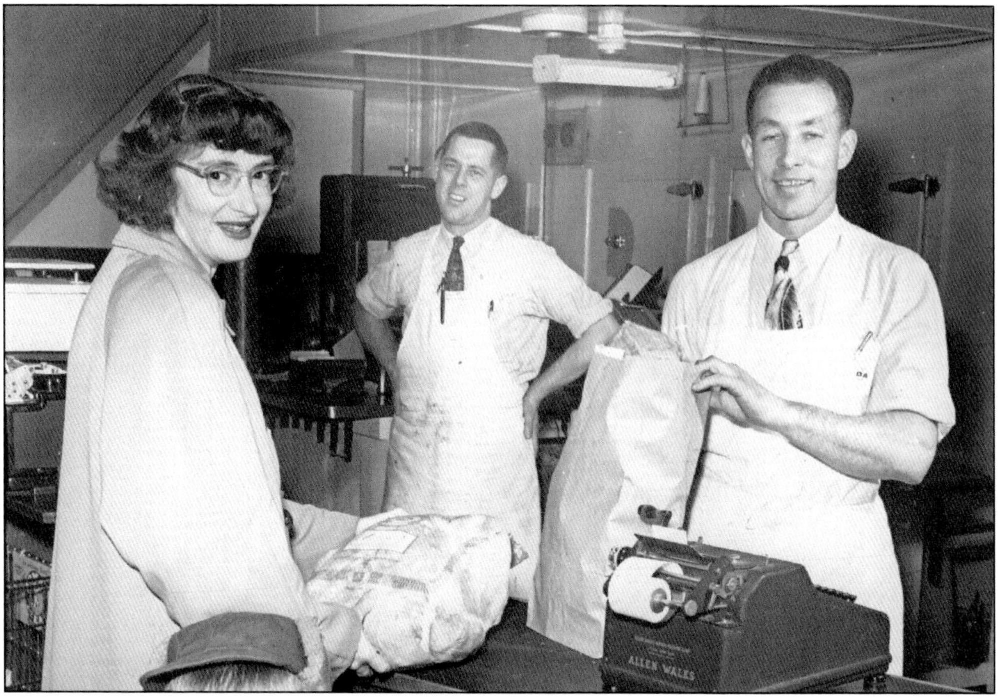

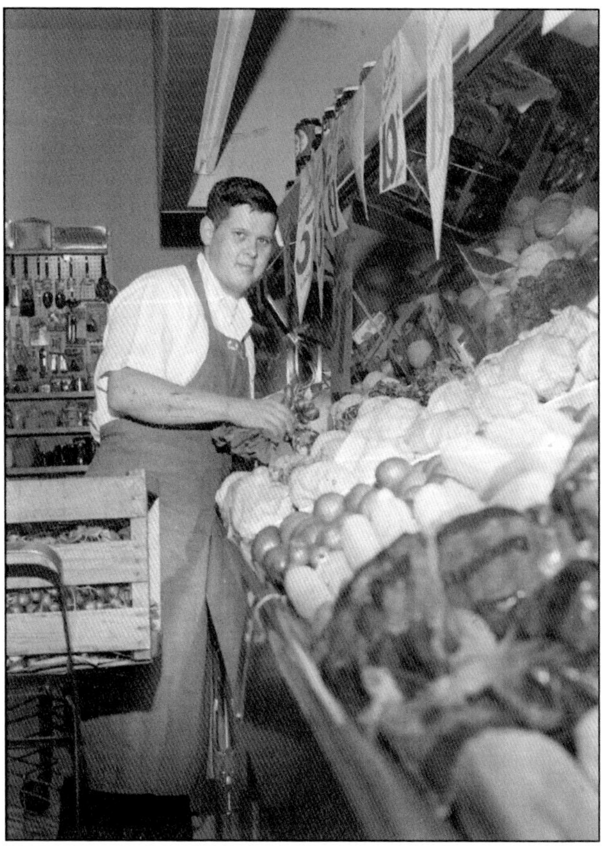

In 1963, Cutsforth's Market moved to a new location on the corner of Second Avenue and Holly Street, where it remained for 12 years. Cutsforth's again relocated in 1975, to its current site at 225 NE Second Avenue in Downtown Canby. Here are Jean Warren and Rene DuPont being assisted by Glenn T. Cutsforth (center) at the new store.

Lifelong Canby resident Frank Cutsforth, Glenn Cutsforth's son, is shown here working at Cutsforth's Market as a young man. After graduating from Canby High School, he studied at the University of Oregon. When Frank became the owner, he became the third generation of his family to own and run Cutsforth Thriftway Marketplace in Canby. Frank is now working with his children to run the business, which has 120 employees.

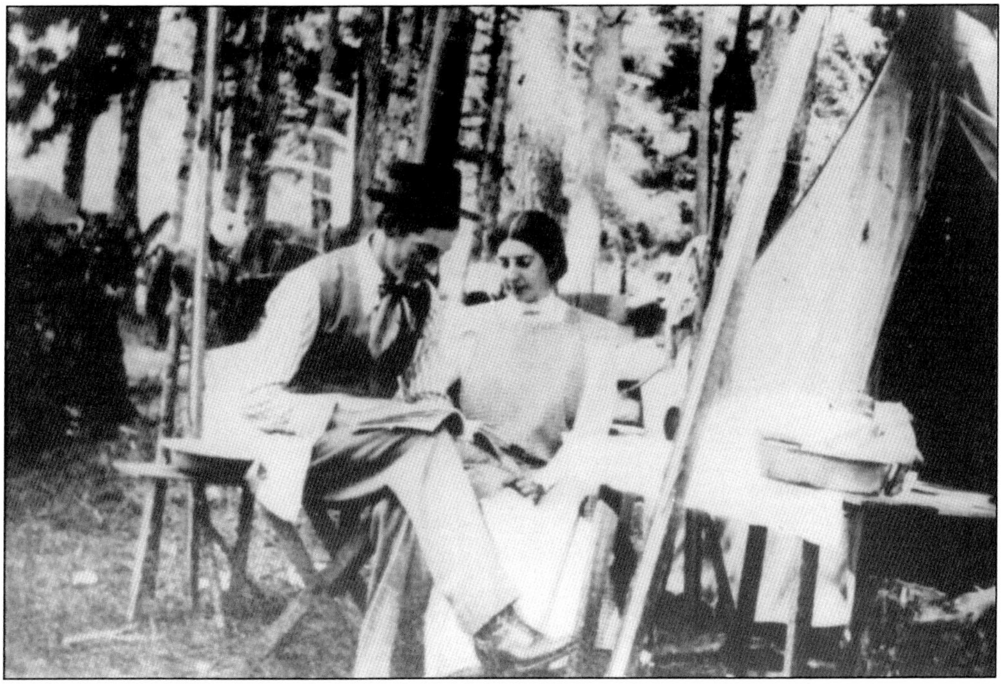

The Yoder family has lived in the Canby area for well over 100 years. They opened their sawmill business, Yoder Mill, in 1889. Yoder is an unincorporated neighborhood just south of Canby. This name comes from the Mennonite family who settled in the area. Here are Ralph and Nell Yoder at the Canby Fairgrounds in 1909.

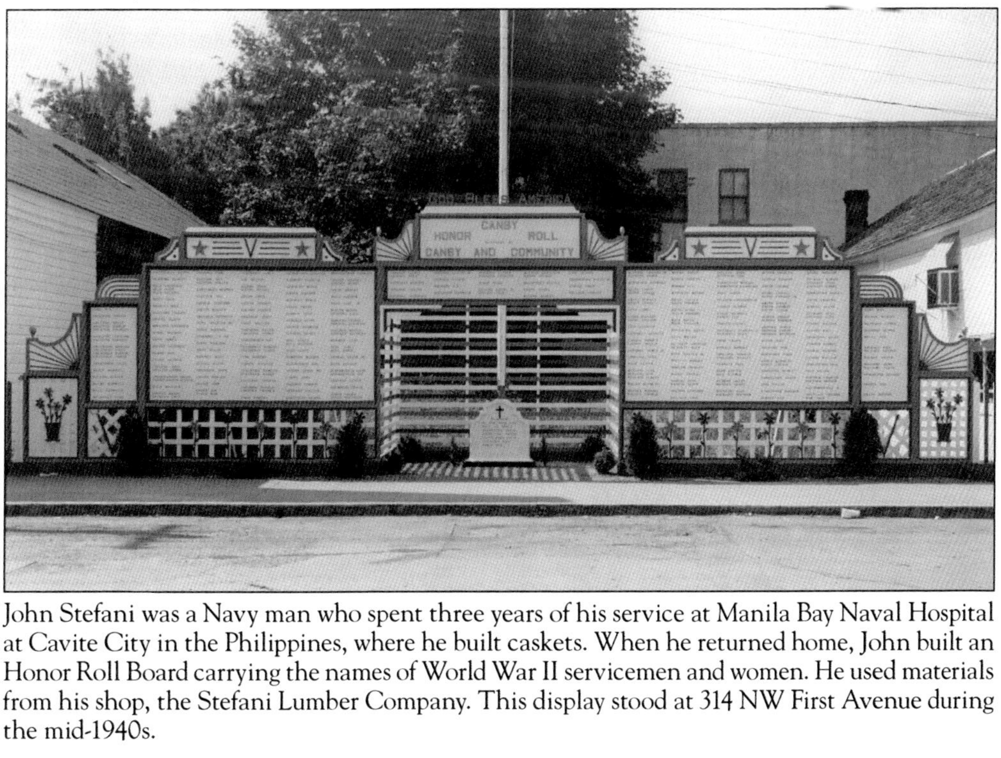

John Stefani was a Navy man who spent three years of his service at Manila Bay Naval Hospital at Cavite City in the Philippines, where he built caskets. When he returned home, John built an Honor Roll Board carrying the names of World War II servicemen and women. He used materials from his shop, the Stefani Lumber Company. This display stood at 314 NW First Avenue during the mid-1940s.

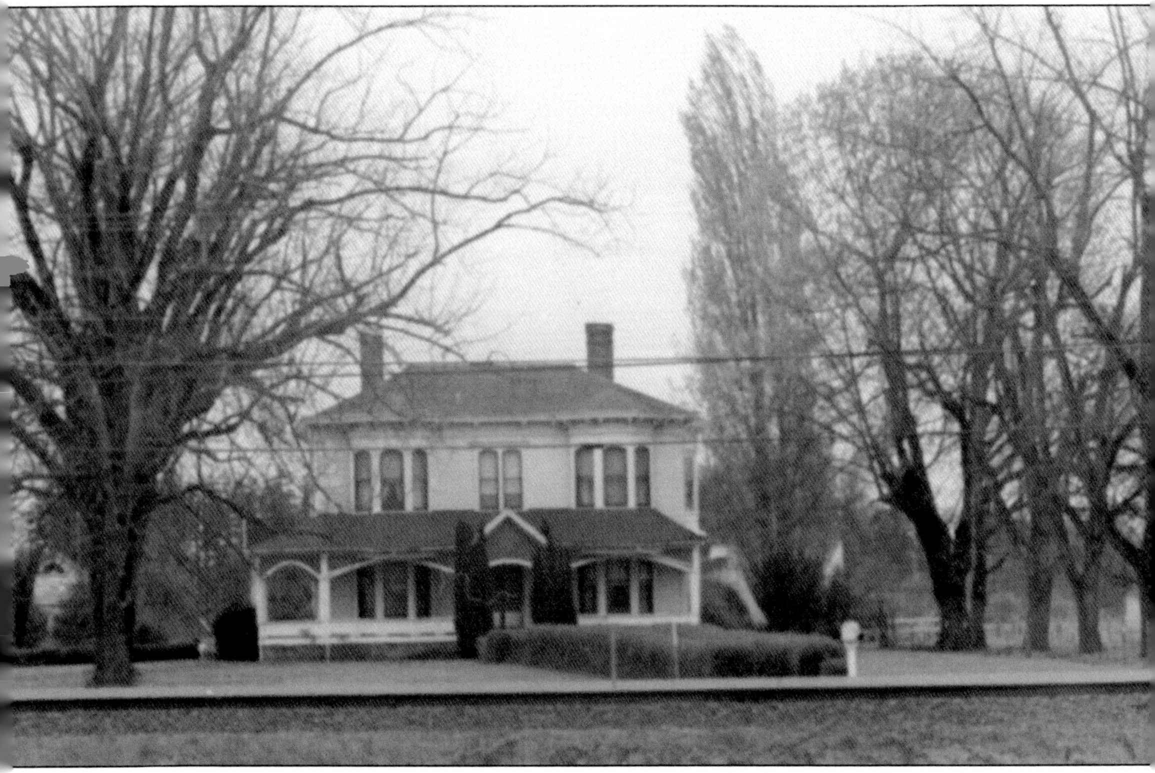

When the railroad came through Canby in 1870, a station was built nearby called Barlow. In 1903, the growing community became the town of Barlow, namesake of William, the son of Samuel K. Barlow, who built the Barlow Road. William Barlow started a sawmill, a gristmill, the first post office, and the Barlow Bank and Land Development Company. The house that had stood on William's property burned down around 1883. In 1885, he built a house on the same spot in the Victorian Italianate style, which was popular from the 1860s through the 1880s. The house passed to William's daughter Mary in 1896, and it was sold out of the family in 1906. William died at 81 years old in 1904. The house still stands as a prominent landmark of Canby. The William Barlow House (or Barlow House) was listed in the National Register of Historic Places on February 15, 1977. It is located along Highway 99E in Barlow, now a Canby address.

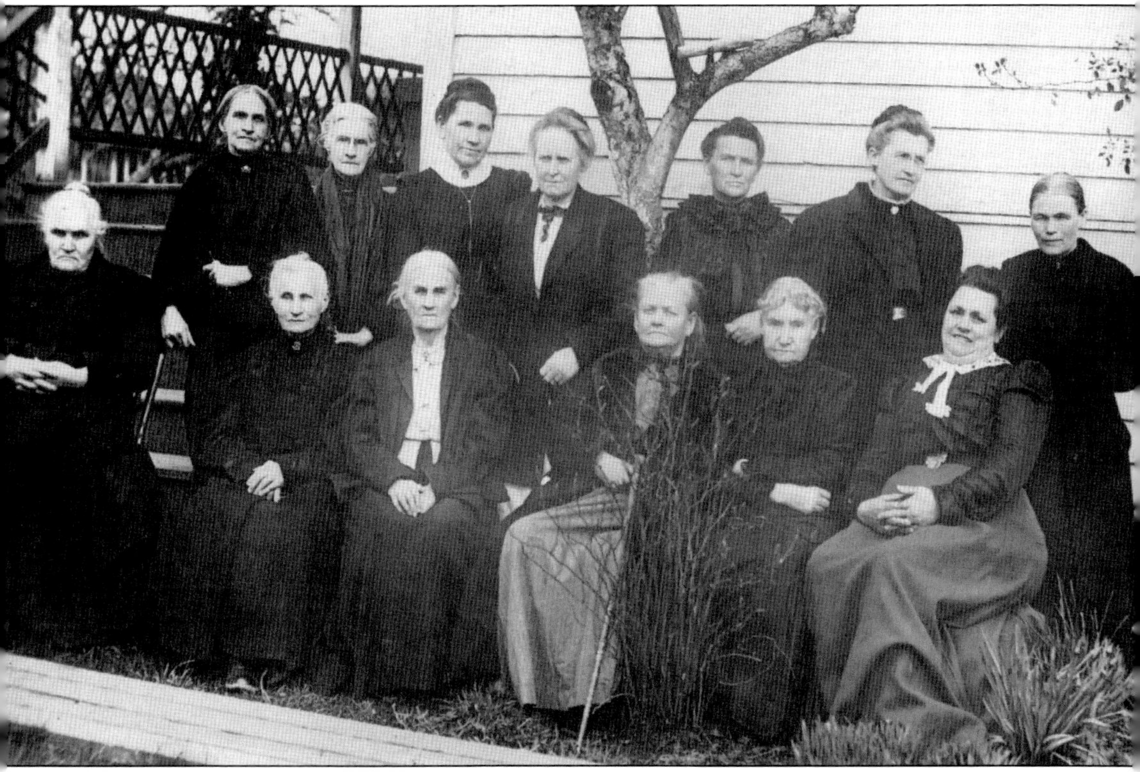

A birthday party for Mrs. O.W. (Harriet) Quint, born in 1833, was held in 1913. Her friends from the Barlow neighborhood joined in for her 80th birthday. Quint was the widow of a Civil War veteran who died October 30, 1899. He was buried in the Barlow Cemetery in Canby. After the war, he had spent his life as a blacksmith in town. Pictured are, from left to right, (first row) Caroline Ausve, Harriet, Mrs. Dement, Mrs. James R. Andrus, Mrs. David J. Parmenter, and Mary Louise Parmenter; (second row) Amanda Jesse, Mrs. Robert Ogle, Mrs. S.B. Berg, Mrs. Rufus E. Irwin (Harriet's daughter), Mrs. VanWinkle, Mrs. Howe, and Mrs. Brudwig. Harriet died on November 27, 1915. She was buried next to her husband. (Courtesy of Virginia Yoder, granddaughter of Mrs. Parmenter.)

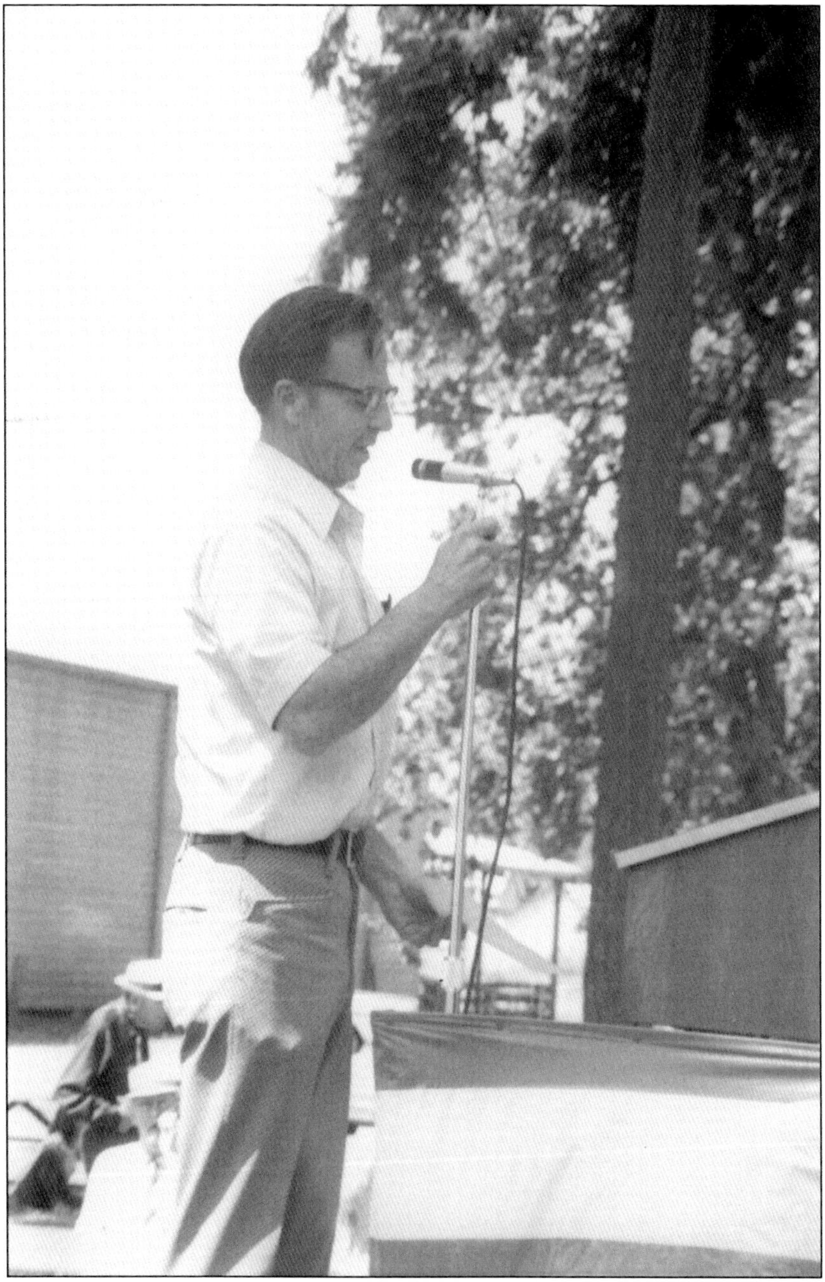

The Canby Historical Society was the idea of John R. Nieland (1911–1982), who initiated the Canby Historical Society on May 15, 1968. He served as the first president, chaired the meetings, and organized the social events, like the annual picnic. He volunteered his time to seek out old, forgotten photographs of historic significance to Canby from families, estates, and charities. John's mother, Anna Louise Haefs Nieland, owned the Maple Corner Restaurant. In 1934, John worked at the Canby Post Office on North Grant Street. He was appointed postmaster on September 30, 1959, and retired after 40 years of service on August 16, 1974. Because of John's passion, time, and diligence, the Canby Depot Museum has been able to document the history of Canby and maintain the train depot and caboose for everyone to enjoy.

BIBLIOGRAPHY

Canby Centennial Celebration Committee. *Canby 1893–1993: A Century to Celebrate*. Canby, OR: Canby Herald, 1993.

Cassell, Bill. *Canby, Oregon: The Early Years*. Portland, OR: Pediment Publishing, 1997.

Leonard, Lois. *A Life for Canby: Elsie Egli Cutsforth 1918–2003*. Canby, OR: Cutsforth Properties, 2007.

Scott, Mike, ed. *Looking Back: The Land at Eden's Gate*. Portland, OR: Pediment Publishing, 2008.

Consistent with our mission to preserve history on a local level, this book was printed in South Carolina on American-made paper and manufactured entirely in the United States. Products carrying the accredited Forest Stewardship Council (FSC) label are printed on 100 percent FSC-certified paper.

MADE IN THE USA